BELGIUM
and the First World War

Henri Pirenne

Translated by Vincent Capelle and Jeff Lipkes

© The Brabant Press, 2014. All rights reserved.

Pirenne, Henri, 1862–1935.
Belgium and the first world war / Henri Pirenne ; translated by Vincent Capelle and Jeff Lipkes [foreword [by] David Nicholas ; introduction [by] Sarah Keymeulen].
p. cm.
ISBN 978-0-9890993-4-9 (pbk.) ISBN 97809890993-5-6 (e-book)
"Translated from the French : La Belgique et la guerre mondiale."
Includes bibliographical references and index.
1. World War, 1914-1918-- Belgium. 2. Belgium --History --German occupation, 1914-1918. 3. War and society --Belgium. I. Capelle, Vincent. II. Lipkes, Jeff. III. Nicholas, David, 1939-. IV. Keymeulen, Sarah. V. Title.
D615 .P57 2014
940.3/493 --dc23 2013956311

ISBN : 97809890993-4-9

front cover photo: Cloth Hall, Ypres, 1918: Archives of Ontario

back cover photo: Portrait of Henri Pirenne, 1925, at University of Bordeaux: Free University of Brussels

typesetting: Diane Collins
cover design: Kachergis Book Design

Contributors

David Nicholas taught at the University of Nebraska-Lincoln for two decades and retired from Clemson University in 2006 as Kathryn and Calhoun Lemon Professor Emeritus of History. A student of Henri Pirenne's biographer, the late Bryce Lyon, his early works concerned economic and family structures in the Flemish cities, particularly Ghent. More recently he has published on comparative urban history in medieval and early modern Europe. His most recent book, reflecting a growing interest in medieval Germany, is *The Northern Lands: Germanic Europe, c. 1270-c. 1500* (Oxford, 2009).

Sarah Keymeulen is completing a dissertation on Henri Pirenne at the University of Ghent, *The Pirenne Phenomenon: the History of a Reputation*. She is the co-author with Jo Tollebeek of *Henri Pirenne, Historian: A Life in Pictures (Leuven, 2011)*

CONTENTS

Preface i
Foreword ix
Translators' Note xlvii
Foreword 1

Chapter I
    Belgium on the eve of the war 7
    § I. — The country and its inhabitants 7
    § II. — Political organization 19
    § III. — State of the country on the eve of the war 28

Chapter II
    The invasion of the country 43
    § I. — Neutrality violated 43
    § II — The invasion 55

Chapter III
    General situation of the country during the occupation . . .65
    § I. — An imprisoned nation 65
    § II. — The attitude of the people 68

Chapter IV

Organization of the Occupation 89
§ I. — Establishing a System 89
§ II — The System in Action 99

Chapter V

The Social and Economic Crisis 109
§ I. — Causes and Progress of the Crisis 109
§ II. — Agriculture 112
§ III. — Industry 117
§ IV. — Banks 123

Chapter VI

The Commission for Relief in Belgium and the *Comité National de Secours et d'Alimentation* 127
§ I. — Establishment and lack of organization 127
§ II — Operation and accomplishments 140

Chapter VII

Exploitation of the Country 157
§ I. — Rational Exploitation and Worker Deportation 157
§ II. — Extreme Exploitation 186

Chapter VIII

Administrative separation 195
§ I. — Until March 21, 1917 .195
§ II. — The Flanders Council .209
§ III. — The Administrative Separation 217

Chapter IX
  Activism 231
  § I. — Until the *"cès de justice"* (February 7–10, 1918) .231
  § II — Activism in Action 240
Chapter X
  The Debacle 257
Chapter XI
  The Diaspora 261
Index 269

PREFACE: HENRI PIRENNE IN THE TWENTY-FIRST CENTURY

David Nicholas

The works of most historians survive their authors only in scholarly footnotes by younger practitioners who feel obliged to cite previous publications on their topics, if only to detail their shortcomings. Even when the factual bases of the older works are unassailable, their interpretations frequently consign them to the dustbin of political or academic "incorrectness."

Henri Pirenne is a major exception to this doleful rule. Pirenne's career in Belgium had been built on scholarly monographs, syntheses, and document editions when the first volume of his *Histoire de Belgique* appeared in 1899. Eventually this history, which commences at a time when there was no Belgium, together with *La Belgique et la Guerre mondiale* (1928), which is translated here, would make him a prominent figure in establishing a Belgian national consciousness. The books by which he is best known in the English-speaking world were anticipated by articles that reinforced his reputation in Belgium. Pirenne was a pioneer in the study of economic history. His work made English-speakers aware for almost the first time of the critical importance of the Low Countries, particularly Flanders, in the commercial economy of medieval Europe.

When "The Pirenne Thesis" is mentioned, medieval scholars are justified in asking "Which one?" The term could be applied to at least five of his major interpretations. Pirenne has been faulted,

i

with some justification, for extrapolating broad applicability from examples derived from the places that eventually became Belgium, especially Flanders. He did not deal with Italy, except to a degree in *Mohammed and Charlemagne*, nor Germany, where the medieval cities and towns offer many parallels and similarities to Flanders that, perhaps for personal reasons, Pirenne refused to admit. For all his grand syntheses, he was convinced not only of the uniqueness of each event, but also of each ideal type as he constructed it. This caused him, as in the case of the German cities, to reject parallels that could have strengthened the case that his theses were generally applicable throughout the north, not only in Flanders.

First and most famously, Pirenne argued for many years before his *Mohammed and Charlemagne* appeared in book form that the Germanic migrations into the Roman Empire did not end the Empire as a Mediterranean-focused commercial network. Rather, the Germans honored the Romans, sought the Mediterranean as an ultimate goal of their migrations, and tried to preserve as much of the Roman achievement as they could. He saw the Muslim conquest of the Mediterranean in the seventh century as the prime mover of Europe from a commercial economy based on cities to an agrarian economy. He thus argued that there had been no rupture of continuity with the Roman commercial world by the invasions of the fifth and sixth centuries, but rather that the nadir of commercial development came in the early Carolingian period, when he thought that long-distance trade in the Mediterranean virtually ceased.

There was an immediate reaction that Pirenne had misread or ignored evidence. The Muslims did not close the Mediterranean, and eastern goods continued to reach the west at all times. More seriously, he underestimated the extent to which long-distance trade was developing on the shores of the North Sea, centered on trading settlements that were linked to the demand markets at the Carolingian courts. The most telling weakness of his thesis—and this is tied to the problem with *Medieval Cities*—is that Pirenne thought of commerce solely in terms of long-distance trade, ignoring the considerable evidence of growing local and regional trade and markets in Carolingian Europe.

Yet the larger question of *Mohammed and Charlemagne* was when Greco-Roman antiquity ended. On this issue much of the detailed work behind Pirenne's thesis has stood the test of time. Most of his predecessors had accepted the idea that there was a sharp break in the fifth century. The great achievement of *Mohammed and Charlemagne* was to note that the changes were gradual, although Pirenne was wrong about the economic depression of the Carolingian period. There was not mass population decline in the wake of the invasions nor wholesale abandonment of sites.

The second Pirenne thesis finds its most concise expression in *Medieval Cities*, which is his most contentious work. He insisted that the "city" can be defined only in economic terms, which put him at odds with scholars of his and more recent times who realized that the cities had political, religious, and military functions as well. Pirenne was not a gradualist. He saw an economic revolution creating genuine towns in the eleventh century and thus argued that the previous period was darker than it was. In fact, this goes back to his thesis that long-distance trade was necessary for true towns, while the trade of the tenth century was focused on local markets.

Scholars have not hesitated to point out logical and scholarly improbabilities in the second Pirenne thesis. Part of the problem is in the English translation of the French original. The word translated as "city" is the French *ville*, which can be rendered in English as either "city" or "town." A city in French is a *grande ville*. Pirenne concentrated on places that developed around an older fortification, in most cases Roman, in others princely or monastic, creating a binuclear city topography. When he used *cité*, he meant the central part of the pre-urban nuclei, most often around a bishopric or a fortress. Pirenne never denied that the cities had non-economic functions at an early stage, and in a late work, interestingly in English ("Northern Towns and Their Commerce," in *The Cambridge Medieval History*, VI (1929)), he gave a broad definition of "medieval town" with which few would disagree. He was actually saying only that the primary characteristic, not the only one, that differentiates a "town" from a "village" is the presence of a market. Unfortunately, Pirenne's personal vehemence against those who questioned his idea of the town as an economic unit had the impact of convincing many contemporary and subsequent scholars that he was narrowly ignoring evidence and refusing to admit the obvious.

Pirenne argued further that the trade that created the medieval city had to be long-distance trade and that the early urban elites consisted entirely of long-distance traders. The latter idea is no longer accepted for any region of Europe. Yet the meaning of "long-distance" evolves. If we define it as more than the distance that a merchant can cover and still return home the same day, it was clearly larger in the twelfth century than in the tenth, when some people who would have passed as long-distance merchants for Pirenne in the tenth century were local in the twelfth. This argument is derived from works of historical geography of which Pirenne could not have been aware, but it provides some posthumous corroboration of his thesis. Similarly, Pirenne and most economic historians of his and the following generation saw the importance of the cities in industrial production, generating capital that could be used to purchase raw materials. More recent work has suggested that the demand market in cities, including those of Flanders, was larger and more important in capital formation than Pirenne thought. Even in the Flemish cities, the most industrialized of northern Europe, the elites made more money through financial services and reshipment to a broader market of goods produced in their environs than in exporting manufactured cloth. In virtually all cities of the north the most prestigious and politically powerful guilds were those of importers of strategic commodities needed to feed and employ the city's masses, not of exporters of manufactured goods.

Pirenne saw the urban and rural worlds as completely separated. He would not accept the argument that farm villages could and often did evolve into cities on the same site. He did not deny the existence of founded towns, but he saw their charters as extending urban liberties to the rural areas and contributing to the dissolution of serfdom. He refused to admit that serfs could be or become townspeople, because they were unfree, and freedom was a mark of the citizen. Nor would he concede that in Germany and the Low Countries the families of the lesser nobility of the environs of the town provided many of the early town patricians. Unsophisticated as this idea seems now, Pirenne had good company at the time; Max Weber, whose work is more highly regarded in some circles than Pirenne's, said something quite similar.

Thirdly, Pirenne's earliest work to achieve wide currency in English, *Belgian Democracy: Its Early History* (1915), is a stirring narrative of the guild revolutions of the late thirteenth and early fourteenth centuries in Flanders and the prince-bishopric of Liège. Pirenne saw the guild regimes as harbingers of democracy. While it is undeniable that the guilds broadened eligibility for city council membership, even in Flanders more recent scholarship has shown that it was more a matter of a commercial elite, often based on extended families, taking power alongside an older landholding patriciate. After coming to power, the guild regimes became more exclusive, reserving seats for specific trades and engineering a *de facto* rotation of offices within a narrow group.

Fourth, the theme of democracy also permeates Pirenne's *Histoire de Belgique*. Shifting the scene somewhat to the territorial principalities, he saw the "democracies" of the late medieval Low Countries as the prototype for a democratic Belgian state. While Pirenne applauded the rebellions of city populations against the

Flemish counts in the early stages, he dismissed their continuations in the Burgundian period as relics of the past, because he thought in terms of a teleology that made the nation-state inevitable. The cities were thus blocking the inexorable march of history. *Histoire de Belgique* got Pirenne into trouble with both Flemings and Walloons, for he insisted that their common experience as Belgians overrode the language barriers. He thus saw more community between Flemings and Walloons in Belgium than between Flemish and Dutch-speakers in the eventual Netherlands. Modern scholarship has been divided on this issue, but considerable recent work has revived this aspect of Pirenne's view for the early Burgundian period (after 1384), although not for the later.

Finally, although Pirenne did not often use the word "capitalism," his article "The Stages in the Social History of Capitalism" (*American Historical Review,* 1914) was important in spreading the understanding that commercial techniques in the late Middle Ages were sophisticated and were an early form of commercial capitalism, defined as the use of money to make money. He was less bound to models in his view of capitalism than were most of his contemporaries, seeing economic behavior as a more accurate indicator of what the medieval moneymen were actually thinking than the strictures of moralists and theologians. Interestingly, Pirenne thought that the thirteenth-century merchants were closer to modern capitalism (which he saw as having a necessary industrial component) than the guild and princely regimes that tried to regulate and restrict moneymaking. He thought that the modern state, specifically the theory of mercantilism that underlay much economic thinking, was inimical to the capitalist spirit of the late Middle Ages. Modern capitalism thus was a new creation, not a revival of medieval capitalism.

The present volume is welcome in making available to an English-speaking readership a crucial work showing Henri Pirenne's reaction to the political conflicts of the twentieth century that so shaped his consciousness and his later scholarly work. Nearly a century after Pirenne's death his works are still read for their content, insights, and analysis, not simply as historical curiosities, and provide a conceptual and analytical framework on which the study of the medieval economic history of northern Europe is still predicated.

INTRODUCTION
Pirenne, Belgium and the First World War*

Sarah Keymeulen

Overview

Henri Pirenne's *La Belgique et la Guerre Mondiale* (1928) was published in the Belgian series of the Economic and Social History of the First World War, an initiative of the Carnegie Endowment for International Peace. Explicitly written from the point of view of the occupied, the book analyzes the German occupation and its effects on Belgium's economy and society. As Pirenne himself acknowledged in the preface, *La Belgique et la Guerre Mondiale* should therefore be read both as an historical account and as a source on Belgium in the First World War.[1] Moreover, the author's proximity to the events inevitably made this study a 'provisionary draft': decades would be necessary before the development of the facts could be retraced with adequate scientific rigor. Pirenne's volume indeed remained the only synthesis written on Belgian history between 1914 and 1918 until the publication in 1997 of Sophie De Schaepdrijver's *De groote oorlog: het koninkrijk België tijdens de Eerste Wereldoorlog*.[2]

---

* The author would like to thank Marc Boone, Walter Prevenier, and Jeff Lipkes for their suggestions and comments.
1 Henri Pirenne, *La Belgique et la guerre mondiale, Histoire économique et sociale de la guerre mondiale. Série belge* (Paris/New Haven: Presses universitaires de France/Yale University Press, 1928), 38.
2 Sophie De Schaepdrijver, *De groote oorlog: het koninkrijk België tijdens de Eerste Wereldoorlog* (Amsterdam: Atlas, 1997).

The context in which it came about is most compelling. *La Belgique et la Guerre Mondiale* testifies to the dramatic impact of the Belgian war experience on Pirenne's life, work and reputation. It also illustrates the methodological reorientation and the internationalization of the historical sciences, and the part played by the Carnegie Endowment in this development. And if it recounts Belgium's many sufferings during the war, the book also demonstrates Pirenne's efforts to reinforce the country's national identity, unity, and international ambitions. Consequently, *La Belgique et la Guerre Mondiale* can also be read as a record of the postwar status of an historian, a discipline, and a nation.

Pirenne and the historical sciences before 1914

Henri Pirenne was born at a critical juncture in history. He observed the triumph and the decline of the liberal bourgeoisie, the rise of socialism and unions, and the advent of mass democracy. He witnessed the upsurge of nationalism in a world of growing international interdependence. Born as the talented son of an industrial entrepreneur, he grew up to be a celebrated national historian and an influential international scholar. Pirenne was a true-born liberal, with a firm belief in progress, reason, and the existence of social laws. With his extensive network, that was particularly influenced by German scholarship, he greatly contributed to the professionalization and internationalization of the historical sciences. He was not only recognized as the patron of a modern historical school but also, to some extent, as a father of the nation. His Histoire de Belgique *gave the nation a glorious past and a promising identity as the microcosm of Europe. The country's booming industrial success predicted an even more glorious future.*

At the beginning of the nineteenth century, Belgium (or at least the territory that was to proclaim its national independence in 1830) was the first industrialized economy on the European continent. A century later it had become the fifth economic power in the world, the fourth trading power, and the country with the densest and, for the propertied classes, perhaps the wealthiest population on earth.[1] The *Belle Époque* was an era of unprecedented capitalist expansion for Belgium, with the acquisition in 1908 of the Congo—a colony about eighty times the size of its territory—as the jewel in its crown. Belgium had the most liberal constitution of its time. The export-oriented entrepreneurs profited from the doctrine of free trade and considered their country as a pivot of the European economy. In the first decades of Belgian independence, this successful liberal-industrial bourgeoisie was the nation's leading class.[2]

However, as social, confessional, and communitarian tensions intensified, its political power declined. The Catholic Party successfully made the change-over to mass politics. The replacement in 1893 of limited suffrage by universal suffrage facilitated the rise of the socialist party. The liberals, in fact an amalgam of competing electoral groups ranging from doctrinaires to progressives, remained a small elitist party that defended the interests of the urban bourgeoisie and represented their enlightened values, their cosmopolitan spirit, and their belief in progress. Somewhat ironically, they were the only party claiming to represent the national or general interest instead of specific regional, religious, or class interests. Although a minority, they did remain a social elite with a political voice to be reckoned with. One of the most prominent members of this social elite was Henri Pirenne (1862–1935), born in the industrial city of Verviers as the eldest of eight children in a family of textile manufacturers.

Pirenne's father Lucien Henri was a successful industrialist and an active municipal councilor for the progressive wing of the liberal party of Verviers.[3] As the city's *échevin* for public instruction (1872–1876), one of his projects was the construction of

---

[1] Ibid., 11.
[2] For a political and cultural history of *Belle Epoque* Belgium, see Gita Deneckere, *1900: België op het breukvlak van twee eeuwen* (Tielt: Lannoo, 2006); Gita Deneckere, *Les turbulences de la Belle Époque, Nouvelle Histoire de Belgique : 1878–1905* (Bruxelles: Le Cri, 2010).
[3] André Zumkir, *La genèse des partis politiques dans l'arrondissement de verviers à l'époque du suffrage censitaire (1831-1893). IV. Les hommes* (Liège: 1997), 138.

the new communal college where his son would receive his education. At the inauguration of the edifice—"one of the prettiest colleges of the nation"—Lucien Henri expressed the hope that the institution would "elevate the soul, give it a higher notion of its moral dignity and prepare it for the conceptions of the mind, the productions of the imagination, and the impressions of sentiment, all while contenting the will under the rule of a natural and legitimate discipline."[1] His speech illustrates the moral values and the ideal of *Bildung* that characterized the liberal bourgeois culture of the late nineteenth century. On a more personal level, it demonstrates the spirit in which the young Pirenne was raised for success: the future historian would share his father's faith in individualism, industriousness, and progress.

In 1878 Pirenne's father became Verviers' *échevin* for public works. For eighteen years he would be one of the driving forces behind the city's modernization. Large boulevards and residential districts were developed, dilapidated houses were demolished, and a tramway system constructed. Most transformations were, of course, undertaken in the interest of the industrial bourgeoisie, which played an important role in the political life of the city. When Leopold II came to dedicate the *Barrage de la Gileppe*, the dam that had been constructed to provide the Verviers factories (including that of *Pirenne Frères*) with water, it was, therefore, probably not just because of his rhetorical talent that the son of the *échevin* responsible, a then fifteen-year-old Pirenne, was chosen to welcome the King on behalf of the city's students.[2]

As the preserved correspondence shows, Pirenne relied on his

---

[1] «[Elle] élève l'âme, lui donne un plus haut sentiment de sa dignité morale et la prépare aux conceptions de l'esprit, aux œuvres de l'imagination, l'impression du sentiment tout en contentant la volonté sous la règle d'une discipline facile et légitime.» *L'Union Liberale* 7-10-1875, in Freddy Joris, *L'Athénée de Verviers et ses devanciers. Deux siècles d'histoire 1807-2007* (Verviers: Athénée Thil Lorrain, 2007), 84.

[2] The anecdote of the young Pirenne's speech to the King is recounted in Bryce Lyon, *Henri Pirenne. A biographical and intellectual study* (Ghent: 1974), 20-21. Numerous other biographical texts on Pirenne appropriately take it up as an example of Pirenne's early ability for written and oral expression. The obvious connection with his father's position and influence is, however, never made.

father's social network at the beginning of his academic career in 1886. However brilliant a historian he had already proven to be during his studies in Liège, France, and Germany, at the height of the conflict between Catholics and liberals over education (the "School War"), it was a rather delicate exercise for the son of a freemason with Protestant sympathies and a conservative Catholic mother to apply for the desired position of university professor.[1] After initial disappointments, he was, thanks to political lobbying, appointed to teach courses in paleography and diplomatics (the study of medieval charters) in Liège and one year later, in 1886, the general history of the Middle Ages and the history of Belgium at the university of Ghent. And so began Pirenne's "dizzyingly fast ascent" to a phenomenal career.[2]

From early on Pirenne emerged as an innovator in higher education and research.[3] He was the architect of the reform program of 1890 in which humanities faculties adopted modern scientific methods. In history, he introduced practical exercises and lectures in auxiliary sciences. In 1893, Pirenne was the first to present a lecture series on social and economic history, which would be the field of his most important publications. Inspired by German historiography, its methodology, its positivist approach, and its consideration for social and economic factors, Pirenne was an intermediary between the German historical school and the Francophone scholarly world, at least for economic history.[4] By around the age of thirty he already enjoyed an enviable reputation, not just within Belgium but also beyond its borders. He was a member of numerous associations, a frequent guest at conferences

---

[1] Ibid., 65-68. See also Walter Prevenier, "Pirenne, Jean, Henri, Otto, Lucien, Marie, gezegd Henri, historicus," in *Nationaal Biografisch Woordenboek, 19* (Brussel: 2009), kol. 753-770.
[2] Jan Dhondt, «Henri Pirenne: historien des institutions urbaines,» in *Hommes et pouvoirs. Les principales études de Jan Dhondt sur l'histoire du 19e et du 20e siècle* (Gent: Fondation Jan Dhondt, 1976), 63.
[3] See Jo Tollebeek and Sarah Keymeulen, *Henri Pirenne, historian: a life in pictures* (Leuven: Lipsius Leuven 2011), 26.
[4] See Erik Thoen and Eric Vanhaute, "Pirenne and economic and social theory: influences, methods and reception," *Belgisch Tijdschrift voor Nieuwste Geschiedenis* XLI, no. 3-4 (2011): 327.

and at the major historical gatherings in Germany and France, a charismatic speaker and a highly productive writer. His marriage to Jenny Vanderhaeghen and the birth of his four sons added the label of 'paterfamilias' to his already impressive curriculum.

In his oeuvre as in his personal life, Pirenne was very much a child of his time and of his social environment. Although always respectful of religious beliefs, he had little ambition to become a 'second Godefroid Kurth' (his devout Catholic mentor at the University of Liège), as his mother ardently hoped for.[1] He was, however, deeply permeated with the spirit of liberalism and the idea of a 'malleable' society. It was the driving force behind Pirenne's eagerness to succeed.[2] It also was the underlying conviction on which his innovative ideas about the history of capitalism and the origins of cities were based.[3] Pirenne had inherited his father's entrepreneurial spirit and applied it with great success to the 'historical entreprise'.[4] He had an intuitive feeling for ideas, methods, and themes on the verge of a general breakthrough. His *L'Origine des constitutions urbaines* (1895), *Les anciennes démocraties des Pays-Bas* (1910) and *Les périodes de l'histoire sociale du capitalisme* (1914) touched the right chords in a rapidly modernizing society that was characterized by a climate of economic

---

[1] See the letter of 29.05.1888 from Pirenne's mother Virginie Duesberg to her son, who was at that time in Paris for an additional year of study: "If only you knew how I pray for you so that you'll always remain faithfully religious and so that your good intentions will grow ever stronger and so that one day you'll become a second Kurth! Oh how happy and proud I would be if one day my prayers would be answered." [my translation] Archives Yves Pirenne, Cernex, *H. Pirenne, Correspondance avec son père et sa mère 1879-1884*.

[2] An interesting anecdote in this respect can be found in a letter dated 25.02.1884 of the young Pirenne to his parents. Admiringly, he recounts the success story of professor Auguste Longnon of the *Ecole Pratique des Hautes Etudes*. The son of a 'miserable shoemaker', his industrious and ambitious character and his passion for history had allowed him to climb his way up to academic (and thus social) prestige. Archives Yves Pirenne, Cernex, *H. Pirenne, Correspondance avec son père et sa mère 1879-1884*. See also Lyon (op. cit.), p. 52

[3] For an assessment of Pirenne's influence on urban history, see Claire Billen and Marc Boone, "L'histoire urbaine en Belgique: construire l'après-Pirenne entre tradition et rénovation," *Città e Storia* 5, no. 1 (2010);Marc Boone, "Cities in late medieval Europe: the promise and the curse of modernity," *Urban History* 39, no. 2 (2012): 332-333.

[4] For an anthropological approach to "the historical trade", see Jo Tollebeek, *De ziel in de fabriek. Over de arbeid van de historicus, 1998* (Amsterdam: 1998).

liberalism, democratization, urbanization, and increasing class struggles.¹ At the same time his work reflected the urban cosmopolitan components of the nineteenth-century liberal bourgeois worldview.² Like Max Weber, Pirenne identified strongly with the economic and political programs of liberal industrial capitalism, and with the ideals of urban culture. In his famous *Medieval Cities* (1925), for instance, urban life was presented as a definition of modern western civilization, with the mercantile bourgeoisie as the inventors of modern capitalist economy, political autonomy, and contemporary civil rights.³

But his growing fame was based not solely on his scholarly work on urban and economic history. With what was to become his magnum opus, the *Histoire de Belgique*, Pirenne gained immediate acclaim both inside and far outside the scholarly world. As early as 1888 Pirenne noted in his diary: "I must also record here the plan I have to write a history of the Low Countries."⁴ When his colleague in Ghent, Paul Fredericq, received an invitation from the German professor Karl Lamprecht to write a Belgian history for his series *Geschichte der europäischen Staaten*, it was only logical that he passed on the job to Pirenne.⁵ The young historian published the first volume of his synthesis of national history in 1899, just as elsewhere in Europe historians were producing overviews of the history of their countries.⁶ According to Pirenne, Belgian history derived its unique character from three

---

1 It is characteristic in this regard that Pirenne's *Les périodes de l'histoire sociale du capitalisme* was re-issued in 1922 in the socialist series of the Librairie du Peuple, together with classics from the workers' movement:, including Marx, Engels, and de Man.
2 Robert John Holton, *Cities, Capitalism and Civilization* (London: Allen and Unwin, 1986), 48 ff.
3 See also Joanna Guldi, *The spatial turn in history* (Institute for Enabling Geospatial Scholarship at the Scholar's Lab at the University of Virginia Library, 01.04.2011 [cited 31.08.2013]).
4 «Il faut que je note ici mon projet d'écrire une hist. des P[ays-] B[as] dont je porte le plan.» Pirenne Archive, Free University of Brussels, ULB 026PP/01/04/003 [My translation].
5 See Tollebeek and Keymeulen, *Henri Pirenne, historian: a life in pictures*, 32-33.
6 Petrus Johannes Blok, *Geschiedenis van het Nederlandsche Volk* (1892-1907); Ernest Lavisse, *Histoire de France depuis les origines jusqu'à la Révolution* (1900-1912); Karl Lamprecht, *Deutsche Geschichte* (1891-1908).

factors: the country's exceptional position at the European crossroads between the Latin and Germanic cultures, the fact that a cultural and social unity in the nation had existed before political unity was achieved, and the so-called *pax belgica*, the peaceful coexistence of the two major ethnic groups, the Flemish and the Walloons. Pirenne's argument provided a powerful legitimization of the Belgian nation that had emerged in 1830. In lectures across the country, the idea was reaffirmed that Belgium was not an artificial nation, but an historical entity that had developed naturally over time: "*La Belgique moderne plonge profondément dans le passé de solides racines.*"[1]

The book's success was immediate. Among colleagues, the work commanded respect for the mastery of the craft, the boldness of the style, and the wideness of scope. The *Histoire de Belgique* was considered Belgium's first 'modern' national history. In contrast to earlier mainly politically oriented Romantic historiography, Pirenne's synthetic view paid considerable attention to economic processes and social structures of the nation's past. Part of the work's approval was also due to the fact that the problems it treated were adapted not only to the scientific but also to the political requirements of the time.[2] Among a wider public, the *Histoire de Belgique* appealed to the desire to give the Belgian state its own history. Pirenne managed to unite Walloons and Flemings by giving them a shared identity—a job for which he, as a native Walloon who lived and worked in Flanders, was perfectly cast. Soon after the first volume of the French edition came out in 1900, Pirenne was—somewhat to his own surprise and embarrassment—proclaimed Belgian's national historian. The four

---

[1] Henri Pirenne, «Les origines de l'état belge,» in *La nation belge 1830–1905. Conférences jubilaires faites à l'exposition universelle et internationale de Liège en 1905* (Liège/Bruxelles: Desoer/Weissenbrucher, 1905), 1.
[2] See Jo Tollebeek, "Historical representation and the nation-state in Romantic Belgium (1830-1850)," *Journal of the History of Ideas* 59, no. 2 (1998): 351-352.

volumes of this national synthesis which appeared before 1914 turned him into the *monstre sacré* of the Belgian intellectual and political establishment.

On May 12, 1912 a large-scale tribute was organized to mark the twenty-fifth anniversary of Pirenne's professorship at the University of Ghent and the completion of his fourth volume of *Histoire de Belgique*. As befitted a national icon, the celebration took place in the prestigious *Palais des Académies* in the nation's capital and in the presence of numerous Belgian and foreign historians, illustrious politicians, and nearly all of Belgian high society. In an acceptance speech he would often look back upon in bitterness during the war, the historian thanked fortune for the happy course his life and work had followed up till now, "like water flowing down a gentle slope, smoothly, without struggle, without obstacles."[1] With the generous support of some affluent members of Pirenne's Brussels progressive liberal network[2], the organizing committee, with Paul Fredericq presiding, established a foundation to consolidate the international prestige of the Belgian academic community.

This *Fondation Pirenne* awarded travel grants for young historians to conduct research in foreign archives and libraries, carrying on Pirenne's self-declared mission of academic diplomacy. Just as Belgium was the crossroads of German and Roman culture, Belgian historians were to assume the role of bridge-builders between the leading scientific nations of the time, Germany

---

1 Quote from H. Pirenne in *Manifestation en l'honneur de M. le professeur Henri Pirenne. Bruxelles, 12 mai 1912*, (Mons: Léon Dequesne, 1912). For Pirenne's regret about his 1912 speech, see e.g. Ghent University Archives, Hs 3704, *Journal of Paul Fredericq*, Notebook 69, 03.11.1915: "I was obviously wrong to say in Brussels, on the day of my tribute, that I was a lucky man. One should never say those things. My mother warned me about it the same day." [my translation]

2 Amongst the most generous donators were Raoul Warocqué (1870–1917), at the time Belgium's richest man and head of a coal mines imperium; Ernest Solvay (1838–1922), whose discovery of the ammonia-soda process had brought him considerable wealth; and the marquise Arconati-Visconti (1840–1923), a well-off widow with a passion for science and liberalism. For a complete list, see Fredericq in ibid., 17.

and France.[1] Through research stays abroad, foreign publishing activities (eg. in the German *Vierteljahrschrift für Sozial-und Wirtschaftsgeschichte*) and participation in international congresses (eg. the German *Historikertage* from as early as 1893 and the International Congresses of Historical Sciences from 1900 onwards), Belgian scholars enhanced their own scientific professionalism and status. While promoting the idea of a European or even a worldwide scholarly guild, they equally reinforced the prestige of their own national historical school. Pirenne, the most illustrious patron of that school, was pleased to notice that Belgium was no longer "only a market and a factory, but played its part in the world of ideas."[2]

This internationalism was not an exclusive feature of the Belgian academic community. The spirit of 'scientific cosmopolitanism' was in fact encouraged by the diplomacy and foreign politics of nations all across the world. International cooperation received state funding because it served national interests. Members of governments attended international scientific conferences to increase their prestige.[3] The beginning of the twentieth century witnessed the emergence of some important new protagonists on the already crowded scene of international relations: large philanthropic organizations were founded, mostly American, with great financial power and a universalist project for peace, democracy, and free trade. The first American foundation to focus its activities on Europe was the Carnegie Endowment for International Peace, a creation of the wealthy steel magnate Andrew Carnegie.

---

[1] Although he wasn't the sole intermediary, Pirenne was generally recognized as the bridge-builder *par excellence* between Germany and France. German's leading economic historian of the time, Gustav Schmoller, wrote to Pirenne in this regard that "*Sie sind in ganz Deutschland hochgeschätzt al seiner der heilsamen und notwendigen Vermittler zwischen deutscher und französischer Wissenschaft.*" See Geneviève Warland, "'Pirenne & Co.': The Internationalization of Belgian Historical Science, 1880s–1920s," *Revue belge de philologie et d'histoire—theme issue: Beyond belgium: ecounters, exchanges and entanglements, 1900–1925* 90, no. 4 (2013): 1240.

[2] Henri Pirenne, *Histoire de Belgique VII. De la révolution de 1830 à la guerre de 1914* (Bruxelles: Lamertin, 1932), 387. [my translation]

[3] See Willem Otterspeer, *Wetenschap en wereldvrede. De Koninklijke Academie van Wetenschappen en het herstel van de internationale wetenschap tijdens het interbellum* (Amsterdam: 1997), 20

It was perfectly in line with Theodore Roosevelt's foreign policy and with the American 'dollar diplomacy' of his successor William Taft.[1] Carnegie's main goal was to promote world peace in order to prevent new large-scale conflicts and to stimulate international commerce—and American commerce in particular. Its strategy was threefold: to work for international justice[2], to propagandize on behalf of peace, and to collect data on the causes of war.

As early as 1911, under the direction of the economist John Bates Clark, the Carnegie Endowment brought together a selection of academics and experts to "stimulate the scientific study of the causes of wars and of the practical methods to foresee and avoid them."[3] The research committee was composed of eighteen members, mainly lawyers and economists. The Belgian delegate was the internationalist senator Henri La Fontaine (1854–1943), who was rewarded for his commitment with the Nobel Prize for Peace in 1913. But despite the efforts, the Carnegie project could not realize its ambitions. Established in 1910, at a time when international tensions were at a height, its impact on governments and public opinion was weak. Although the Endowment did create new international and transnational networks between academic and pacifist circles, its objective to federate the various European pacifist movements failed. Not long after it began an ambitious scientific survey on the causes of war, the greatest war in history broke out. As a report on the Carnegie Endowment's activities aptly concluded in 1941, "the scientific study of the effects of former wars upon modern life suddenly gave place to

---

1 Ludovic Tournès, «La Dotation Carnegie pour la Paix Internationale et l'invention de la diplomatie philantropique (1880–1914),» in *L'argent de l'influence. Les fondations américains et leurs réseaux européens*, ed. Ludovic Tournès (Paris: Les Editions Autrement, 2010), 38.
2 As a symbol of the project a Palace of Peace was erected in The Hague in 1913. After the war, it accommodated the permanent Court of International Justice, created in 1921 in the slipstream of the League of Nations.
3 Jules J. Prudhommeaux, *Le centre européen de la Dotation Carnegie pour la Paix Internationale, 1911–1921* (Paris: Centre européen de la dotation carnegie pour la Paix Internationale, 1921). Quoted in Alain Chatriot, «Une véritable encyclopédie économique et sociale de la guerre: Les séries de la Dotation Carnegie pour la Paix Internationale (1910–1940),» in *L'Atelier du Centre de recherches historiques*, acrh.revues.org (2009).

the study of history in the making."¹

Above: The solemn *'Grande Salle'* of the *Palais des Académies*, the heart of the Belgian scientific world, anno 1918–1919: "an incredible pile of beds and dirty linens. [The German soldiers] had installed machine guns there.... Pots filled with excrement everywhere, and leftover foods in decay."²

Below: The same hall restored to its original prewar grandeur, at the time of the Pirenne tribute in 1921 organized by the *Ligue Nationale du Souvenir*.³

---

1 Carnegie Endowment for International Peace, *Summary of organization and work, 1911–1941* (Washington: 1941). Quoted in Chatriot, «Une véritable encyclopédie économique et sociale de la guerre: Les séries de la Dotation Carnegie pour la Paix Internationale (1910–1940).»
2 «Invraisemblable amas de lits, linges sales. On y avait installé des mitrailleuses.... Partout des vases remplis d'excréments, des restes de victuailles en décomposition.» Académie Royale de Belgique, *Bulletins de la Classe des Lettres et des Sciences Morales et Politiques* (Bruxelles: Lamertin, 1919), 35–36.
3 Pirenne Archive, Free University of Brussels, ULB 026PP/01/07/018, Manifestation du 30 avril 1921

The watershed of the war

War came as a surprise. *The loss of a son in battle and two years of exile in a German prison camp (and later in an isolated village) made Pirenne rethink his pre-war network and reject German historical science and its representatives. The optimistic spirit of international scientific cooperation was shattered. Anti-German resentment continued to affect international congresses and reviews (e.g. Annales) throughout the 1920's. The Carnegie Endowment's project was to be adjusted to these new circumstances. The German occupation of neutral Belgium, the war atrocities and the resulting economic and social crisis transformed the country from a strong and flourishing nation into a dependent and suffering one. Although the war experience initially strengthened national pride and patriotism, it also increased existing tensions between the linguistic communities in Belgium. 1914 was, in other words, a dramatic turning point for the country, for the historical discipline and for the historian who served both with great energy and success. Pirenne's pre-war personal, academic, and national life was history, so to speak.*

On the eve of 1914, Pirenne was working diligently on the fifth volume of *Histoire de Belgique*. He maintained his friendship with German historians such as Lamprecht and Fritz Arnheim, who had undertaken the German translation of *Histoire de Belgique*. Although he was well aware of increasing international tensions, he attached little credit to the warnings of his eldest son Henri-Edouard, studying in Berlin and Heidelberg in 1913, on the growing nationalism and imperialism of German *Kultur*. Like so many of his contemporaries, he was trapped in the 'great illusion'. "We neither wanted nor dared to believe the prophetic signals prefiguring the catastrophe," Pirenne later admitted.[1] When in August 1914 a rapid sequence of events led to the German declaration of war on Belgium, "the country inevitably became what

---

1 Pirenne, *Histoire de Belgique VII. De la révolution de 1830 à la guerre de 1914*, 393-394. [my translation]

it had been so often in the course of its history: the battlefield of Europe."[1] King Albert's proclamation to his army at the beginning of the war emphasized Belgium's historical military prowess: "Caesar said about your ancestors: 'of all the people in Gallia, the Belgians are the bravest.'... Remember, Flemings, the Battle of the Golden Spurs and you, Walloons of Liège, that of the 600 Franchimonts!"[2] One can easily see why Fredericq was convinced that at least part of the text had been written by Pirenne.[3] At the same time, the King's address reflected the country's increasing communitarian divide. In 1914 the indignation about the German invasion still united the Flemish and Walloon causes

---

1 Ibid., 371–372. [my translation]
2 Reproduced in Paul Hymans, *La neutralité de la Belgique* (Paris: Librairie Militaire Berger-Levrault, 1915).
3 Ghent University Archives, Hs 3704, *Journal of Paul Fredericq*, Notebook 38, 09.08.1914. Not only the contents of the speech suggested that Pirenne was its ghostwriter. As volume after volume of *Histoire de Belgique* was published, bonds between Belgium's national historian and (the future) King Albert grew tighter, to a point at where Pirenne was frequently summoned to the Royal house for advice and confidential meetings. On Henri and Jacques Pirenne's close ties with the King, see Lyon, *Henri Pirenne. A biographical and intellectual study*, 385–386. However, a former student of Pirenne, Leo Picard, claimed to have heard 'from informed sources' that the King's reference to the history of Flemings and Walloons was in fact the idea of Emile Waxweiler (see Leo Picard, *De vrijzinnigheid in Vlaanderen en de Vlaamse beweging*, Diogenes Cahier 3 (Antwerpen: Humanistisch Verbond van België, 1963), 33.) Picard (not to be confused with Edmond Picard, the inventor of the 'âme belge'-concept) was a private student of Pirenne and one of the first to openly contest the authority of his patron. In 1915 he announced his participation in the foundation of the Pan-German inspired journal *Vlaamsche Avondpost* and denounced Belgium's reason for existence. Pirenne was flabbergasted by Picard's disloyalty to his master and his country (see Ghent University Archives, Hs 3704, *Journal of Paul Fredericq*, Notebook 45, 06.02.1915). All the same, Picard might have been right about Waxweiler's input in the King's 1914 address: Waxweiler was indeed a confidant of King Albert at that time. He even acted as a go-between between Albert and his brother-in-law Hans Törring, a German diplomat, during secret peace negotiations in 1915. Naturally, Pirenne and Waxweiler were no strangers to each other. Waxweiler was a prominent member of Pirenne's influential Brussels network and the director of the *Institut de Sociologie Solvay* (see Kaat Wils, "Everyman his own sociologist. Henri Pirenne and disciplinary boundaries around 1900," *Belgisch Tijdschrift voor Nieuwste Geschiedenis* XLI, no. 3–4 (2011): 364–365.) As a friend of the historian, Waxweiler co-organized the Pirenne celebration of 1912. He also helped furthering the career of Pirenne's most talented pupil Guillaume Des Marez by assigning him a chair at the Solvay Institute (see Claire Billen and Marc Boone, "Pirenne in Brussels before 1930. Guillaume Des Marez and the relationship between a master and his student," *Belgisch Tijdschrift voor Eigentijdse Geschiedenis* XLI, no. 3–4 (2011).) Another member of Waxweiler's Social Sciences Institute, its secretary Fernand Van Langenhove, would participate in the Carnegie project with the publication in 1916 of a remarkable study of the fears in the German army that had caused the civilian massacres of 1914: Fernand Van Langenhove, *Comment naît un cycle de légendes, francs-tireurs et atrocités en Belgique* (Lausanne/Paris: Payot, 1916).

in a joint patriotic discourse. During and after the occupation, however, the idea of a historical and shared 'Belgian civilization' increasingly lost ground.[1]

It was painful to realize that Belgian neutrality had been nothing more than a makeshift measure for the protection of a European equilibrium that no longer existed. Pirenne knew from his own experience how "everyone felt almost like a personal injury the shame of the German proposal" to permit its troops free passage through Belgium.[2] But even more shocking was his sudden recognition that the German scientific world was as responsible for the injustice as its government. Pirenne had to admit that his son Henri-Edouard had been right to portray his German professors as "nothing more than learned brutes."[3] As the famous Manifesto of the Ninety-Three attested, even renowned historians justified the war as a sacred mission to spread the superior German *Kultur* across Europe.[4] Pirenne's former German colleagues and friends now had revealed their true nature: that of dangerous Pan-Germanists with imperialist ambitions towards Belgium.[5] For the author of the *Histoire de Belgique*, who had put considerable effort into stressing the nation's historical roots, its sovereignty, its political importance, and therefore its very right to exist, this was nothing less than a smack in the face. The prewar historical sciences had been dominated by an optimistic faith in the benefits of international scientific cooperation and the

---

[1] See e.g. the chapter "De afbrokkeling van de 'idée belge' – ondanks Pirenne", in Marnix Beyen, *Oorlog en verleden. Nationale geschiedenis in België en Nederland, 1938–1947* (Amsterdam: Amsterdam University Press, 2002), 44.
[2] Pirenne, *Histoire de Belgique VII. De la révolution de 1830 à la guerre de 1914*, 395. [my translation]
[3] Lyon, *Henri Pirenne. A biographical and intellectual study*, 217.
[4] This proclamation was endorsed in October 1914 by 93 prominent German artists, scientists and scholars, amongst whom were Lamprecht and Schmoller, to declare their unequivocal support of German military actions. For Pirenne's attitude towards Lamprecht during the war, see De Schaepdrijver, *De groote oorlog: het koninkrijk België tijdens de Eerste Wereldoorlog*, 144–147. See also Hans Van Werveke, «Karl Lamprecht et Henri Pirenne,» *Bulletin de la Commission royale d'Histoire* 88 (1972).
[5] See Tollebeek and Keymeulen, *Henri Pirenne, historian: a life in pictures*, 43.

propagation of universal scholarly standards, which would not only contribute to the advancement of knowledge, but would eventually lead to world peace. Now, on an unprecedented scale, science had embraced the war.[1]

However great was Pirenne's indignation as a citizen, a patriot, and a historian—according to Fredericq he was "like a volcano of anger against Germany and its militarism"[2]—it was nothing compared to the anguish that overpowered him as a father and as a husband. Three of his sons—Henri-Edouard, Jacques, and Pierre—were conscripted into military service. In November 1914, Pierre fell in battle at the Yser at the age of nineteen. It took until October 1915 for his death to be officially confirmed. In the agony of doubt, Pirenne confided to his mother that "he was my favorite son, as you know. He had so much uprightness, honesty, intelligence and heart. If he is no longer there, it will be a loss for the country."[3] And the country suffered catastrophic losses during the four years of its occupation. Its economy was paralyzed and its press censored, its historical towns were ruined, its streets were packed with German soldiers and its houses were sacked. In spite of the ambitious food aid program of the Committee for Relief in Belgium, people suffered from hunger and cold.[4] An estimated 50,000 Belgians—soldiers and civilians—lost their lives, and another 50,000 soldiers returned home injured.[5] Apart from the 'industrial' warfare, with its dramatic material impact,

---

[1] See Otterspeer, *Wetenschap en wereldvrede. De Koninklijke Academie van Wetenschappen en het herstel van de internationale wetenschap tijdens het interbellum*, 21.
[2] Ghent University Archives, Hs 3704, *Journal of Paul Fredericq*, Notebook 40, 07.10.1914. [my translation]
[3] [my translation] Archives Françoise Pirenne, Waterloo, *H. Pirenne. Lettres à sa mère*, 1911–1922, 21.12.1914.
[4] The CRB was an international, predominantly American organization under the aegis of the future American president Herbert Hoover, that arranged for the supply of food to German-occupied Belgium and France.
[5] See De Schaepdrijver, *De groote oorlog: het koninkrijk België tijdens de Eerste Wereldoorlog*, 295. The In Flanders Fields Museum (IFFM) is currently working on an extensive Name List of all victims linked to the First World War in Belgium. They aim to publish the list as from August 4th, 2014. More information on http://www.inflandersfields.be/en/educational-activities/name-list- www.inflandersfields.be.

'psychological' warfare was also carried on. One of Germany's propaganda-offensives to increase loyalty to the occupying regime amongst a strategically important part of the Belgian population was the installation of a Dutch-only policy at the University of Ghent—for a long time one of the central demands of the Flemish movement.

After the German invasion the largely francophone Ghent University had closed its doors, but as early as September 1915 the occupiers sounded out its professors on their individual willingness to resume lectures the following academic year. Mainly under the influence of Pirenne, Fredericq, and the classical philologist Joseph Bidez, the Ghent Academic Council categorically refused. In late 1915 the German governor-general Moritz von Bissing officially announced a Dutch-only policy for the institution. The decision, part of Germany's strategy ('*Flamenpolitik*') to detach the Flemish from Belgium and hence weaken the country, immediately provoked sharp protests on the French-speaking side. When in early February 1916 a survey was conducted among Ghent's professors to learn whether they were capable of teaching in Dutch, even most Flemish professors answered with a resounding 'no'. The German authorities now began to suspect Pirenne and Fredericq of orchestrating resistance, even though they found it hard to believe that their country's 'greatest friends' in the prewar era now seemed to be amongst their most formidable 'enemies'.[1] The two historians indeed prevailed upon a large number of professors to hold periodic, secret meetings where they passionately reiterated the moral, legal, and political reasons why the university should remain closed.[2] Pirenne, however, became increasingly worried about the risks of his actions.

---

1 See Peter Schöttler, «Henri Pirenne face à l'Allemagne de l'après-guerre ou la (re)naissance du comparatisme en histoire» (paper presented at the Une guerre totale? La Belgique dans la Première Guerre Mondiale. Nouvelles tendances de la recherche historique, Actes du colloque international organisé à l'ULB du 15 au 17 janvier 2003, Brussels, 2005), 508–509.
2 See Bryce Lyon and Mary Lyon, *The Journal de guerre of Henri Pirenne* (Amsterdam/New York/Oxford: 1976), 1. Fredericq's war journal also attests to their intellectual resistance.

"Can you guarantee me there is no danger?" he asked before he was to address a patriotic lecture to some soldiers—"You know that nothing scares me, but for my wife and for my son I can't risk being deported to Germany right now."[1]

Only three weeks later, on 18 March 1916, Pirenne and Fredericq were arrested in an attempt to break the resistance against the opening of the 'Vlaamsche Hoogeschool'. For Germany, the measure proved to be counterproductive. Both in Belgium and internationally, a storm of protest erupted that was not to diminish before the return of the two war heroes in 1918. For Pirenne, the more than two-and-a-half-year-long exile disrupted the work schedule he had tried to maintain, took him away from his family and colleagues, and profoundly affected his way of thinking. But, as he had taught his son Jacques earlier in the war, "sadness does not exclude energy".[2] With an almost boyish enthusiasm Pirenne engaged in the curious routines of camp life, first in Krefeld, then in Holzminden. Naturally, there was grief over the separation from his wife and children, but there was also excitement over his encounters with Russian officers, circus artists, and everything in between: "I have the feeling I'm living in a Dickens novel", he wrote to his wife.[3] And there were new intellectual challenges, as well.

A group of fellow prisoners in Holzminden talked him into setting up a lecture series on the social and economic history of Europe. He also taught a course on Belgian history for his compatriots. All through his exile Pirenne would study the Russian language and culture. At first this was only occupational therapy, but by the end of war, to his own surprise—"Who would have

---

[1] Ghent University Archives, Hs 3704, *Journal of Paul Fredericq*, Notebook 81, 24.02.1916. [my translation] In his diary Fredericq made fun of Pirenne's 'faint-heartedness', neglecting the fact that he as a confirmed bachelor had less to lose.
[2] Archives Yves Pirenne, Cernex, *H. Pirenne, Correspondance avec son père et sa mère 1879–1884*, 07.04.1915. [my translation]
[3] Ibid., 24.05.1916. [my translation]

thought that at my age I could still learn a new language!"[1]—he was able to read Russian historians fluently. The newly gained knowledge extended his historical perspective beyond the frontiers of Western Europe and aroused his interest in comparative studies of Byzantine and Western civilizations. This approach was to lie at the basis of *Mahomet et Charlemagne*[2], the main argument of which he already set out in a chapter of the *Histoire de l'Europe*[3] that he began to write in Creuzburg.[4] Isolated from his compatriots or other allies and at the insistence of his wife, he decided to write an economic history of Europe from the Germanic invasions up to the present day. The project helped him to relieve his boredom and melancholy and allowed him to elaborate further on the hypotheses and ideas that he had developed during his lectures at Holzminden. The fact that reading matter was difficult to come by – he could borrow books from the University of Jena, but this service was limited and delivery took a while[5]—turned out to be a blessing. It obliged Pirenne to generalize more than he normally did and stimulated his ideas about historiography and its methods, value, and meaning. The reflections that he recorded on these subjects were later collected in *Réflexions d'un solitaire*.[6]

After his return, Pirenne's status as an emblem of national resistance turned him into a spokesman of 'poor little Belgium' and an advocate of the cause of democratic civilization on the world stage. His life in the immediate post-war years seemed to

---

1 Ibid., 03.02.1918. [my translation]
2 Henri Pirenne, *Mahomet et Charlemagne* (Bruxelles: Nouvelle Société d'Edition, 1937).
3 Henri Pirenne, *Histoire de l'Europe. Des invasions au XVIe siècle* (Paris: Alcan, 1936).
4 After a short reunion in Jena with his colleague Fredericq, the remote town of Creuzburg became Pirenne's final involuntary residence. He would stay there during the last twenty-two months of his captivity, the last four of which his wife Jenny and his youngest son Robert were permitted to join him.
5 For a 'demystification' of the persistent myth that Pirenne had conceived *Histoire de l'Europe* 'entirely from his memory and from powerful reflection by his matured spirit', see Geneviève Warland, «L'Histoire de l'Europe de Henri Pirenne: Genèse de l'oeuvre et représentation en miroir de l'Allemagne et de la Belgique,» *Textyles. Revue des Lettres belges de langue française*, no. 24 (2004): 40–41.
6 Bryce & Mary Lyon and Jacques-Henri Pirenne, ««Réflexions d'un solitaire» by Henri Pirenne,» *Bulletin de la Commission Royale d'Histoire* CLX (1994).

be a succession of solemn ceremonies, prestigious honorary tributes, and exciting new commitments in the field of international scientific cooperation.[1] It was a time for Pirenne to assume, even more distinctly than before the war, the role of public intellectual.[2] In his lectures as in his work, he now would elaborate explicitly on his ideas, matured in exile, about the causes of war and the ideological aberrations of Germany. Exactly one year after the Armistice, on November 11, 1919, the University of Ghent was reopened. As the institution's new rector, Pirenne used the programmatic commencement speech at the start of each academic year to sharply denounce Germany's pernicious theory of races and its ideological abuse of science. His last and most outspoken inaugural speech, in 1921, was published as *'Ce que nous devons désapprendre de l'Allemagne'* ('What we must unlearn from Germany'), a highly symbolic title coming from a historian whose pre-war practices, methodology and professional network owed so much to Germany.

In the past two decades the so-called 'anti-German resentment' of Pirenne has been the object of a lively scholarly debate, reflecting opinions as diverse as the idea that Pirenne's entire post-war oeuvre was a "virulent settling of scores with Germany, its history and its historians"[3] and, on the other hand, the opinion that his criticism of German *Kultur* was not only 'constructive', but the *condition sine qua non* for the postwar historiographic revolution

---

[1] For an overview, see Tollebeek and Keymeulen, *Henri Pirenne, historian: a life in pictures*, 59–64.
[2] Naturally, as Belgium's national historian, Pirenne to a certain extent had already fulfilled a public function. Moreover, on two occasions Pirenne has been close to a political mandate: in 1912 he was proposed for a ministerial post in a caretaker cabinet, but elections brought disappointment for the liberals. In 1919 he was asked to occupy the first place on the list of the *Parti de Renaissance National*, but his position as rector of the University of Ghent did not allow him to take up a position in Parliament. See ibid., 40, 61.
[3] See Adriaan Verhulst, «Marc Bloch and Henri Pirenne on comparative history. A biographical note.,» *Revue belge de philologie et d'histoire* 79, no. 2 (2001): 510. Adriaan Verhulst, «Henri Pirenne en de Universiteit Gent,» *Revue belge de philologie et d'histoire* 76, no. 4 (1998): 872. Quoted in Sophie De Schaepdrijver, "'That theory of races'. Henri Pirenne on the unfinished business of the Great War," *Belgisch Tijdschrift voor Nieuwste Geschiedenis* XLI, no. 3–4 (2011): 537.

towards comparative and total history.¹ As is often the case, the truth is somewhere in between. Pirenne did not target German culture or German historians per se so much as the new direction taken by German scholarship in the course of the late nineteenth century.² To Pirenne, the earlier German historiographical methods remained valid: apart from some reflections on the role of 'le hazard en histoire', he still adhered to the study of large structures and collective phenomena and a focus on 'the general' over the 'individual' in history. His 'volte-face vis-à-vis Germany'³ was solely directed against the country's new völkish-nationalist perspective, its narrow essentialist vision on history and its 'Pan-German' racial focus. Consequently, Pirenne's postwar attitude and oeuvre consisted less of a 'travail de deuil on the German part of his culture'⁴ than of a continuous disassociation from the *new* evolution of German historiography. One could say that, after the war, Pirenne considered himself a better 'German' historian than the German historians, who had deviated from the scientific path of objectivism and critical thinking – even though they had been the first to pave it. Pirenne's work on his wartime experiences, and on the lessons drawn from it, time and again reaffirmed this opposition between wrong and right.⁵ Against the aggression of Germany's conservative and authoritarian government, he celebrated the triumph of Belgium's liberal-democratic regime. Against the narrow-minded German conception of nationality

---

1 Schöttler, «Henri Pirenne face à l'Allemagne de l'après-guerre ou la (re)naissance du comparatisme en histoire». This historiographic revolution would eventually lead to the creation of the influential *Annales* revue by two self-declared spiritual heirs of Pirenne, Marc Bloch and Lucien Fèbvre.
2 See De Schaepdrijver, "'That theory of races'. Henri Pirenne on the unfinished business of the Great War," 537. Bryce Lyon, "The war of 1914 and Henri Pirenne's revision of his methodology," in *De lectuur van het verleden. Opstellen over de geschiedenis van de geschiedschrijving aangeboden aan Reginald De Schryver*, ed. Jo Tollebeek, Georgi Verbeeck, and Tom Verschaffel (Leuven: 1998), 511.
3 Term borrowed from Lyon, "The war of 1914 and Henri Pirenne's revision of his methodology," 511.
4 See Cinzio Violante, *La fina della 'grande illusione': uno storico europeo tra guerra e dopoguerra, Henri Pirenne (1914–1923)* (Bologna: 1997).
5 For an overview of Pirenne's work on the war and it's consequences, see Schöttler, «Henri Pirenne face à l'Allemagne de l'après-guerre ou la (re)naissance du comparatisme en histoire», 510–511.

along ethnic lines, he exalted the internationalist and voluntarist character of the Belgian nation.

In his postwar scientific oeuvre, Pirenne tried to explain the origin of the *'théories fumeuses'* of German scholarship by showing how ever since the ninth century Germany had been lagging behind Western Europe, and more particularly France.[6] On occasion Pirenne had opposed German historiography before on this matter, for instance with regards to the Germanisation of the Roman Empire or the resurgence of cities in the Middle Ages.[7] However, the war experiences had markedly sharpened Pirenne's tone towards Germany[8] and intensified his minimization of the role of the German invasions and the concept of 'germanisation' itself, with *Mahomet et Charlemagne* as the most striking example.[9] And so subjectivity after 1914 affected Pirenne's account of the events and his presentation of historical tendencies, by systematically exaggerating Germany's 'backwardness' while, at the same time, drawing an overly positive picture of its 'mirror-image,' Belgium.[10] Pirenne felt the need to update some of his prewar writings in accordance with these new insights. Before 1914 he had consistently presented Belgium as a syncretism of German

---

6 Warland, «L'Histoire de l'Europe de Henri Pirenne: Genèse de l'oeuvre et représentation en miroir de l'Allemagne et de la Belgique,» 46, note 48.
7 Ibid., 43. Thoen and Vanhaute, "Pirenne and economic and social theory: influences, methods and reception." As the authors show, even Pirenne's famous plea for comparative history was expressed as early as 1898, in his article "Villes, marchés et marchands au Moyen Age".
8 Warland even uses the word "aggressive". See Warland, «L'Histoire de l'Europe de Henri Pirenne: Genèse de l'oeuvre et représentation en miroir de l'Allemagne et de la Belgique,» 45, note 48.
9 Pierre Toubert, «Henri Pirenne et l'Allemagne (1914–1923),» *Le Moyen Age*, no. 107 (2001): 319. Numerous notes in the Pirenne-archives attest to Pirenne's attempts to minimize the impact of the German invasions. See for instance his assertion that "Instead of claiming that Europe was Germanized, it would be more exact to say that it was Byzantinized or, if you like, that it was Orientalized. Germanization by the Carolingians was a consequence of the Islamic invasion." (Pirenne Archives, ULB 026PP/01/06/006—my translation), or that "The Germans have barbarized the Empire, not Germanized. Their influence has been enormously exaggerated by the German School whose doctrines we have accepted too fully." (National Archives of Belgium, I 115, 4533—my translation) More information on the genesis of Pirenne's *Mahomet et Charlemagne*-thesis can be found on the website www.henripirenne.be [only in Dutch], conceived as part of the 2009 exposition *Mahomet et Charlemagne: genèse et aventures d'une hypothèse historique* (UGent/ULB).
10 Warland, «L'Histoire de l'Europe de Henri Pirenne: Genèse de l'oeuvre et représentation en miroir de l'Allemagne et de la Belgique,» 55.

and Roman influences—it was the central idea of *Histoire de Belgique*. In *Histoire de l'Europe* he argued that Belgians had actually always been more attracted to the superior Western (French) culture than to the Eastern (German) culture; had not the patricians in the large Flemish cities preferred to use the French language ever since the twelfth century?[1] Striking also is the semantic revision of the pre-war volumes of *Histoire de Belgique,* a result of Pirenne's resolute condemnation of nationalism and racist theories after the war. Comparison with their re-editions after 1918 has shown that Pirenne systematically rewrote all passages that contained the notion of 'race'.[2]

In the patriotic atmosphere of post-war Belgium, Pirenne was lauded in 1921 by King Albert and the *Ligue Nationale du Souvenir* as 'one of the handful of people who truly embodied the national ideal.' In subsequent months and years, he was sent abroad to speak about the origins of the Belgian nation-state and its historical and political importance. He countered the claims of German (and 'Greater Netherlands') historians that Belgium was an 'artificial nation'.[3] Pirenne's post-war oeuvre reflects this patriotic mission, both by over-emphasizing the role played by Belgium in European history and in the First World War, and by reiterating time and again the uniqueness of Belgian civilization and the superiority of its culture.

Within Belgium, too, it was important to reaffirm the strong unity of Flemings and Walloons. When the initial wave of patriotism had abated in the early 1920's, communitarian tensions rose to new heights. In Ghent, the Flemish continued to demand the adoption of Dutch as the official language.[4] In this context

---

1 Ibid., 54, note 98.
2 Schöttler, «Henri Pirenne face à l'Allemagne de l'après-guerre ou la (re)naissance du comparatisme en histoire», 514–515.
3 Tollebeek and Keymeulen, *Henri Pirenne, historian: a life in pictures*, 64.
4 On Pirenne's self-serving distortions with regards to the communitarian question, see De Schaepdrijver, "'That theory of races'. Henri Pirenne on the unfinished business of the Great War," 535. Much to Pirenne's bitterness, in 1930 the protests would lead to the complete imposition of Dutch throughout Ghent University. He moved to Uccle, Brussels that same year.

of growing national antagonism, Pirenne's interpretation of the war as a confirmation of his theory on the harmonious unity of the Belgian nation became all the more significant.[1] Pirenne has sharply observed how, in German historiography, "the historical literature produced by the war has been a literature dominated by sentiment or by the willingness to serve political or national goals.... Its value essentially consists in revealing a certain state of mind."[2] However, the 'dynamic of human weakness' is also applicable to his own post-war writings. Like so many historians during and after the conflict, he fought his own war, using and abusing the weapons of his profession.[3] Regrettably, this fact has obscured somewhat the relevance of Pirenne's perceptive analysis of the mechanisms of war: at least in Belgium, his work on the First World War is generally regarded nowadays as 'marred by nationalism.'[4]

In fact, these criticisms already began to undermine Pirenne's reputation in his own time. His reputation as a patriot and war hero, indeed a national icon, added to his post-war status as one of the most important historians of his time. However, it also tarnished to some extent from his image as an historical innovator. The association with national history had become poisonous after the war. In his own country, both the Flemish and, although less weighty, the Walloon movement progressively undermined the Belgian idea. As demands for autonomy grew, Pirenne's *Histoire de Belgique* was increasingly criticized and caricaturized. For the Walloon opponents, Pirenne's work systematically overstressed

---

[1] Christophe Bechet, «La révision pacifiste des manuels scolaires. Les enjeux de la mémoire de la guerre 14–18 dans l'enseignement belge de l'Entre-deux-guerres,» *Bijdragen tot de Eigentijdse Geschiedenis*, no. 20 (2008): 96–97.
[2] Henri Pirenne, «Une histoire économique et sociale de la guerre,» *Bulletin de la classe des lettres et des sciences morales et politiques de l'Académie Royale de Belgique* 4 (1924): 113–114.
[3] Marcello Verga, «Manuels d'histoire pour la paix en Europe, 1923–1938,» in *Pour la paix en Europe. Institutions et société civile dans l'entre-deux-guerres*, ed. Marta Petriciolo and Donatella Cherubini (Bruxelles: Peter Lang, 2007), 506.
[4] De Schaepdrijver, "'That theory of races'. Henri Pirenne on the unfinished business of the Great War," 546.

the historical importance of the Flemish cities and neglected the historical ties of Wallonia with France. The Flemish nationalists considered Pirenne as the representative of the maligned Francophone University of Ghent, who had projected back his long cherished dream of a unified Belgium onto history.[1] It was yet another reason for Pirenne to redirect his field of study out of the national framework. From now on, comparativism and *'histoire total'* became his historiographical leitmotifs. As he put it in his influential plea for comparative history at the International Conference of Historical Sciences in Brussels, 1923: "Only the comparative method enables historians to avoid the pitfalls that surround them.... Through that method, and only through that method, history can become a science and free itself from the idolatry of sentiment. It will succeed in so far as it will adopt for national history the perspective of universal history. From that moment, it will not only become more exact, it will also become more human."[2] His scholarly oeuvre of the 1920's and '30's was marked by this methodological reorientation. It earned him the title of the father of the *Annales* and of modern historiography. Nevertheless, Pirenne's work and engagements would continue to reflect his somewhat paradoxical dual identity of modern, innovative scholar and Belgian national icon, of convinced internationalist and fervent opponent of German participation in international scientific cooperation.

La Belgique et la Guerre Mondiale

With his experience as a social and economic historian and his postwar predilection for international, comparative research, the Carnegie assignment seemed to be cut out for Pirenne. However, the

---

1 See Beyen, *Oorlog en verleden. Nationale geschiedenis in België en Nederland, 1938–1947*, 396.
2 Henri Pirenne, «De la méthode comparative en histoire, discours d'ouverture du cinquième Congrès international des Sciences historiques,» in *Compte-rendu du cinquième Congrès international des Sciences historiques*, ed. Guillaume Des Marez and F. L. Ganshof (Bruxelles: M. Weissenbruch, 1923);Schöttler, «Henri Pirenne face à l'Allemagne de l'après-guerre ou la (re)naissance du comparatisme en histoire», 513. [my translation]

First World War had not yet been sufficiently 'culturally demobilized' for a truly scientific project. The prefaces of most volumes already made clear that they would be a mix of scientific aspirations and subjective accounts of the authors' experiences. In La Belgique et la Guerre Mondiale, *as well, Pirenne's role as a spokesman of 'poor little Belgium' and as the country's national historian prevented him from developing a fully objective analysis. The volume was not just a synthesis of earlier published monographs on the Belgian war experience. Pirenne also employed it to reconfirm the specificity of the Belgian history and its identity within Europe, and to denounce German nationalism and imperialism. In this sense, the Carnegie Series' greatest relevance might lie in the fact that it provoked and still provokes historians to think about the role of their own 'passions and prejudices' in history writing. The old historiographic ideal of objectivity, too, would never be the same again.*

After the liberation, it was not only countries that had to be rebuilt. Slowly but surely, meetings were organized, letters were exchanged and projects were launched to reestablish international scientific cooperation. The work was difficult. The postwar climate of exacerbated patriotism and nationalism had turned Europe into a minefield of national sensitivities, ambitions, and prejudices that had to be taken into account. The most delicate question was that of the participation of Germany and the Central Powers in the new "international republic" of historical research.[1] The different reactions depended naturally on the extent to which the nation had suffered during the war: in Belgium and France the hostility towards Germany made any reconciliation difficult. In England this was less the case, whereas the United States for purely pragmatic reasons wished to

---

[1] Pirenne on the Vth International Conference of the Historical Sciences in Brussels, 1923 made a plea for such an "international republic" of the historical sciences. See Bechet, «La révision pacifiste des manuels scolaires. Les enjeux de la mémoire de la guerre 14–18 dans l'enseignement belge de l'Entre-deux-guerres,» 88.

see Germany reintegrated into the international scholarly guild.[1] Intertwined with the place of Germany in after-war international cooperation, the objectivity question was at the heart of the debates surrounding the important V[th] International Congress of the Historical Sciences, organized in Brussels under the presidency of Henri Pirenne.

"When it was announced…that the Belgian scholars…were to undertake to organize the fifth international gathering of historians," the American president of the *Union Académique Internationale*, Waldo G. Leland, admitted, "there was some shaking of heads and not a little doubt as to the success or even the possibility of the undertaking. Obviously a congress to be held in Brussels could not be organized on the same basis of inclusion as those which had been held before the war, and it was feared that a congress organized on any other basis might serve to perpetuate the division among historians which had been made inevitable by the disaster of 1914." Pirenne, however, had been able to convince the Americans by urging that, "history being a subject-matter as full of high explosives as was formerly theology, and the historian being of like passions with the rest of mankind…, an ecumenical congress, even if it were held in a part of the world so detached from the current of affairs as Easter Island, might not be the best means of restoring harmony", and that the choice appeared to lie "between a congress that should be as nearly 'one hundred percent' international as it might be possible to make it, or no congress at all."[2] So Brussels it was, and according to Leland the congress was "animated by a pronounced sentiment that a new epoch of international co-operation among historians should be inaugurated."[3]

---

[1] Otterspeer, *Wetenschap en wereldvrede. De Koninklijke Academie van Wetenschappen en het herstel van de internationale wetenschap tijdens het interbellum*, 26.
[2] Waldo G. Leland, "The International Congress of Historical Sciences, held at Brussels," *The American Historical Review* 28, no. 4 (1923): 639–640.
[3] Ibid., 651.

Even more ardently than before 1914, Pirenne now presented himself as a convinced internationalist. He was Belgian President of the Carnegie Endowment for International Peace (1919–1924) and of the *Union Académique Internationale* (1919–1923), he helped found the International Committee of Historical Science (1926), he was asked by Bloch and Fèbvre to become chairman of the new international historical revue *Annales*, he was the first Belgian professor to be invited by the Belgian American Educational Foundation to give a series of lectures at American universities, etc. The list of Pirenne's international engagements is endless. However, like most other participants present at the Congress of 1923 (with the notable exception of the Americans), he categorically opposed the participation of the Central Powers. To Pirenne, it had been clear as early as 1915 that any form of post-war scientific cooperation with Germany would be impossible "for at least a few generations".[1] He kept word: already during the war, he broke of all personal contacts with his former German colleagues, and when the Royal Academy of Belgium resumed its sessions in 1919 under his presidency, its first act was the suspension of all signatories of the Manifesto of the 93 amongst its foreign correspondents.

Some have argued that given his definitive rupture with many of his German colleagues tempered his self-declared internationalism, and that his pledge at the 1923 conference for an 'international republic' of historical research was, therefore, somewhat paradoxical.[2] However, Pirenne's 'abortive internationalism'[3] was, again, not so much the result of a general 'anti-German resentment', but of a deep-rooted suspicion against the essentialist and racialist perspective on nationality that had come into fashion

---

[1] "Alle toenadering onmogelijk voor eenige geslachten"; see Ghent University Archives, Hs 3704, *Journal of Paul Fredericq*, Notebook 56, 05.06.1915.
[2] See for example Bechet, «La révision pacifiste des manuels scolaires. Les enjeux de la mémoire de la guerre 14–18 dans l'enseignement belge de l'Entre-deux-guerres,» 88.
[3] Term borrowed from Jo Tollebeek, "The hyphen of national culture. The paradox of national distinctiveness in Belgium and the Netherlands, 1860–1918," *European Review* 18, no. 2 (2010): 222.

in German historiography, and of the difficulty finding German historians after the war who hadn't embraced 'Pan-Germanism'.[1] Pirenne abhorred the part German historians had played as ideologists of the war. "Two sciences have been decisively brought into requisition during the World War", he wrote, "history and chemistry. To the latter, the aggressors asked for explosives and gas. To the first, they asked for pretexts, justifications, and excuses."[2] While chemistry, in the service of the army, had made considerable progress during the war, Pirenne warned that history had "all too often lost its true essence: critical thinking and objectivity." The attitude of German historians during the war had indeed caused "a terrible crisis of civilization" and had opened a wider debate on the political and social role of scientists and intellectuals.[3] Pirenne's personal dilemma in the crucial nine years between the beginning of the war and the International Congress of the Historical Sciences in Brussels in 1923 reflected the general crises that affected the culture and the consciousness of European historiography.[4] In the post-war climate of peace negotiations and international cooperation, historians were forced to reflect on their proper occupation.

Pirenne devoted his opening address to this problem, by defining the task by which historians of his time were confronted: "This task is of a special character and of great difficulty; the historian must strive ever to be objective; he has not the right to consider only his own part, his own religion, his own country. Above all he must endeavor to be critical and impartial." In his bold and

---

[1] See John Horne, «Contentieux—Verwerking,» in *Une guerre totale? La Belgique dans la première guerre mondiale*, ed. Serge Jaumain, et al. (Bruxelles: Archives générales du Royaume, 2005), 451; Schöttler, «Henri Pirenne face à l'Allemagne de l'après-guerre ou la (re)naissance du comparatisme en histoire», 509–510.
[2] Pirenne, «Une histoire économique et sociale de la guerre,» 112. [my translation] Also quoted in Marcello Verga, «Manuels d'histoire pour la paix en Europe, 1923–1938,» in *Pour la paix en Europe. institutions et société civile dans l'entre-deux-guerres*, ed. Marta Petriciolo and donatella Cherubini (Bruxelles: Peter Lang, 2007), 503–504.
[3] Verga, «Manuels d'histoire pour la paix en Europe, 1923–1938,» 507–508.
[4] See Toubert, «Henri Pirenne et l'Allemagne (1914–1923),» 317.

stimulating style, he compared the relevance of the Great War for historians to that of a great seismic disturbance for the geologist: "It has laid before him problems heretofore unforeseen, it has presented facts which refute well-established theories, and it has upset certain scientific prejudices, especially that of race... The ancient historians had some notion of the synthesis which we now find to be essential, but the last century, which has been called the century of history, has been in fact more learned than scientific; and the national point of view in history must now give way to one that is objective and impartial."[1] As Belgium's national historian, there would be plenty of opportunities for Pirenne to put his own principle into practice—his Carnegie-contribution *La Belgique et la Guerre Mondiale* (1928) being a case in point.

The initial plan of the Carnegie Endowment for a collective international study of the causes of war had been adjusted little by little in light of the events of 1914–1918. John Bates Clark had proposed a detailed study of the First World War. However, it was a professor of history at Columbia University and the coordinator of the project from 1919 onwards, James Thompson Shotwell, who suggested "that the study should not restrict itself to diplomacy, military history, and economics, but should include all the social and political sciences in an interdisciplinary attempt to explain the meaning and consequences of the war."[2] Shotwell, influenced by the American New History that originated at the beginning of the twentieth century, thus converted the scientific project into an enormous enterprise with an explicit

---
1 Leland, "The International Congress of Historical Sciences, held at Brussels," 644–645.
2 Harold Josephson, *James T. Shotwell and the rise of internationalism in America* (London: Fairleigh Dickinson University Press/Associated University Press, 1975), 303–304, quoted in Chatriot, «Une véritable encyclopédie économique et sociale de la guerre: Les séries de la Dotation Carnegie pour la Paix Internationale (1910–1940).»

socio-economic focus, *L'Histoire économique et sociale de la guerre mondiale*.[1]

Nevertheless, there were some pressing methodological problems to be solved. First, the idea for a comparative approach to the events had to be abandoned in favor of independent studies conducted by national editorial committees. "As long", Shotwell regretted in his general preface to every volume of the series, "as the facts concerning the history of each nation are not perfectly known, it will be useless to perform comparative analyses."[2] For the direction of the Belgian committee, the choice almost naturally fell on Henri Pirenne, who could draw on his experience with social and economic history, his reputation as one of the world's finest historians and his position as a 'privileged' witness of the war atrocities. Pirenne was a member of the *Commission d'enquête sur l'invasion et l'occupation* which collected a vast documentation on the subject.[3] This rich depot of war archives, created in 1919, was well employed for writing the various Belgian volumes that appeared in the Carnegie series. Apart from his coordinating function over these individual volumes, Pirenne was also charged with writing a general synthesis of the different Belgian volumes that had appeared in the series.

Secondly, in the immediate aftermath of the events it was impossible in most countries to obtain the source material necessary for serious scientific research. To overcome this problem, it

---

[1] More information on this series can be found in Alain Chatriot, «Comprendre la Guerre. L'histoire économique et sociale de la guerre mondiale. Les séries de la Dotation Carnegie pour la Paix Internationale,» in *Histoire culturelle de la Grande Guerre*, ed. Jean-Jacques Becker (Paris: Armand Collin, 2005);Chatriot, «Une véritable encyclopédie économique et sociale de la guerre: Les séries de la Dotation Carnegie pour la Paix Internationale (1910–1940).»;Fabio Degli Espositi, «Grande guerra e storiographia. La storia economica e socialle delle Fondazione Carnegie,» *Italia Contemporanea* 224 (2005). For Shotwell's role in the New History movement, see Josephson, *op. cit.*, 37–38, 41, 46.

[2] Quoted from the preface by James T. Shotwell in every volume of the *Histoire économique et sociale de la guerre mondiale*. In Pirenne's *La Belgique et la guerre mondiale*, the quote can be found on p. vii.

[3] Pierre Alain Tallier, *Inventaire des archives de la commission d'enquête sur la violation des règles du droit des gens, des lois et des coutumes de la guerre (1914–1926)* (Bruxelles: Archives Générales du Royaume, 2001).

was decided to organize the volumes not around the documents but around the experiences of the contributors, most of whom had been eye-witnesses during the war. Naturally this solution raised questions about the historical accuracy and the objectivity of the texts. Shotwell was clever enough to anticipate possible critiques in his general preface, concluding that "this very partiality is in many cases an integral part of history, as the appreciation of the facts by contemporaries is as instructive as those facts are themselves."[1] He took trouble to underline the efforts for impartiality the authors had deployed, even if they had been actors in the conflict themselves. Nevertheless, the objectivity question continued to provoke heated discussions amongst members of the Carnegie Endowment, to the extent that, in the early 1920's, some even wondered whether a pacifist organization should actually finance volumes that seemed to glorify the war against Germany.

As for the authors themselves, many hastened to emphasize the care they took to suppress their own perspective on the events. Others openly defended their right to subjectivity, stating that "no man who has lived through this war will lay claim to be able to see it objectively."[2] Pirenne, in the preface to his volume, tried to transcend the two positions. On the one hand, he cleverly ducked out of the objectivity debate by pointing out his role as a historian. "The main goal of the author," he remarked, "has been to paint a concrete picture of the nation's existence during the four years that without any doubt have been the cruelest of its history.... *As was his task*, he has placed himself in the perspective of the occupied, not of the occupier. It is not his fault if the facts he *had to* report throw a rather gloomy shade on his description." [translation and italics mine] On the other hand, he openly admitted his subjectivity. "Historian by profession, he doesn't disguise all that

---

1 Ibid., x.
2 Albrecht Mendelssohn-Bartholdy, *The war and German society, the testament of a liberal* (New Haven: Yale University Press, 1937), 4, quoted in Chatriot, «Une véritable encyclopédie économique et sociale de la guerre: Les séries de la Dotation Carnegie pour la Paix Internationale (1910–1940).»

his work leaves to be desired. At the most, it can be considered as a provisional draft. Tens of years will be necessary before we will be able to retrace the development of the facts with enough scientific rigor, enabled by the complete knowledge of the sources and the inevitable softening of the passions and prejudices."[1] It was simply not possible at this point in history, Pirenne emphasized, to write anything more than some specific monographs. Yet he had agreed to write a synthesis because he was "convinced that every attempt at synthesis, however insufficient,…has the merit to arouse critique and lead to new investigations. Besides, this little book that reflects the impressions of an eye-witness of the events can to some extent pass for a source itself."

It worked. Pirenne's *La Belgique et la Guerre Mondiale* was received with admiration, not only for its historiographical mastery, but primarily because of its "rare human mastery", as Lucien Fèbvre observed when reviewing the book in *Annales* two years after its publication.[2] "Let's not forget," Fèbvre warned the readers, "how dangerous the enterprise must have been for the historian. The facts dated only from yesterday. What memories, what emotions will they not have brought to life again?… And how many technical difficulties! Almost no sources,…passionate testimonies, where one needs to be able to dispose of passion…and an injured national sentiment as the worst enemy of the objectivity with which a historian should observe the facts with." But Pirenne, Fèbvre admired, "never gave way to violent language or thoughts, nor to a passionate injustice towards the enemy of his country." All in all, Fèbvre concluded, the book was a veritable *tour de force*, not just as a preliminary syntheses provoking further research, but first and foremost "as a testimony, a testimony

---

[1] See Pirenne's similar acknowledgement in *Histoire de Belgique*, vol. 7, ix: «Pour pouvoir scientifiquement se rendre compte d'une époque, il faut qu'elle soit morte et que l'on puisse fouiller les entrailles comme l'anatomiste qui dissèque un cadavre.» ("In order to scientifically give an account of an era, it needs to be dead so one can probe into its bowels like the anatomist dissects a cadaver.")
[2] Lucien Fèbvre, «M. Henri Pirenne, la Belgique et la guerre mondiale,» *Annales d'histoire économique et sociale* 2, no. 5 (1930): 148–150.

before History; and there is none more serene, none more cautious, and, consequently, none more convincing."[1]

Pirenne's *La Belgique et la Guerre Mondiale* strongly reaffirmed the country's unique political *raison d'être*, claiming that on the fate of Belgium during the war had depended the fate of Europe, and therefore the fate of the world. Belgium had not just fought for its own existence; it had fought for the value of international treaties and for the right of international justice. "Never," Pirenne concluded, "has the international character of the nation been more firmly affirmed than in the Great War, from which it emerged wounded but glorious, to begin a new era in its history."[2] It was yet another proof of the intense entwinement of the historian and the nation: both had suffered much during the war, both had emerged from it stronger and more ambitious than ever. With Pirenne as its spokesman, Belgium now presented itself as the "nerve center" of Europe, the place where international networks were initiated and came together. The role Pirenne played in post-war Europe was exactly the same: that of a mediating figure who worked hard to promote international exchanges of knowledge and cooperation. But despite the tidal wave of scientific tributes and public acknowledgements, Pirenne's life ended in somewhat of a malaise. On the international stage, the onward march of national socialism in the 1930s made clear that Germany still hadn't learned its lesson. In Belgium, the total imposition of Dutch on the University of Ghent—for Pirenne the symbol of radical Flemish nationalism—had, in his eyes, marked the beginning of the end of the Belgian unity he had exalted time and again in his writings and lectures. In this sense, when Pirenne died in 1935, the old idea of 'Belgium' died, too.

The world has dramatically changed in the course of the eighty years separating us from that day, and so has historiography.

---

1 Ibid., 150.
2 Pirenne, *Histoire de Belgique VII. De la révolution de 1830 à la guerre de 1914*, 393.

However, the thought-provoking ideas Pirenne developed during and after his wartime experiences can still inspire historians today to reflect about their own prejudices, their critical thinking, and their responsibility towards humanity.

References

Christophe Bechet, «La révision pacifiste des manuels scolaires. Les enjeux de la mémoire de la guerre 14–18 dans l'enseignement belge de l'Entre-deux-guerres,» *Bijdragen tot de Eigentijdse Geschiedenis* (2008), 49–101.

Académie Royale de Belgique, *Bulletins de la Classe des Lettres et des Sciences Morales et Politiques* (Bruxelles: Lamertin, 1919).

Marnix Beyen, *Oorlog en verleden. Nationale geschiedenis in België en Nederland, 1938–1947* (Amsterdam: Amsterdam University Press, 2002).

Claire Billen, and Marc Boone, «L'histoire urbaine en Belgique: construire l'après-Pirenne entre tradition et rénovation,» *Città e Storia* 5 (2010), 3–22.

Claire Billen, and Marc Boone, "Pirenne in Brussels before 1930. Guillaume Des Marez and the relationship between a master and his student," *Belgisch Tijdschrift voor Eigentijdse Geschiedenis* XLI (2011), 459–485.

Marc Boone, "Cities in late medieval Europe: the promise and the curse of modernity," *Urban History* 39 (2012), 329–349.

Alain Chatriot, «Comprendre la Guerre. L'histoire économique et sociale de la guerre mondiale. Les séries de la Dotation Carnegie pour la Paix Internationale,» in *Histoire culturelle de la Grande Guerre*, ed. Jean-Jacques Becker (Paris: Armand Collin, 2005), 33–44.

Alain Chatriot, «Une véritable encyclopédie économique et sociale de la guerre: Les séries de la Dotation Carnegie pour la Paix Internationale (1910–1940),» in *L'Atelier du Centre de recherches historiques*, 2009).

Sophie De Schaepdrijver, *De groote oorlog: het koninkrijk België tijdens de Eerste Wereldoorlog* (Amsterdam: Atlas, 1997).

Sophie De Schaepdrijver, "'That theory of races'. Henri Pirenne on the unfinished business of the Great War," *Belgisch Tijdschrift voor Nieuwste Geschiedenis* XLI (2011), 533–552.

Fabio Degli Espositi, "Grande guerra e storiographia. La storia economica e socialle delle Fondazione Carnegie," *Italia Contemporanea* 224 (2005), 413–444.

Gita Deneckere, *1900 : België op het breukvlak van twee eeuwen* (Tielt: Lannoo, 2006).

Gita Deneckere, *Les turbulences de la Belle Epoque, Nouvelle Histoire de Belgique : 1878–1905* (Bruxelles: Le Cri, 2010).

Jan Dhondt, «Henri Pirenne: historien des institutions urbaines,» in *Hommes et pouvoirs. Les principales études de Jan Dhondt sur l'histoire du 19e et du 20e siècle* (Gent: Fondation Jan Dhondt, 1976), 53–119.

Lucien Fèbvre, «Mr Henri Pirenne, la Belgique et la guerre mondiale,» *Annales d'histoire économique et sociale* 2 (1930), 148–150.

Joanna Guldi, The spatial turn in history, In, Institute for Enabling Geospatial Scholarship at the Scholar's Lab at the University of Virginia Library, (accessed 31.08.2013].

Robert John Holton, *Cities, Capitalism and Civilization* (London: Allen and Unwin, 1986).

John Horne, «Contentieux—Verwerking,» in *Une guerre totale? La Belgique dans la première guerre mondiale*, eds. Serge Jaumain, Michaël Amara, Benoit Majerus and Antoon Vrints (Bruxelles: Archives générales du Royaume, 2005), 445–451.

Paul Hymans, *La neutralité de la Belgique* (Paris: Librairie Militaire Berger-Levrault, 1915).

Freddy Joris, *L'Athénée de Verviers et ses devanciers. Deux siècles d'histoire 1807–2007* (Verviers: Athénée Thil Lorrain, 2007).

Waldo G. Leland, "The International Congress of Historical Sciences, held at Brussels," *The American Historical Review* 28 (1923), 639–655.

Bryce Lyon, *Henri Pirenne. A biographical and intellectual study* (Ghent, 1974).
Bryce Lyon, "The war of 1914 and Henri Pirenne's revision of his methodology," in *De lectuur van het verleden. Opstellen over de geschiedenis van de geschiedschrijving aangeboden aan Reginald De Schryver*, eds. Jo Tollebeek, Georgi Verbeeck and Tom Verschaffel (Leuven, 1998), 507–516.
Bryce & Mary Lyon, and Jacques-Henri Pirenne, "'Réflexions d'un solitaire' by Henri Pirenne," *Bulletin de la Commission Royale d'Histoire* CLX (1994), 143–257.
Bryce Lyon, and Mary Lyon, *The Journal de guerre of Henri Pirenne* (Amsterdam/New York/Oxford, 1976).
Manifestation en l'honneur de M. le professeur Henri Pirenne. Bruxelles, 12 mai 1912, (Mons: Léon Dequesne, 1912).
Willem Otterspeer, *Wetenschap en wereldvrede. De Koninklijke Academie van Wetenschappen en het herstel van de internationale wetenschap tijdens het interbellum* (Amsterdam, 1997).
Carnegie Endowment for International Peace, *Summary of organization and work, 1911–1941* (Washington, 1941).
Leo Picard, *De vrijzinnigheid in Vlaanderen en de Vlaamse beweging, Diogenes Cahier 3* (Antwerpen: Humanistisch Verbond van België, 1963).
Henri Pirenne, «De la méthode comparative en histoire, discours d'ouverture du cinquième Congrès international des Sciences historiques,» in *Compte-rendu du cinquième Congrès international des Sciences historiques*, eds. Guillaume Des Marez and F. L. Ganshof (Bruxelles: M. Weissenbruch, 1923).
Henri Pirenne, *Histoire de Belgique VII. De la révolution de 1830 à la guerre de 1914* (Bruxelles: Lamertin, 1932).
Henri Pirenne, *Histoire de l'Europe. Des invasions au XVIe siècle* (Paris: Alcan, 1936).
Henri Pirenne, *La Belgique et la guerre mondiale, Histoire économique et sociale de la guerre mondiale. Série belge* (Paris/New Haven: Presses universitaires de France/Yale University Press, 1928).
Henri Pirenne, «Les origines de l'état belge,» in *La nation belge 1830–1905. Conférences jubilaires faites à l'exposition universelle et internationale de Liège en 1905* (Liège/Bruxelles: Desoer/Weissenbrucher, 1905), 1–21.
Henri Pirenne, *Mahomet et Charlemagne* (Bruxelles: Nouvelle Société d'Edition, 1937).
Henri Pirenne, «Une histoire économique et sociale de la guerre,» *Bulletin de la classe des lettres et des sciences morales et politiques de l'Académie Royale de Belgique* 4 (1924), 112–129.
Walter Prevenier, "Pirenne, Jean, Henri, Otto, Lucien, Marie, gezegd Henri, historicus," in *Nationaal Biografisch Woordenboek, 19* (Brussel, 2009), kol. 753–770.
Peter Schöttler, «Henri Pirenne face à l'Allemagne de l'après-guerre ou la (re)naissance du comparatisme en histoire» Paper presented at the Une guerre totale? La Belgique dans la Première Guerre Mondiale. Nouvelles tendances de la recherche historique, Actes du colloque international organisé à l'ULB du 15 au 17 janvier 2003, Brussels 2005.
Pierre Alain Tallier, *Inventaire des archives de la commission d'enquête sur la violation des règles du droit des gens, des lois et des coutumes de la guerre (1914–1926)* (Bruxelles: Archives Générales du Royaume, 2001).
Erik Thoen, and Eric Vanhaute, «Pirenne and economic and social theory: influences, methods and reception,» *Belgisch Tijdschrift voor Nieuwste Geschiedenis* XLI (2011), 323–353.
Jo Tollebeek, *De ziel in de fabriek. Over de arbeid van de historicus, 1998* (Amsterdam, 1998).
Jo Tollebeek, "Historical representation and the nation-state in Romantic Belgium (1830–1850)," *Journal of the History of Ideas* 59 (1998), 329–353.
Jo Tollebeek, "The hyphen of national culture. The paradox of national distinctiveness in Belgium and the Netherlands, 1860–1918," *European Review* 18 (2010), 207–225.
Jo Tollebeek, and Sarah Keymeulen, *Henri Pirenne, historian: a life in pictures* (Leuven: Lipsius Leuven 2011).
Pierre Toubert, «Henri Pirenne et l'Allemagne (1914–1923),» *Le Moyen Age* (2001), 317–320.

Ludovic Tournès, «La Dotation Carnegie pour la Paix Internationale et l'invention de la diplomatie philantropique (1880–1914),» in *L'argent de l'influence. Les fondations américains et leurs réseaux européens*, ed. Ludovic Tournès (Paris: Les Editions Autrement, 2010), 25–44.

Fernand Van Langenhove, *Comment naît un cycle de légendes, francs-tireurs et atrocités en Belgique* (Lausanne/Paris: Payot, 1916).

Hans Van Werveke, «Karl Lamprecht et Henri Pirenne,» *Bulletin de la Commission royale d'Histoire* 88 (1972), 39–60.

Marcello Verga, «Manuels d'histoire pour la paix en Europe, 1923–1938,» in *Pour la paix en Europe. Institutions et société civile dans l'entre-deux-guerres*, eds. Marta Petriciolo and Donatella Cherubini (Bruxelles: Peter Lang, 2007).

Marcello Verga, «Manuels d'histoire pour la paix en Europe, 1923–1938,» in *Pour la paix en Europe. institutions et société civile dans l'entre-deux-guerres*, eds. Marta Petriciolo and donatella Cherubini (Bruxelles: Peter Lang, 2007), 503–524.

Adriaan Verhulst, «Henri Pirenne en de Universiteit Gent,» *Revue belge de philologie et d'histoire* 76 (1998), 871–874.

Adriaan Verhulst, "Marc Bloch and Henri Pirenne on comparative history. A biographical note.," *Revue belge de philologie et d'histoire* 79 (2001), 507–510.

Cinzio Violante, *La fina della 'grande illusione': uno storico europeo tra guerra e dopoguerra, Henri Pirenne (1914–1923)* (Bologna, 1997).

Geneviève Warland, «L'Histoire de l'Europe de Henri Pirenne: Genèse de l'oeuvre et représentation en mirroir de l'Allemagne et de la Belgique,» *Textyles. Revue des Lettres belges de langue française* (2004), 38–51.

Geneviève Warland, «"Pirenne & Co.": The Internationalization of Belgian Historical Science, 1880s–1920s,» *Revue belge de philologie et d'histoire—theme issue: Beyond belgium: ecounters, exchanges and entanglements, 1900–1925* 90 (2013).

Kaat Wils, «Everyman his own sociologist. Henri Pirenne and disciplinary boundaries around 1900,» *Belgisch Tijdschrift voor Nieuwste Geschiedenis* XLI (2011), 355–380.

André Zumkir, *La genèse des partis politiques dans l'arrondissement de Verviers à l'époque du suffrage censitaire (1831–1893). IV. Les hommes* (Liège, 1997).

TRANSLATORS' NOTE

For cities and towns in the Dutch-speaking provinces, the Flemish name has been used, along with the spelling of Liège adopted after World War II. Belgium, Brussels, Ghent, and Antwerp are referred to by their English names, as is the Yser River, and "England" is called Britain when appropriate. Following Pirenne, "Flanders" occasionally refers to all of the Dutch-speaking provinces, and Dutch and Flemish, in reference to the language, are used interchangeably. Full names are given for individuals the first time they are mentioned, and a few are identified in footnotes.

Other notes occasionally translate sentences or phrases in German and Dutch, or amplify Pirenne's observations, particularly those likely to be of interest to American and British readers. These footnotes are in italics. Several small errors have been corrected in the text itself, but no attempt has been made to use the notes to systematically update *Belgium and the First World War*.

A few of Pirenne's observations have been rendered more concisely, and some redundancies eliminated. This is therefore a slightly abridged version. The preface by Columbia University professor James Shotwell, director of the Carnegie Endowment series in which this volume appeared, has also been omitted.

Pirenne writes in his Foreword that his book must be considered "a provisional sketch," as "dozens of years will be necessary" before "passions and prejudices subside." As Sarah Keymeuen notes in the Introduction, this is perhaps truer than he knew.

The passion that moves him, and, occasionally colors his account, is not, however, as readers may assume, an animus against Germany.[1] Though there are invidious comparisons most historians would not make today between the Belgian and German national characters (Pirenne of course does not regard these *sub specie aeternitatis*), an unlikely hero of Pirenne's narrative is, in fact, Moritz von Bissing, Governor General of Belgium from December 1914 until his death in April 1917. Von Bissing, "the incarnation of the military traditions of the Prussian nobility," stoutly resisted pressure from the *Oberste Heeresleitung* (OHL), the German High Command, to exploit Belgium more ruthlessly. Needless to say, the "conservation" policy he pursued, as Pirenne notes several times, was not undertaken out of sympathy for Belgium, but exclusively in the interest of Germany. Von Bissing is almost a tragic figure, dying shortly after failing to persuade the Emperor not "to squeeze the lemon dry," in his words.[2]

Though they were unable to appreciate the character of the Belgians, so different from their own, other civilian administrators also win high marks: they "worked with the zeal, dedication, and ability one would expect of German administrators. The praise they constantly received from the German press was

---

[1] Pirenne's reputation as an enemy of Germany comes less from his writings–*Mohammed and Charlemagne*, after all, exculpates the German tribes from the traditional charge of having destroyed the Roman Empire (though at the cost of renouncing their "Germanness")–as from his post-war activities as the doyen of European historians. As Keymeulen writes, he excluded his German colleagues from conferences and other academic gatherings. Most had never retracted the accusations they made against Belgium in the opening weeks of the war, and their defense of the invasion and occupation was unforgivable for Pirenne.

[2] Shotwell, who was unhappy at what he considered the anti-German bias of the five other volumes in the series on Belgium, was delighted with Pirenne's portrayal of von Bissing.

certainly deserved, despite the eulogistic tone."[1]

Readers familiar with the invasion may be surprised at the cursory treatment of the massacres of civilians committed by the German Army between August 5 and August 26. Over 5,500 men, women, and children were executed as franc-tireurs, guerilla fighters. Pirenne follows the sociologist Fernand van Langenhove in believing that the killings were the result of panic on the part of soldiers, influenced by the conviction that they were facing armed resistance from civilians, organized by the Belgian government. But he does not explain how the troops came by this conviction, apart from references to the topography of Liège and the gun workshops, dovecotes, and the language and religion of the inhabitants, and the fact that the Belgian Army was defending the country's neutrality. At times he seems to dismiss the killings and arson as an inevitable consequence of the invasion.[2] The conscription of workers that began in 1917 created more outrage and dug a lasting "abyss of hatred," Pirenne believes.[3] He devotes several times the number of pages to the deportation of workers as to the executions of civilians.

However, the failure of the Germans to win much support among the Flemish population by promoting its language and culture owed something to the bitter memories of the killings in Leuven, Aarschot, and the villages south of Mechelen. These, along with the behavior of German troops in the provinces of

---

[1] The quotation from von Bissing and those about the Governor General and his subordinates appear on pages 100, 105, and 162.
[2] Page 90. Pirenne's lack of interest is especially curious given that his first book was on Dinant, where 672 civilians were shot, and that a number of mass executions took place just to the northwest of Verviers, his home town. It is surprising also that the destruction of the Leuven University library and much of the central town, and the killing of 248 civilians in "the Oxford of Belgium," did not leave more of an impression. The deliberate burning of the library is mentioned only in passing as one more difficulty faced by scholars during the occupation. Pirenne's mentor at the University of Liège, Godefroid Kurth, along with most Belgian and French intellectuals, viewed the violence directed against civilians as the result of convictions that had become widespread among the upper classes and military in Germany by 1900, rather than spontaneous outbreaks of panic on the part of paranoid soldiers. While Pirenne, as noted, believed in a distinctive Prussian *Weltanschauung*, this had repercussions for the occupation only and not the invasion.
[3] Page 179

Liège, Luxembourg, and Namur are documented in detail in the first two volumes of the *Rapports et Documents d'Enquête* of the post-war commission investigating German war crimes. Though Pirenne was a member of the *Commission d'Enquête* and draws extensively on its third volume, he never refers to any of the evidence in volumes 1 and 2.[1]

If the OHL, imbued with the idea of spreading *Kultur* and eager to conscript Belgian workers and to requisition machinery, and the civilian German administrators, doing their best in difficult circumstances, are treated with some understanding, if not sympathy, Pirenne nonetheless has a bête noir about which he feels passionately. This is the "activist" movement, those *flamingants* who welcomed the language reforms introduced by the Germans, and worked with Berlin to create an autonomous Flanders, governed by the *Raad van Vlaanderen*, the Council of Flanders.

Pirenne does not disguise his hostility to the movement or his contempt for its leaders, and occasionally descriptions degenerate into denunciations, and invective is substituted for evidence.

It is also in the chapters on the administrative separation and on activism that Pirenne's adherence to a sociological approach, his reluctance to describe the actions and words of specific individuals, is regrettable. The activists are roundly abused, but only occasionally quoted, and then the quotes are unattributed.[2] Also

---

[1] An even more thorough and detailed account, covering only the provinces of Namur and Luxembourg, is J. Schmitz and N. Nieuwland's seven-volume *Documents pour servir a l'histoire de l'invasion allemenade dans les provinces de Namur et de Luxembourg.* (Brussels, 1919–1924).

[2] Cardinal Mercier is quoted, and the King and Queen, Adolphe Max, Émile Franqui, Ernest Solvay, Louis Franck, and Herbert Hoover, and the American, Spanish, and Dutch ministers are mentioned briefly.

The Council declared Flanders independent on December 22, 1917. However much they may share Pirenne's disgust with those who collaborated with an oppressive regime that systematically exploited the country, it will not be easy for most American and British readers to sympathize with his feelings on the subject of Flemish autonomy. No matter how many times he repeats one of the principle theses of his seven-volume *Histoire de Belgique*, that French influence spread into Flanders peaceably and voluntarily, the idea that government officials and judges should be required to use the language spoken by the local population seems unexceptionable, as does the idea that education should be provided in the native language, including higher education. Pirenne minimizes the

regrettable is his repeated accusation that activists suffered from a "war psychosis." The historian could not have anticipated how promiscuous would become the strategy of discrediting one's ideological opponents by attributing their convictions to a psychological disorder.

Pirenne's strong feelings on the subject may have nearly as much to do with the revival of the language question in the early 1920s as with the collaboration itself, and particularly with the renewed attempt to convert the University of Ghent into an entirely Dutch-speaking institution. When this finally came to pass in 1930, Pirenne resigned his professorship.

If the activists are the villains, the true hero of Pirenne's book is the Belgian people collectively, but more specifically the *Comité National de Secours et d'Alimentation*. The organization was responsible for distributing the grain brought into Belgium via Rotterdam by the American-run Commission for Relief in Belgium, which also receives well-deserved accolades. As Pirenne makes clear, the *Comité* not only helped keep

---

resistance these demands met with on the part of the francophone upper middle-class that ruled Belgium from its inception. Tellingly, one of the first acts the Germans took to win support in Flanders was simply to enforce a Belgian law that had been on the books since 1878 requiring government officials to communicate in Dutch with individuals and local administrations in the Dutch-speaking regions.

The historian is bemused that the Germans required that tram stops in Brussels be announced in both languages, and that they designated Namur, "a second-class city," the capital of the Walloon region. The *Wallons* of course, selected Namur themselves as their capital after Belgium became a federal state in 1993. The administrative separation he attacks with such vehemence has been a reality for several decades. (Key reforms were enacted in 1970–1, 1980, 1988–9, and 1993.) The haute-bourgeois *franscillons* of Ghent, Bruges, and Antwerp–Pirenne married into one prominent family–were not representative of public opinion in the Flemish-speaking provinces. In retrospect, the two World Wars only delayed the inevitable, because of the association of some Flemish nationalists with the German invaders, though it can also be argued that the reforms of 1914–1918 sharpened the desire of *flamingants* that Dutch be granted full parity with French.

Chapter 1, Pirenne's admirable *tour d'horizon* of Belgium in 1914, includes a fair-minded overview of the language question. But for a more balanced treatment of the activists and Flemish nationalism one should consult in English S. Clough, *A History of the Flemish Movement in Belgium* (New York, 1968 [1930]) and the introduction in T. Hermans, L. Vos, and L. Wils, *The Flemish Movement* (London, 1992), and also L. Wils, *Flamenpolitik en aktivisme* (Leuven, 1974) and Chapters V and VIII of S. Schaepdrijver, *De Groote Oorlog : het koninkrijk België tijdens de Eerste Wereldoorlog* (Amsterdam, 1998) (French translation: *La Belgique et la Premier Guerre Mondiale* (Brussels, 2012))

Belgians from starving, but it was the heart of the resistance to the occupation, along with municipal administrators. Hastily granted immunities by the first Governor General of Belgium, Wilhelm Colmar von der Golz, who was anxious to avert a food crisis and the disorder that would follow, tenaciously protected by the ministers[1] of the U.S., Spain, and the Netherlands—the food coming from America was legally the personal property of Brand Whitlock, the U.S. Minister—the *Comité* provided a central organization through which policy decisions regarding German initiatives could be made and a network through which they could be communicated. It was, as Pirenne says, quoting von Bissing, a state within a state. In his account of the activities of the *Comité*, the tone may occasionally become overly celebratory, but his pride in its work is understandable.

Despite its biases, *Belgium in the First World War* is a valuable work. Though from a post-World War II perspective, the behavior of the Germans seems comparatively civilized,[2] the suffering the country endured during the war, so vivid to Americans and British at the time, has been largely forgotten. The hunger, the deprivations, the unemployment, the deportations, the indignities of home invasions and confiscations, the censorship (perhaps the deprivation felt most keenly by educated Belgians), and, finally, the conscription of labor and the dismantling and

---

[1] The papacy had an ambassador in Brussels, but until after the First World War all other foreign diplomats were ministers heading legations, not embassies.

[2] The fact that occupied Poland during World War II was, like Belgium during World War I, called the *Generalgouvernement*, General Government, underscores the contrast. Fewer than 100 Belgians were killed from September 1914 until November 1918, excluding those convicted of espionage and those attempting to escape to the Netherlands. Around 6 million Poles and Polish Jews lost their lives in World War II. About 120,000 Belgian men were conscripted by the Germans after October, 1916. During the Second World War, the number of slave laborers working for the Third Reich is estimated at 12 to 15 million. Germans had a great many more scruples in 1914 than they would have twenty-five years later.

destruction of factories, are all clearly described and analyzed.[1]

Belgium and the First World War chronicles, with great passion and eloquence, the depth of the catastrophe and the stoicism and the resiliency with which Belgians responded.

---

[1] Chapter VII should be required reading for journalists and teachers who still today repeat the myth about "punitive" reparations demanded of the Germans in the Versailles Treaty. The Germans themselves estimated in October 1917 that, if they won the war, they ought to reimburse Belgium between 5 and 8.5 billion francs, and the war still had one more year to run, in which the destruction of factories and the seizure of equipment accelerated. The German Chancellor, after all, had declared on August 4, 1914, that the invasion of Belgium was "a wrong" that "we will try to make good."

After the war, the Belgian government calculated that Germany owed $2.22 billion (about $25.8 billion today) for damages inflicted on the country and another $537.5 million in war contributions it had levied on towns and provinces. The devastation in northern France was more extensive, and was calculated at over $16 billion. Of this total, Germany paid $5.375 billion, relying on American loans that were never repaid. Because of British claims as well as French, Belgium wound up receiving only about $500 million in reparations.

BELGIUM
and the First
World War

FOREWORD

Belgium's situation during the war differed radically from that of the other belligerents. Invaded at the beginning of the war, the country was entirely occupied by the enemy from October 1914, except for a narrow strip of land south of the Yser River. The King established himself there with the army, over which he exercised supreme command. As its territory was entirely filled with troops and military support services, the government was obliged to relocate on October 13 to Sainte-Adresse, near Le Havre. After this date, the state existed only beyond Belgium's boundaries. It was obliged to abandon its citizens to the foreign power that had seized the country.

Thus, with the exception of the ten weeks after the violation of neutrality until the middle of October (August 4–October 13, 1914), the history of Belgium during the World War is simply the story of its occupation by Germany. As a result of the state of war, social services, industrial and commercial regulation, and policing and administration were no longer provided by the government, but by either the invader or the population itself.

The Belgian series in this collection of studies is thus distinguished by the special nature of its case. Whereas the other series are primarily dedicated to analyzing the war-time economic policies of the various governments, one volume was all was required to describe the efforts of the government at Sainte-Adresse, given the extraordinary conditions imposed on it, to assist those Belgians who had emigrated, to relieve the conditions of those remaining under German occupation, and to prepare for the country's postwar economic recovery.[1] All the other works in this series concern the regime imposed by the occupier. Some describe the legislation and administrative changes introduced by Germany[2] or, more specifically, regulations concerning work[3] and industry[4], while others trace the initiatives taken by the people themselves to meet their most pressing needs—provisioning[5] and unemployment[6]. Taken as a whole, they give the reader an excellent picture of a nation subjugated to the rigors of modern warfare. The studies explore not only economic or social phenomena, but psychological and ethical questions. Historians and politicians would do well to study the spontaneous reaction of the nation against foreign domination.

Unlike previous works in the Belgian series, all conceived as monographs, this is an attempt at a synthesis. It's an effort not only to combine in a single survey the data so carefully collected by previous authors, but to provide a general overview of the occupation.

It is necessary to begin by summarizing the economic, political, and social conditions of Belgium at the time of the invasion. This is the subject of the first chapter. It begins early in the country's history, as it's impossible to understand the attitude of the conquered toward their conquerors without entering into some detail into the historical reasons for their incompatible temperaments. In comparing Germany to Belgium, the author, needless to say, is referring not to the German people, but rather to imperial and official Germany, as it existed until the armistice.

The following chapters cover, respectively, the invasion of the country, the general conditions during the occupation, the

---

1 F. G. Van Langenhove, *L'Action du government belge en matière économique pendant la guerre*.
2 J. Pirenne and M. Vauthier, *La Législation et l'administration allemandes en Belgique*.
3 F. Passelecq, *La Déportation e le travail forcé des ouvriers et de la population civile*
4 Ch. De Kerchove, *L'industrie belge pendant l'occupation allemande*.
5 A. Henry, *La Ravitaillement de la Belgique pendant l'occupation allemande*.
6 E. Mahaim, *Le Secours-chômage en Belgique pendant l'occupation allemande*.

organization of the occupation, the economic and social crisis that resulted from it, the activity of the Commission for Relief in Belgium and the *Comité National de secours et d'alimentation*, the exploitation of the country, the administrative division and, lastly, the role of "activism." Of the final two chapters, the second to last traces very rapidly the downfall of the German regime, while the last one attempts to describe, unfortunately in a very incomplete way, the condition of the hundreds of thousands of Belgians forced by the war to live abroad.[1]

The main purpose of the author has been to provide a detailed picture of the nation during the four years that have certainly been the cruelest in its history. More than describing the German regime itself, he wanted to explore its impact. In other words, he adopted the point of view of the occupied rather than the occupier.[2] It's not his fault if the facts that he has had to report give his description a rather somber tone.

As a professional historian, he does not at all conceal what's missing in his work. It can be considered, more than anything, a provisional sketch. Dozens of years will be necessary before we can retrace events with sufficient scientific rigor, through a thorough study of the sources and after passions and prejudices subside, as they inevitably will. Although it is possible to write special monographs now, it is certainly still too soon to go beyond that. However, if the author took a risk, it's because he is convinced that all attempts at synthesis, however inadequate, are worthwhile if only for the information they pull together and the hypotheses they offer. They provoke critiques and inspire new investigations. Moreover this little book, which includes the author's reflections on events to which he was an eye-witness, can, to a certain degree,

---

1 For the period following the war, one should consult *La Belgique restaurèe*, a sociological study published under the direction of Ernest Mahaim, Brussels.
2 Conversely, M. L. Von Köler, *Die Staatsverwaltung der Besetzten Gabiete in Belgien*, 1927 (German series of this collection) describes the system of German institutions, their purpose and how they functioned, but without discussing the consequences for the population.

itself serve as a primary source.¹ If it has no other merit, in this way at least the book fulfills the desiderata of an economic and social history of the World War.

The author does not claim to have read the enormous quantity of printed material that appeared on this subject both during and after the war. He did not even consider this impossible and pointless task. He limited himself, in addition, to the official documents published by the Belgian and German governments, to the reports of the *Comité National de secours et d'alimentation,* those of the Commission for Relief in Belgium, those of the (Belgian) Commission of Inquiry on Human Rights Violations, as well as the monographs already cited in the Belgian series of this collection and a certain number of studies, memoirs, and publications of every kind whose number continues to proliferate. It would have been useless to add to this volume to a bibliography, for which it is sufficient to consult the *Bulletin of War Archives* (Brussels, since 1922) and the *Belgian Review of Books, Documents and War Archives* (Brussels, since 1924).

The extensive collection of *War Archives,* created in Brussels by the German government on November 15, 1919, has naturally contributed. The excellent classification of it by its curator, Mr. J. Vannérus, has provided a thread through the thousands of documents that it contains, including papers abandoned in Belgium by the German authorities upon the evacuation from the country that provide irrefutable documentation of the Reich's policies and practices. The archives of the Council of Flanders, of which an analytical edition has appeared, were also consulted.²

Lastly, the author was fortunate enough to have benefited from valuable notes and information that several people were

---

1 The author lived in Ghent from the beginning of the war until his deportation to Germany on March 16, 1916. During that time, he was authorized twice to spend a day in Brussels and, another time, to spend two days in Verviers
2 The Archives of the Council of Flanders (*Raad van Vlaanderen*), published by the National League for Belgian Unity (*Brussels, 1928, 551 pages in-4 vol.*) These archives, property of the National League for Belgian Unity, will eventually be deposited into the War Archives.

kind enough to provide. He wishes to express his deep gratitude to his friends Mr. J. Cuvelier and Mr. J. Vannérus. The former shared a collection of material of the utmost importance, while the latter guided the author through archives with endless good cheer. Also, Mr. Louis Franck was kind enough to share details on the activity of the Belgian parliament representatives who lived inside the country during the war, and the author is indebted to Mr. A. de Ridder for abundant bibliographical assistance.

CHAPTER ONE

Belgium on the eve of the war

§ 1. — The Country And Its Inhabitants

A quick look at the map will reveal that Belgium has no geographical coherence. Except for the west, where the sea meets the coast of Flanders, Belgium is without natural boundaries. Nothing but a customs line separates the country's territory from that of the three states that border it: Holland on the north, Germany on the east, and France on the south. Geographically, Belgium is an extension of the other territories. Its entire north region belongs to Europe's Great Plains, which extends from the Baltic Sea to the North Sea, while in the south, the hills of Condroz and the Ardennes are the last undulations of a mountain chain extending to the Alps. Nature has therefore contributed nothing to the formation of Belgium. The country owes its existence entirely to history: wars and international treaties led to its creation. The current boundaries are similar to those imposed on the country during the 17th century by the victorious wars of the United Provinces and France against the kings of Spain, successors of Charles V.[1]

---

1 Charles V, 'natural prince' of the Netherlands, inherited on January 23, 1516 the Spanish kingdoms that had been ruled by his mother, Joan of Castille. The dynastic union created by this event between the Netherlands and Spain affected Belgium. The Northern provinces (the United Provinces) separated at the end of Philip II's reign, until the death of Charles II (1700). As a result of the War of the Spanish Succession, the Austrian branch of the House of Hapsburg assumed sovereignty over Belgium (the Treaty of Utrecht, 1713). The dynastic union, inaugurated in the 16th century, continued, but, in a real sense, there was no more an "Austrian domination" than there had been a "Spanish domination." The country's autonomy did not disappear until it was annexed to France after the battle of Fleurus (1794). With the fall of the French Empire, the European Powers recognized Belgium as an independent and perpetually neutral state by the treaties of 1839.

The treaties of 1839, which ratified the existence of modern Belgium, perpetuated and contributed even further to the oddities of a configuration that owed everything to politics. Among these are the strip of land imposed between Flanders and the maritime Scheldt River provinces, the long corridor by which Holland stretches along the Meuse to Visé and, lastly, the extension of the Grand Duchy of Luxembourg into Belgian Luxembourg.[1] Belgium is thus the result of the politics of equilibrium played by the Great Powers during the modern era. Its borders have been assigned to it in virtue of diplomatic considerations unrelated to the interests of its inhabitants.

This lack of geographic unity is matched by a no less striking absence of linguistic unity. Like Switzerland, Belgium contains different language groups. A nearly straight line running from La Panne to Visé separates the Flemish population in the north from the Walloon population in the south. To the east and south of Verviers and around Arlon, about 17,000 inhabitants speak German. According to the latest census, in 1920, out of a total population of 7,405,569, 2,855,835 spoke only French and 3,187,073 spoke only Flemish.[2]

The literary language of the Flemish is Dutch, that of the Walloons, French. In daily life, both the former and the latter often use dialects that are sometimes rather different. While in Switzerland the knowledge of German is almost as widespread as a second language among the French-speaking Swiss as French is among the Germanic Swiss, in Belgium the knowledge of Flemish is as rare among the Walloons as that of French is widespread in the Flemish-speaking part of the country. Of

---

1 The treaties of 1839 cut the territory of Luxembourg in two. The Western part was assigned to the Kingdom of Belgium, while the Eastern part was set up as a Grand Duchy for the benefit of the oldest branch of the House of Nassau.
2 These figures include the entire population. The linguistic competency of children is based on the language spoken by their parents. If we look at inhabitants age 21 and older in the 1920 census, 1,988,469 people spoke exclusively French and 1,892,606 spoke only Flemish. In 1910, those numbers were respectively 1,823,825 and 1,760,656. From 1910 to 1920, the number of German-speaking inhabitants decreased from 31,415 in 1910 to 16,877 in 1920.

the 960,960 bilingual Belgians reported in the 1920 statistics[1] nine-tenths are probably of Flemish origin. Therefore it is not correct to say that Belgium is bilingual, if by "bilingual" one means a country where the knowledge of the two languages is very widespread. This *is* true, however, of the Flemish part of the country. Since the 12th century, French has been increasingly used in the northern provinces. This was not the result of conquest or violence. Unlike the situation in Bohemia or Poland, where the Germans subjugated or expelled the Slavs, neither one of Belgium's populations has ever attempted to dominate the other politically or linguistically. So-called race struggles have not occurred in the country. With the exception of the Brussels urban area, the language split is still today for all intents and purposes what it was during the time of the Salian Franks, the ancestors of the Flemish, in 5th century Roman Belgium. French was introduced to Flanders only by political and economic relations with France and the Walloon territories, beginning in the Middle Ages. It's worth noting that the introduction of French has for the most part affected only the upper classes of society: the nobility and bourgeoisie.

The great majority of people continued, as they continue today, to use their national language exclusively. The adoption of French by the privileged minority had already made such great progress by the 18th century that a certain number of its members considered Flemish as merely a dialect used by the lower classes. This state of things was even more accentuated during the union of Belgium and France from 1794 to 1815. Measures taken by the government of the Netherlands during the fifteen years of its rule (1815–1830) did not succeed in modifying it. After the revolution of 1830, the use of French continued to expand, so much so that by around 1848 it provoked a reaction: the movement known as *flamingant*, the importance of which has steadily increased.

---

[1] This figure shrinks to 728,738 if we consider inhabitants ages 21 and above.

The failure of the Flemish language to penetrate Walloon Belgium is as understandable as the rapid introduction of French into Flemish Belgium. The limited extent to which Dutch has spread throughout the world does not encourage its acquisition by those other than native speakers of the language. For a Flemish Belgian, French is the means of communication not only with its fellow countryman, but also with the rest of civilization. On the other hand, the Walloon Belgian feels no necessity to learn Dutch unless he wishes to pursue a profession in Flanders. He would prefer, among the Germanic languages, German or English. Each of these, with an infinitely greater number of speakers, would be of more use to him. As remarkable as Dutch literature has been in times past and still is today, conditions have not permitted the language to spread widely even in Belgium. Religious differences between Catholic Belgians and Calvininst Dutch have obstructed, and continue to obstruct, though less strongly, the diffusion of Flemish.

It is important to restate that the various languages have encountered no opposition in Belgium. Of course, one observes between the two parts of the country a range of customs and sentiments. However, this never translates into hostility. There is no antipathy among these populations which, through the centuries, have shared a common destiny, faced the same enemies, suffered the same catastrophes, and lived under similar institutions. Besides, intermarriage is so widespread, especially among middle-class citizens, that it would be quite difficult today to determine who belongs to this or that group. Traveling around the country, one sees how much less marked are the contrasts in Belgium than in Switzerland. Although there are considerable differences, for example, between Liège and Ghent, they are much less obvious than those one initially observes between Geneva and Basel.

The country's linguistic diversity is counterbalanced by religious, economic, and political unity.

For the most part, Belgians belong to the Catholic faith. There is hardly another country, if any at all, where the number of dissenters is so low. Protestants amount to just 15,000 to 20,000 and there are 3,000 to 4,000 Jews. Of course faith is not the same thing as religious fervor. Although almost all Belgians are baptized, many of them abstain from religious practices and many more regard the Church with distinct antipathy. Free thinkers and lapsed Catholics abound in the big cities. Nonetheless, in Flanders most people attend church faithfully, and perhaps this is what most distinguishes it from Walloon Belgium. The influence of the clergy, particularly in rural areas, is as strong today as a century ago. However, as the country becomes more industrialized and workers embrace socialism, skepticism advances. But if Catholicism is waning, it is not making way for another church. Those who leave the Church do not seek a replacement. Protestant propaganda has achieved results that are hardly proportional to its efforts. Recently, a devotionist cult, the *Antoinistes* has gained some followers in certain parts of the Walloon regions. All in all, religious sentiment, as inevitably happens in Catholic countries, seems to be nourished only by the Church. This is true throughout the country. It's not accurate to say that the Flemish are more religious than Walloons. The Church has simply done a better job at maintaining its hold on the former. However, in both groups, if people leave the Church, they don't replace their faith with a different one.

At the beginning of the 20th century, economic activity was more intense in Belgium than in any other country in the world. Remarkably, one can observe the same phenomenon at the beginning of the Middle Ages. From the start of the 12th century to the end of the 16th century, no other region in Europe had cities so large. The ports of Bruges and Antwerp were the North's international trade centers par excellence and no industry rivaled the cloth trade of Flanders and Brabant. By the 13th century, the population of Flanders was so dense that it needed to import part of its food supply. Then as now, Belgium's prosperity depended on its exports.[1] Trade networks were extraordinarily well-developed, and the investment of capital in production much more intensive than anywhere else north of the Alps. The geographical location of the territory is undoubtedly responsible for the vigorous growth of commerce and industry. Criss-crossed by numerous navigable rivers, in direct communication with the sea, placed at the crossroads of the commercial routes of France, Germany, and England, Belgium was destined by nature for rapid and intense development. However, by the same token, it was also vulnerable to the rivalries of the Powers that surrounded it. As soon as the conflict between the great states began, Belgium saw itself drawn into their wars. The workshop and the marketplace of Europe became its battlefield. Politics deprived it of the favors that nature had so abundantly provided. The closing of the Scheldt River in 1648 condemned it to decadence, and England and the United Provinces strove jealously to prevent its revival. The protectionism of its neighbors suffocated its commercial activity. However, with remarkable tenacity, Belgium's population fought relentlessly against its bad luck. The technical skills and industriousness bequeathed by its long prosperity kept the country from giving up. Some channels were built at Ostend; in 1722 an "Indies Company" was forced to shut down by maritime powers disturbed by its progress. The lace and linen industries remained important, favored by the abundance of raw materials and the skills of their workers, passed on from generation to generation. The country survived in this anomalous situation. Though equipped with everything that would have permitted trade and industry to flourish, the Belgium was forced by external constraints to stagnate and wait for better times.

Its annexation to the French Republic, then the Empire, (1794–1815) released Belgium's captive energy. Suddenly, the

---

[1] It is of course anachronistic to refer to the territory of modern Belgium by that name before 1830, but Pirenne felt it too cumbersome to do otherwise.

immense markets of the state into which it had been incorporated were opened up to it.

Industry revived right away. Cotton spinning, wool manufacture, and sugar beet production spread. At the same time the coal deposits of Liège and Hainaut began to be actively exploited. Metallurgy, machine construction, weapons manufacture, and the glass industry developed with surprising speed. The fall of the French Empire did not put an end to this renewed prosperity. Reunited with Holland to form with it the Kingdom of the Netherlands, Belgium experienced a period of new progress thanks to the outlets supplied to its industry from the Dutch colonies and the intelligent policies of King William. However, it seemed that the revolution of 1830 would deal a fatal blow. Once again the Scheldt was closed, or at least traffic on the river was subject to heavy tolls. The Dutch ports attracted German commerce. The relationship with Southeast Asia was no longer possible. French protectionism on the one hand and British competition on the other seemed to portend a new period of decline.

However, the same energy that had supported the nation during the 17th and 18th centuries came to its rescue once more. To keep foreign trade in Antwerp, the government of Leopold I, in 1834, commissioned the first railroads on the European continent. A free-trade policy, boldly adopted despite the protectionism of neighboring states, managed to procure raw materials at low prices. The county's vast coal deposits gave it an incalculable advantage. Much thought was put into promoting the circulation of goods by developing a network of navigable waterways, roads, and railroads. These efforts have not slowed since then. On the eve of the war, Belgium was crisscrossed by 4,700 kilometers of large-gauge railroad transporting annually more than 210 million travelers and around 70 million tons of merchandise. This does not include a network of about 4,000 kilometers of small-gauge railroad that transported around 100 million travelers and more than 7 million tons. To this network of railroads, one must add around 10,000 kilometers of major roadways and a dense network of local roads. Lastly, there were around 2,200 kilometers of navigable waterways, channels, or re-channeled rivers. More ships crowded into Antwerp than at any other time, and its docks competed with those of rivals such as Rotterdam and Hamburg. As in the 16th century, it regained the rank of a great cosmopolitan port. The revoking of the river toll in 1863 facilitated its ascent, together with the railroads and development of industries along its wharves that provided return freight for the ships.

By 1914 more than 7,000 vessels and 14 million tons of goods arrived and departed annually. The general activity of the country revived the secondary ports of Ostend and Nieuwpoort. That of Zeebrugge was completed in 1905. In the interior, Brussels, Ghent, and Bruges, connected to the sea by large-section channels, received important maritime installations. The economic revival triggered rapid population growth. The number of inhabitants went from 3,785,814 in 1831 to 7,451,903 in 1909. According to the 1910 census, 1,551,950 individuals were farmers or agricultural workers, while 3,249,184 were employed in the industrial sector, respectively 20 percent and 43 percent of the total population.

Farming was no less effective than industry. Wherever one looks, they develop in concert. A hotchpotch of factories and cultivated fields, with furrows and crops extending right to the factory walls, is a distinctive feature of the Belgian landscape. Except in the sandy regions of Campine or the marshy fens and the shale plateaus of the the Ardennes, not an inch of soil goes uncultivated. In places where the soil is too poor to produce other things, fir plantations have proliferated, providing timber for the underground tunnels of mines. Before the war there were fewer than 1,000 square kilometers of uncultivated land. Cereal for human consumption and feed for cattle were the dominant crops, together with potatoes. Soil yield was unsurpassed, except in Denmark, with 2,500 kilograms of wheat per hectare. Livestock included 1,800,000 head of cattle, 1,400,000 pigs, and 320,000 horses, and were higher by surface area than any in other country.

Yet agricultural production was far from sufficient to feed Belgium's population. In this respect, the situation of Belgium was comparable to that of Britain, even though Belgium had superior farming.

One has only to consider the country's extraordinary population density. As in the Middle Ages, but with much higher numbers, Belgium, with 252 inhabitants per square kilometer, led every other country in the world. In 1913 Belgium had to import 4 million tons of foodstuff, of which three-fourths were grain, to offset the deficit of indigenous production, which provided only 22 percent of the nation's requirements.

In Hainaut and the countryside around Liège, the exploitation of coal had brought about a great proliferation of metallurgical facilities, high-intensity kilns, machine construction shops, electrical plants, etc. The manufacture of windows and glassware enjoyed an unrivaled reputation. Located at the entrance of Liège province, Verviers was a first class center of the weaving, washing, and knitting of wool. Deprived of the collieries that transformed the basins of Mons, Charleroi, and Liège into exclusively industrial regions, Flanders did not experience such a vigorous development of linen and cotton works. Such works have nonetheless proliferated in the countryside around Ghent, Kortrijk, Sint-Nikolaas, and Lokeren. But as a whole, the Flemish part of the country is less heavily industrialized than Wallonia. Approximately half of the population is employed in agriculture, whereas farming employs only a quarter of the population in Hainaut and the province of Liège.

Except for coal, industry must import raw materials from foreign countries (cotton, wool, iron), so one can see how complex and delicate Belgium's economic situation is. All the parts of the economy are linked in a general equilibrium. None of these parts can lag without others being affected, as well. In this respect, the country is tightly cohesive. Its abundant population depends continuously on exchanges of goods and services. Belgium somewhat resembles a single large city. Even in the 16th century, Spanish soldiers remarked on this. In reality, a number of regions are nothing but suburbs radiating out from a center into other suburbs. Most of the inhabitants live in the cities or in industrial towns. The purely rural municipalities hold less than one-third of the population. Belgium hardly has any true peasants, the type that one still encouters in many regions of France or Germany, whose life revolves around the interests of the village and whose outlook contrasts so starkly with that of city-dwellers.

The economy has led to the proliferation of a particular type of worker, part-rural and part-urban. These are the laborers who ride the low-cost trains from their villages to the factories and then go home at the end of the day. In the morning and in the evening there is a true population exodus on the "workers' trains." In 1906, it was estimated that these trains transported more than 125,000 people per day. The mobility of workers is matched by that of businesspeople, traveling salesmen, and all sorts of brokers and agents who also enjoy the ease of transportation and the affordable travel passes. On Wednesdays, the day the stock exchange opens, Brussels is the meeting point of all Belgium.

No other capital city displays a similar character. One might almost imagine that Brussels' location was selected by a compass, as it lies in the exact center of the nation: fifty minutes by rail from Antwerp and Ghent; one and a half hours from Liège. The metropolitan area of Brussels, with its 770,000 inhabitants, contains ten percent of the total population of Belgium. Moreover, established astride the language frontier, it is equally convenient for both Flemish and Walloons. It is truly ecumenical. The original Flemish base of its population continues to receive immigrants from all parts of the country. Compared to the other large cities, which preserve their regional character, Flemish or Walloon, Brussels seems to be uniquely Belgian. Its originality surprises or shocks observers. It is too Flemish for the Walloons and too Walloon for the Flemish. This is to say, it's neither one nor the other. The capital of the Brabant, it lost its provincial nature and became the capital of Belgium. It is not only the residence of the king and the seat of Parliament and of the central administration, but it has also become and continues to be the center of national activity. Most of the large banks and industrial and commercial companies are based there. Artistic and scientific movements gravitate to Brussels and the major political parties have established their headquarters in the city.

However, Brussels is still very far from achieving the dominance that Paris exercises over France. Provincial and regional life remains very active in Belgium. Cities such as Antwerp, Ghent, and Liège preserve a striking originality that they work carefully to maintain. Those who know only Brussels do not know Belgium. A great many of the country's foremost artists, writers, and scholars work in the provinces. The universities of Ghent, Liège, and Leuven have as many resources and activities as their sister university in the capital. Many social initiatives and movements, the *Vooruit* in Ghent, the *Boerenbonden*, the farmers unions, and the *Université de Travail* in Charleroi have been created without the participation of Brussels. Although the most important newspapers and journals are published in the capital, there are also influential papers in the provinces. It is true, though, that Brussels exercises a heavy intellectual and psychological influence over the country, and that it serves as a uniquely energetic agent of unity and cohesion. The multiple relationships that the rest of the country has with Brussels have created a national identity and outlook opposed to particularistic tendencies and regional exclusiveness.

If one wouldn't wish to compare the capital of Belgium to the brain of an animal, it's appropriate to compare it to the nucleus of a complex molecule.

All this to say that, among other European states, Belgium has a distinctive physiognomy. Since the country appears to lack both geographic unity and unity of language, it's tempting to refuse to call it a nation and to consider it the artificial creation of international politics. But one must be careful not to confuse politics with history. Of course for four centuries the Great Powers have determined its fate, intervening in a heavy-handed way in the affairs of a country whose territory is in some ways the key to European equilibrium. But to refuse to acknowledge the country's right to exist is to ignore that day in the 15th century when the seventeen provinces of the Netherlands were united under the rule of the Duke of Burgundy, establishing a new state along the North Sea that modern Belgium and Holland represent today. Their separation in the 16th century was but the consequence of a religious revolution. On one hand, by adopting Protestantism, Holland at the same time shook off the sovereignty of Spain, to which it had been subject, just like Belgium, since the reign of Charles V. On the other hand, Belgium, remaining faithful to Catholicism, preserved the hereditary sovereigns, the Hapsburgs of Spain and then, after the Treaty of Utrecht, the Hapsburgs of Austria. Under both it retained its own constitution. Nothing could be more false than considering Belgium, before the 19th century, as submitting to foreign domination. It was governed by a regime of personal union, not by a regime of conquest. The country recognized the Hapsburg sovereigns as they truly were: the legitimate successors of the Dukes of Burgundy who continued to respect the country's autonomy. Belgium remained faithful to them despite the misfortunes inflicted on it by their wars. It was only at the end of the 18th century, when Joseph II claimed the right to impose his "enlightened despotism" on the country, that Belgium rebelled, in a movement joined by all provinces, and established a federal republic. In this respect, its revolution against Austria in 1788 closely resembled the revolution of the colonies of North America against England. Afterward, despite its annexation by France and subsequent "amalgamation" with Holland in the Kingdom of the Netherlands, Belgium never abandoned hope of recovering its independence.

Despite their linguistic differences, the institutions, interests, social status, and suffering they've shared have given Belgium's inhabitants a common national consciousness. The Revolution of 1830 was the brilliant affirmation of this to the rest of Europe. The Powers recognized it as a fait accompli to avoid a general war. They certainly didn't create a Belgian nationality; they only unwillingly acknowledged it. What is artificial is not its existence, but the conditions with which Europe encumbered it. The permanent neutrality that the treaties of 1839 imposed on Belgium and the guarantee that they give to its independence are only a consequence of the proclamation of this independence by Belgium itself. Far from being the creation of diplomacy, as is so often said, the country owes its existence to the will of its people, rising in opposition to diplomacy.

§ II. — POLITICAL ORGANIZATION

As with most Western European states, the political organization of Belgium is closely connected to the principles proclaimed and put into practice by the French Revolution. None of the institutions of the old regime were preserved in the Constitution of 1830, except a few traditional names. The French conquest of 1794 had made a clean sweep of the past, making it impossible to restore anything after Waterloo. The "fundamental law" that governed the Belgians during their reunion with Holland in the Kingdom of the Netherlands kept pretty much intact the Napoleonic administration system. It reserved the government for the king. The Estates General, a parliament with limited prerogatives, exercised no real power.

The revolution of 1830 targeted this monarchic regime. Its goal and its outcome were to give the country a constitution that no longer rested on the sovereignty of the crown, but on national sovereignty, in a purely parliamentary form. It reserved only executive power for the king. As far as the legislative power, the king cooperates with the two chambers, the Senate and House of Representatives. His ministers, who answer to the Constitution, must be chosen by the parties that win the electoral majority. Parliament can otherwise reject the budget, making it impossible to perform the functions of government.[1]

The Belgian Constitution is as liberal as it is parliamentary. A product of the parties that united against the King of Holland, the Catholic Party and the Liberal Party, it promulgates the liberties to which each of the parties aspired, so that in the end it promulgates all. On behalf of the Catholics, it established freedom of religion and teaching; on behalf of the Liberals, it established freedom of the press. No other constitution guaranteed such a wide range of individual rights. It advanced them to the point of weakening executive power. The men who drafted the Constitution were clearly inspired by a keen hostility to administrative rule and to the state. They believed that freedom, which in their eyes was beneficial in itself, could be restricted only in respect to the freedom of others. The state appeared to them as a "necessary evil" and its sphere of action was reduced to a minimum.

Truly they enacted legislation not from the point of view of the national community, but from the standpoint of the citizens that made up such a community. Their extreme liberalism followed from their extreme individualism. All precautions were taken to reduce as much as possible the powers of the government. The Constitution abstains from establishing a State Council and although it places a High Chamber, the Senate, ahead of the Chamber of Representatives, it takes care to make it purely elective and to keep the king from exercising any influence over the selection of its members. The Senate and the Chamber of Representatives come from the same electoral body; the only

---

[1] P. Voy, P. Errera, *Traité de droit public belge* (Paris, 1909); M. H. Reed, *Government and politics of Belgium* (New York, 1924); M. Vauthier, *Précis du droit administratif de la Belgique* (Brussels, 1928)

difference between them is that the Senators are elected by voters paying a higher poll tax. This constitutes a conservative guarantee and does not in the least buttress the crown.

The extraordinary liberalism of the Belgian Constitution is explained not only by the fact that it was the work of a coalition of parties, but also by the fact that those two parties were recruited from the middle class. If the revolution of 1830 was the work of the people, it was the middle class that directed it. At the time the revolution broke out, the social question was not discussed and modern class consciousness didn't exist. The people did not demand universal suffrage. Following the ideas of the time, the essential guarantee of all free government lay in the independence of the elector. By making the right to vote subject to the payment of a fee, members of the National Congress didn't intend that the middle class dominate the government. Rather, they simply believed that those living on the brink of poverty ought not to have the right to vote. In a true parliamentary government, only those who were sufficiently well off could become sufficiently well-informed to be granted full citizenship—this seemed to the Founders the apex of political wisdom.

Their perspective was clearly influenced by the fact that Belgium is a small country. A Great Power, forced to defend multiple outside interests must possess an imposing army or fleet in order to intimidate its neighbors and maintain its status.

It could never reduce the authority of the executive power to the same degree as does the Belgian Constitution. But a nation that asked only to develop freely within its borders, without ambitions ranging beyond them, and to which war appeared as both the greatest of evils and a form of insanity, could forego an army and fleet without fear—at least if it believed in a political system that allowed its citizens unlimited individualism. All in all, the Belgian Constitution established a pure parliamentary government, compatible with the Liberal spirit in which the middle class of the 19th century interpreted the principles of the French

Revolution. The Constitution was greeted with enthusiasm by Europe's liberals and with hostility by the governments of the Holy Alliance. Metternich considered it an act of madness and the King of Prussia, in 1840, predicted that it wouldn't last much longer.

It survived, however, and Belgium is still governed by it today. The changes that were introduced in 1893 and 1919 simply made it more democratic, expanding the right to vote. If in its actual application it largely differs from what its authors intended it, it remains the foundation of the country's political organization. Out of all the continental states of the West, Belgium's constitutional system has best withstood the test of time. It's the only country among them that kept its institutions intact through the crisis of 1848. Since then, no other danger has threatened it. The Constitution has always been accepted by the country's warring political parties. Over time it has become a part of the nation's being, and a powerful source of cohesion. As it gave Belgians the conviction that they were the freest people in Europe, it fostered their attachment to independence, which guaranteed their liberty. In 1853, Prime Minister Henri de Brouckère wrote, "What gives today's Belgium a unique physiognomy and a distinctive character is primarily this regime of free discussion, of self-government... Remove this system from Belgium, even weaken it, and this young state will lose all its virility, all its self-confidence... You will eliminate its moral fibre and its raison d'etre. From that moment on, it will become a body without soul, a loose aggregate without energy or a future, prey to anyone who comes along and offers to satisfy and secure its material interests."[1]

The persistence of a Constitution that at first sight appears incompatible with the normal operation of a state, and most of all of a state so complex as is Belgium, can be explained by several factors.

---

1 A. De Ridder, *Le Mariage du Roi Léopold II,* p. 186 (Brussels, 1925).

First is the happy circumstance that the three kings who have led the country each ruled for a long time and were admirably suited for their respective roles. Leopold I (1790–1865), summoned by the vote of the National Congress to inaugurate a 'Republican Monarchy,' was as tactful as he was intelligent, and drew on both virtues to pursue an English-style parliamentarianism. By the time of his death, a political tradition had been founded. His successor, Leopold II (1865–1909) adhered to it. He succeeded, reining in his great genius, in avoiding all clashes with the nation, whose position and influence in the world he sought to increase. He persuaded the country to want what he wanted, and eventually led Parliament to approve the annexation of the Congo and to sanction essential measures for the defense of the country. Finally, Albert I, (1909–1934), in the grave crisis of the Great War, made of the crown itself the symbol of the country, and became not merely the constitutional monarch but king of the nation. In this way, from reign to reign, the monarchy, faithfully respecting the Constitution, has increasingly legitimized its authority in the eyes of the people, and thereby has played an increasing role in their destiny[1]. If any republicans live in Belgium, they are theoretical republicans. In reality, the monarchic question never comes up. And how would it when the king is essentially nothing but the hereditary president of a republic?

The two political parties also contributed significantly to the success of the Constitution. The union of Catholics and Liberals that made the revolution of 1830 possible survived for only a few years. Since 1847 the allies have gone their separate ways. As in all Catholic countries, they fought over the question of the relationship between Church and State. Reneging on the mutual concessions that they had initially granted each other, the Liberals expected the Church to submit to the supervision of the state,

---

[1] These sanitized assessments are of course not shared by recent biographers of Belgium's first three kings, particularly of the second, nor confirmed by collections of their correspondence edited by C. Bronne, G. Janssens and J. Stengers, and M-R. Thielmans and E. Vandewoude.

while the Catholics wanted the state to abstain from any intervention in the domains where the Church claimed the right to pursue its mission. In reality, both were quite liberal in political matters. Neither dreamt of replacing parliamentary government with another form of government. But while agreeing to maintain the rights guaranteed by the Constitution, they began disagreeing on their interpretation of those rights. The liberalism of the true Liberals was essentially anticlerical. For them, the interests of society required, above all, official neutrality in matters of religion. They demanded a government that was completely secular in spirit and expected to remove all religious influences from education, defense, and justice as incompatible with tolerance. For Liberals, the Church was tarnished by its complicity with the *Ancien Régime* and its opposition to the principles of civil society. Conversely, the Catholics, dubbed "clericals" by their adversaries, reproached Liberals for opposing the Church solely out of hostility to the faith. Invoking as well the interests of society and confusing religion with morals, they sought to rescue the people from the yoke of the "laicizers" in order to prevent the latter from compromising the safety of their souls. As long as the right to vote was confined to the middle class, the two parties succeeded each other in power. From 1857 to 1884, Liberal ministers were in office for nineteen years, while Catholic ministries governed for eight. This balance of two parties, both formidable in all parts of the country, enabled Parliament and the Constitutional system to which it was closely linked to function properly.

This situation was ended by the agitation in favor of extending the right to vote. In the elections of 1884, the Liberals, who were divided on this question, were turned out of office. From that time until the constitutional revolution of 1893, they were never able to recover a majority in the House and Senate. The legislation that introduced universal suffrage, tempering it by plural votes, enormously increased the parliamentary power of the Catholics, while introducing along side them in Parliament a minority of elected Socialists. Three parties thus replaced the two historical parties. On the anti-clerical question, the Liberals and Socialists united against the Catholic majority. Conversely, on the issue of social reforms, which became increasingly important during this time, the Liberals voted more often with the Catholics. These two began to resemble a single a conservative party and they adopted platforms that increasingly conciliated moderate public opinion. After 1884, they continued to provide the personnel for the ministries that succeeded each other until 1914. The parliamentary system then underwent a transformation just like Britain's when, next to Liberals and Conservatives, new parties assumed a place in the House of Commons. However, also as in the United Kingdom, traditions and political customs were so well adapted to this system that it continued functioning normally despite the much more difficult conditions that were imposed on it.

To fully comprehend the political organization of Belgium, one must note that the administrative system that the Constitution of 1830 allowed to persist is older than it and not inspired by the same principles. In general terms, it conforms to the regime introduced in the country by the French conquest. The nine provinces among which the territory is divided are nothing but the continuation of nine departments established in 1795 by the Convention. Only their names have changed. Governors replaced the Prefects and District Police Chiefs replaced the Sub-Prefects. The general layout of the organization of the ministries, of public finance, taxes, the justice system, corps of civil engineers, corps of mines, and the military, despite the countless modifications that have been introduced, still rests on these Napoleonic foundations. The Kingdom of the Netherlands carefully respected them and they were transferred to Belgium. In this way, the executive power, as weak as the Constitution intended it, found itself administering institutions created by the strongest executive power that had ever existed.

However, if the forms of this system have remained intact for the most part, its effectiveness in centralizing government has been singularly reduced by the autonomy granted to municipalities. In this the electors of 1830 remained faithful to historical tradition. Since the Middle Ages the municipal spirit has been more highly developed in Belgium than in any other country on the continent. Nowhere was the urban population so numerous and nowhere else did it enjoy such extensive autonomy. Under the Old Regime, politics, for Belgians, centered entirely on municipal life. They were not interested in issues other than communal affairs. The annexation of the country by France eliminated local autonomy without erasing its memory or the regret at having lost it. The Kingdom of the Netherlands restored it, but imposed an electoral system that subordinated it to the central government. Communal rights were re-established by a municipal law passed in 1836. Municipalities remained under the control of the state and were prevented from encroaching on matters beyond their sphere; but in return they were otherwise left alone. Each town has a communal council, a sort of small parliament in which the burgomaster and the *échevains*[1] form the ministry. Its oversight extends to all the branches of the administration: schools, public works, hygiene, church councils, etc.

The Civic Guard, created by the Constitution alongside the regular army, is organized by the municipality and it provides the burgomaster with an armed force in case of need.[2] Communal autonomy is an article of faith for the national government, which carefully avoids all occasions for conflict with local authorities, and associates itself with them in its activities. The burgomasters of large cities are among the most important officials in the country. The burgomaster of Brussels is a prominent national figure whose power the government has to take into account. It

---

[1] *This office, sometimes translated as "alderman," does not exactly correspond to that or to a councilman, in so far as the échevain has administrative responsibilities, something like a cabinet minister.*
[2] I am speaking only of the situation before 1914. The Civic Guard is suppressed today and the attitude of the government in regards to municipal autonomy has changed due to the circumstances and the needs of post-war period.

is by joining the municipal council that an individual ordinarily enters public life. Local politics excites a lot of interest, and the factions are divided as they are in Parliament. Catholics, Liberals, and Socialists fight relentlessly to maintain or win power.

The party spirit is present in all of public life. Citizens align themselves with clear-cut factions. Neutrals, or those who will not commit to a "label," hardly exist. It seems quite natural that the party in power exploits it to its advantage and offers administrative positions only to its friends. The influence of political associations weighs on Parliament. Representatives pressure the ministry, seeking to dictate policy and reward their constituents. The intervention of the representatives of the majority party almost always determines the choice of administrators. In fact, the legislative power dominates the executive. A minister is simply considered the beneficiary of the victory of his party, and he is obliged to use his office to reward his supporters. This explains the intensity of electoral campaigns: the stakes are not only the triumph of one's policies but the satisfaction of a multitude of special interests. The small size of the country increases the constant mixing of issues of principle with personalities, and of general with local interests.

The neutrality imposed on the country by the treaties of 1839 itself contributed to this by focusing politics on Belgium itself. Foreign policy, which can offer a common ground for the various parties, never consisted of much beyond the negotiating of commercial treaties. Public opinion was diverted from foreign relations; it was not of much interest. The ignorance and indifference of the public contrasted starkly with the passion with which it followed domestic politics.

During the years that preceded the war, significant social, economic and political changes began to alter the traditional character of the country. Indeed, something of a crisis was looming. To understand how the country reacted from 1914 to 1918, it is essential to illustrate this briefly.

§ III. — STATE OF THE COUNTRY ON THE EVE OF THE WAR

National prosperity was never greater than at the beginning of the 20th century. One can cite several causes. First was the annexation of the Congo, approved by Parliament in 1908. If the direct advantages of owning a colony were not felt immediately, the indirect advantages were immense. Capitalists became bolder and began increasingly to look beyond Belgium's borders. Banks began focusing more on industrial enterprises. After a period in which Belgium was mostly content to sell its products to traditional customers, it began seeking new markets. In any case, the growth of foreign competition and the development of economic imperialism required a change in the means by which success was to be achieved. Belgian capital, sometimes alone and sometimes allied with the French capital, was invested in several distant enterprises. In Russia, Spain, and Italy and even in the Far East, it engaged in all sorts of businesses: railroads, tram lines, metallurgic facilities, glass factories, sugar refineries, spinning mills, electricity, etc. On the eve of the war, it was estimated that the total assets of Belgian companies that owned facilities abroad amounted to 3 billion francs and the amount of foreign or Congolian securities held in Belgium was estimated to amount to 8.5 billion. In reality, this figure was probably higher. In 1914 Belgian investments in Russia alone, in various industrial enterprises, amounted to about 3 billion francs. Broadly speaking, commercial activity doubled from 1900 to 1913. In that last year, imports totaled some equal 32,656,282 tons, exports, 20,885,182, and shipping 7,803,734.

The future looked bright. A new coal reserve had just been discovered in Campine; it was abundant in the bituminous coal that the country had hitherto been obliged to import. In Congo, the Katanga was discovered to be overflowing with mineral wealth and so abundant in radium that Belgium could be assured of a monopoly.

The national economy was based increasingly on industry. Its extreme vitality is undoubtedly explained by the traditional technical ability of the workers, their zeal, the excellent transportation system, but especially by the cheapness of labor. In no other Western European country was the cost of living as low as in Belgium; nowhere were taxes as low. But nothing was quite as low as salaries. It is in this way that the country could acquire what it needed from elsewhere and maintain its rank against rivals that had taken away everything through their political power. Since 1830 the preoccupation of the government, in accord with middle class opinion, had been to continually increase production by reducing expenses to a minimum through a customs policy and system of tariffs that favored importing raw materials and exporting manufactured products. It's hardly surprising that workers struggled to keep their wages above a subsistence level.

If Belgium was late to enact social legislation, this is because it did not control any foreign markets, so essential for its exports, and was obliged to maintain lower prices than those of its competitors. The middle class, which alone exercised political power, wished only to increase production. Faithfully adhering to the dogma of economic liberalism, it condemned any type of intervention by the state between employer and employee. It believed it sufficed to guarantee workers access to welfare offices in cases of need, to hospitals in cases of illness, and to shelters and other facilities in cases of disability or old age. In fact, the working class lived in deplorable conditions. It was rare to find factory owners who showed much interest in the welfare of their employees. The hygienic conditions of the shops and workers' homes left much to be desired. Child labor was as injurious to the education of the young workers as to their health. Female labor brought about consequences no less deplorable.

For a long time, the masses of workers accepted a state of things that their lack of organization kept them from improving. It was only around 1880 that the first associations of workers were founded. They were opposed by legislation, however, and subject to the hostility of business owners. A little later a campaign began, which grew increasingly violent, to obtain universal suffrage. Large strikes that triggered bloody repressions proliferated in 1896, and Parliament ordered an investigation of the conditions of work. This revealed facts so painful and abuses so grave that laws were enacted mandating the inspection of workshops, and limiting the use of female and child labor. But these were modest in scope. Meanwhile, thanks to the unrest of workers, socialism progressed rapidly. Its violent and revolutionary tendencies were soon succeeded by an effort to organize workers. This resulted in the creation of labor unions and cooperatives, of which *Voorit* in Ghent is the best example. After a few years, there were similar institutions throughout the country, and they were linked to a central organization, the Labor Commission. At the same time a socialist party, the Workers' Party, was founded.[1] Union dues enabled it to fund newspapers and propaganda. With the support of the advanced section (progressive or radical) of the Liberal Party, the movement in favor of revising the Constitution finally succeeded in 1893. Universal suffrage pure and simple was achieved after a troubling period that seemed the prelude to a revolution. A compromise was reached among the parties, which, while giving a vote to each adult in Belgium, gave one or two additional votes to those with a certain income or education. By 1899, when proportional representation assured each party a parliamentary influence that corresponded to its electoral strength, the periodic return to power of the Catholics and Liberals was no longer possible. The Catholic Party, accused by its adversaries of having organized the plural vote to its own advantage, was sufficiently powerful to command a majority over the two opposition parties.

Since then, the Workers' Party has played an ever more important role in Belgian politics. The number of members attracted by

---

[1] Its constitution dates to 1885.

the advantages of affiliation with the labor unions has continued to increase. In response, the Catholic Party established some Christian labor unions alongside the Socialist labor unions, modeling these on the latter. The *Boerenbonden*, the Farmers' Unions, huge associations of peasants in the Flemish-speaking part of the country, won over the rural classes. These institutions, however, were created largely to counter the propaganda of socialism and slipped little by little under the control of conservatives. A "Christian democratic movement" was launched, on which the Catholic Party increasingly counted. Under the threat of secession, the old Catholic associations were obliged to include on the electoral lists candidates designed by the Christian syndicates and the farmers' unions. The unity of the party was preserved by these concessions. Only the Liberal Party, which attracted mostly industrialists, members of the liberal professions, and the middle classes, preserved its bourgeoisie identity.

The organization and progress of socialism are thus the essential facts of political life in the 20th century. If they did not guide it, they at least propelled it in new directions. The transformation of the Catholic Party is but a consequence and confirmation of its strength. This strength extends beyond the Workers' Party. Moved by the Belgian sprit of realism, socialism subordinates theoretical and distant demands to immediate reforms. It has become a financial power that manages hundreds of labor union groups, owns factories, one bank, some hospitals, some clinics, some institutions of learning, entertainment establishments, athletic teams, print shops, bookshops, and even a fishing fleet.

This party is naturally most widely represented in parts of the country where large industry is most widespread. It follows that the Walloon provinces, particularly Hainaut and the city of Liège, are its base of power. The Flemish Socialists depend on the support that they provide. In this way the workers' movement, as it grew, contributed to the cohesion of the country by associating the entire working class in one movement. In any case, being true to its internationalist tendencies, the party by nature resists the regionalist spirit and is unlikely to permit the linguistic conflict to divide it.

During the last few years before the war, this conflict intensified. Although the Belgian Constitution proclaims freedom of language and the government never enacted any sort of measure repressing Flemish, it was fatal that the Frenchified bourgeoisie who governed had the same indifference toward the popular language of the Flemish provinces as it did toward the proletariat. The use of Flemish was not persecuted; the government just acted as if the language didn't exist. The entire administration of the country was conducted exclusively in French. To be ignorant of that language barred one from any sort of public career. Sooner of later, protests were bound to erupt against a state of things so little compatible with the liberal principles that had inspired the country's institutions. Around 1848, writers, linguists, and teachers began demanding for the Flemish language a treatment worthy of its literary past and of the rights of those who spoke it. An official Commission of Grievances was instituted in 1865. However, it was not until 1870 that the Flemish issue began surfacing in election campaigns. The first success of the *flamingants* was the enactment, in 1873, of a law in matters of criminal procedure. Then, in 1883, another law introduced mandatory teaching in the Flemish language in a certain number of secondary schools, acknowledging this language's equality—at least in theory—with French. The law was applicable only to the Fleming provinces. The *flamingants* had no wish to impose on their Walloon fellow citizens the knowledge of their language.

The linguistic question was addressed in Belgium quite differently than in Germany. Here neither one of the two parties wanted to assimilate the other by forcing it to speak their language. Faithful to their principle "*In Vlaanderen Vlaamsch,*" the *flamingants* demanded reforms only for Flanders. Their adversaries were not the Walloons, but that part of the Fleming population that they labeled "*fransquillons*" on account of their attachment to the French language. However, the *fransquillons* were as Flemish as the Flemish themselves. Among them were the oldest families in the country.

They include the aristocracy and well-to-do middle class for whom, over the centuries, not by violence but by a natural rapport with France and the Walloon provinces, French had become, if not the sole language, the language of "Society" and of business. Therefore the problem existed in a completely different form than in Bohemia, Poland, or the Balkan countries, where the various languages correspond to different nationalities.[1] The French speakers of Flanders were neither foreign conquerors nor immigrants. They were simply a portion of the people who by tradition, choice, and interest had preferred the more popular language to another language and they expected not to be inferred with if they chose to use it.

Thus the issue was very delicate and very complicated. One could not invoke, in favor of the case for Flemish, the mystical principle of race, which appeals increasingly to emotions as it becomes more impervious to reason. The practical usefulness of the knowledge of French for the population constituted another obstacle for the *flamingants*. They rested their case on the interests of society and on pedagogic grounds. The former, they claimed, was harmed by the linguistic isolation of the upper classes, while children in the Flemish provinces were taught from an early age in a foreign language, to the detriment of the national language. The most fervent *flamingants*, won over by current theories in Germany, went on to proclaim the superiority of the Germanic languages over Romance languages, of dolichocephalic blonds over the dark-haired brachycephalics, of blue eyes over brown eyes, and they abandoned themselves to a pseudo-scientific

---

[1] The situation is in fact similar to that in Finland, where all the inhabitants who speak French or Swedish are of Finnish origin.

romanticism in which language appeared as something like a human being, possessing inalienable rights over and above the will and desires of men.

The Flemish movement, moreover, though it prided itself on being Germanic, was not at all oriented towards Germany. Members of this movement who wanted closer relations with Germany were extremely rare. A Pan-German magazine, *Germania*, founded in 1898, had disappeared by 1905 for lack of readers. It was not to Germany but to the Netherlands that Flemish-speaking Belgium looked for a cultural revival. In any case, believers did not have a specific foreign policy agenda. *Flamingantisme* was only influential in as much as it was Belgian and, except for some exceptions so rare that they didn't matter, it was entirely and completely Belgian.

For as long as the Constitution restricted the franchise, the linguistic conflict was only of secondary political importance. Only the middle class voted and governed, and it was largely Francophile and assured of the support of Walloons and *Bruxellois*, for whom Flemish was nothing but a dialect of no consequence. So it was only as a result of log-rolling and horse-trading that the few *flamingant* deputies occasionally got some concessions. But the situation changed after the expansion of the right to vote in 1893. From that point on the Flemish language question took on an increasingly large role in campaigns. *Flamingantisme* changed both its nature and methods. To win over the masses, it assumed a democratic tone. The *franquillons* were depicted as a proud and privileged minority, indifferent to the destiny of the people, disdaining their language because they disdained themselves. The appeal to economic interests by the *flamingants* increased the impact of their propaganda ten-fold. The desire for social legislation that the people of the Flemish-speaking provinces began to voice, following the example of urban workers, naturally intermingled with their demands for linguistic reforms. The Catholic Party, whose electoral base was mainly in the rural districts, could not remain indifferent to this new trend. The clergy in Flanders especially favored the cause. They hoped to use the *flamingant* movement as a dam to contain anticlerical socialism. The democratic organizations that they set up were at one and the same time both Christian and Flemish. The Catholic associations were obliged to align themselves with the *Boerenbonden*, and the support the latter provided was directly proportional to the concessions it was granted. In this way the *flamingant* question quickly took on a scope and a radicalism which surprised only those who had not foreseen how it would inevitably develop in a democracy. The linguistic minority found itself suddenly overwhelmed. The motto *In Vlaanderen Vlaamsch* was no longer a distant ideal but an urgent need. In 1912 a bill to transform the University of Ghent into a Flemish language university was introduced to the House of Representatives.

Unlike the Flemish, the Walloons did not have linguistic grievances. Nevertheless, it was natural that the *flamingant* agitation provoked a certain reaction. Incapable of understanding their motives, they attributed the demands of Flemish activists to the ambition of some leaders, and worried about the danger they posed to the unity of the nation. They were irritated by the occasional use of intemperate language extolling the superiority of German over Latin civilization. Recent laws obliging administrators in Flanders to speak the Flemish language made Walloons apprehensive about the extension of a bi-lingual system into the rest of the country. Regional sentiment that had been maintained by Walloon literary societies intensified. There were outbursts of bad temper against the centralization imposed by Brussels. A small group of *walloonisants* adopted the formula: "Flanders to the Flemings, Wallonia to the Walloons, and Brussels to Belgium." In the House, a representative from Liège yelled out, "Long live administrative separation!" An open letter addressed to the king began with the words, "Sire, there are no 'Belgians.'"[1]

Social agitation thus went hand in hand with linguistic agitation. Under their double influence, the press, accustomed to unlimited freedom, adopted increasingly violent language. It reached the point that some foreigners began to believe that the country was on the brink of a revolution.

In reality the country was adapting to the new democratic regime imposed by the constitutional changes. This adaptation was difficult and its difficulty caused agitation even more tumultuous than regulations permitted: in speeches, newspapers and pamphlets, public gatherings and demonstrations. But militants raged against the government, not against the law. All types of protests were undertaken, but no one dreamt of using force to bring about the changes he sought. For Belgians, the red flag wasn't the symbol of revolution, but only the banner of a party.

The universal right to suffrage had not much modified, at least superficially, the appearance of the Parliament. Socialists had taken seats in the House, but next to them sat representatives of the two traditional parties, the Catholics and the Liberals. The robustness of the Constitution they'd created enabled the latter two parties to surmount the crisis. They saved themselves by accommodating reform movements or linguistic claims. The old conflict of clericalism and anti-clericalism continued to provide a political platform for politicians. It was so deeply rooted that it still prevailed over everything else, if not within the nation at least in Parliament. For half a century the education question had been the battlefield par excellence between Catholics and Liberals. The confessional or non-confessional character of the schools had been of much greater interest than the need to reorganize and standardize schools. The attempt by Liberals to create a completely secular primary school system entirely under the control

---

[1] *This famous letter was written by Jules Destrée (1863–1936), a prominent Socialist representative for Charleroi.*

of the state had been the cause of their defeat in 1884. Since then the public school system had remained, to its detriment, an apple of discord. The education question, to switch metaphors, was like a shuttlecock flying back and forth between the two traditional parties. It was impossible to satisfy at one and the same time the desire of the Catholics to be conceded complete freedom of religion while not subjecting the system to domination by the Church. Public education suffered from a paralyzing instability, in contrast to the vigorous activity of the nation. In 1900, 19 percent of inhabitants over eight years old were illiterate, despite the progress achieved over the previous twenty years.

Although they held opposite views on economic reforms, Socialists and Liberals agreed on creating an educational system that met the needs of the people. In 1913 a law was proposed making attendance compulsory for boys and girls and mandating secondary school education as well. The onset of war prevented the enactment of this law. The same can be said for a law passed in 1914 regulating female and child labor.

The army as well as the schools had the misfortune to be a victim of party conflict. In a country where the cost of living was a vital question, the army was accused of being too expensive for the minimal services it rendered. According to public opinion, the neutrality guaranteed Belgium by the Powers assured perpetual peace. The good fortune that had preserved the country's territory from attack during the war of 1870 made people believe that things would always remain so. The traditional repugnance of Belgians for the military was further strengthened by the clergy's aversion to barracks life. In the end, after passionate debate, credits needed to fortify Antwerp (1859) were approved, and then, in 1888, to allow the construction of the forts designed to defend the passage of the Meuse, at Liège against Germany and at Namur against France. But it was impossible for a long time to undertake the reorganization of the army, and even longer to increase the total strength of the country's forces. Soldiers were recruited by a lottery among militia members and the state sanctioned a system of "replacement," by which the upper classes could purchase the exemption of their sons. This made military service appear to the people as an especially odious obligation because it was so unjust. In vain, the Liberal Party had included universal military service in its program and in vain King Leopold II had intervened personally in its favor. Special interests always prevented its realization. However, it gave progressives such an obvious grievance that an attempt was made to substitute a volunteer army. The result was so pathetic that, without further reforms, the army seemed about to disappear. In 1893, a law was passed that finally ended special privileges, and another in 1909 re-organized the draft. Leopold II had the great satisfaction of signing it on his deathbed. Domestic politics was responsible for the new laws: they were inspired much more by concerns for social justice than for the country's defense. Voters did not want to strengthen the army, but only to eliminate the iniquitous privileges of the middle classes. The total number of effectives was not increased and recruitment continued to be based on lotteries. Many conservatives embraced the reforms because they appeared to guarantee the discipline of the troops in case of domestic disturbances. It was the rare individual who was sufficiently knowledgeable about the state of affairs in Europe as to conceive of the possibility of war, and particularly one that might involve Belgium. There was complete confidence and complete blindness. This view perfectly reflected the rapport that the country enjoyed with its two large neighbors, France and Germany.

After the Republic was proclaimed in Paris, worries about France that had troubled Belgians during the reign of Napoleon III disappeared. There was a revival of France's centuries-old influence. Since the beginning of the Middle Ages, its language, literature, arts, social life, and economic activity had deeply impressed Belgians. Intellectual and cultural relations between the countries were even tighter than economic relations. The proximity of Paris further contributed to French influence. Parisian newspapers were read in all major Belgian cities on the same day they were published. French books filled Belgian bookshops. Parisian plays were staged and its actors performed in all theaters; its political restlessness, the sensational episodes of its feverish existence, were the object of constant interest. No doubt this interest was not always sympathetic. Especially after the separation of Church and state, a part of the clergy regarded French influence with a profound mistrust, which for other reasons, was shared by some *flamingants*.

The rapport was a result also of Belgium's dependency on its large neighbor. Thousands of Belgians worked in the factories of France's *département du Nord*. At the time of the harvest, Flemish villagers, "*les Fransmannen*," went off to find work in the farms of Champagne, Picardie, and Normandy. Belgian and French capital was jointly invested in a great many businesses. France responded to Belgium's trust with an appreciation that flattered public opinion. It admired the young literary schools that came together around Maurice Maeterlinck and Emile Verhaeren,[1] who had both been warmly received in Paris. At every Belgian convention, literary or scientific meeting, art expo or industry trade show, no country was better represented than France. In 1913, France participated with éclat in the universal exposition of Ghent. Newspaper readers were thrilled by the visits the President of the Republic paid King Albert. All in all, the close friendship between France and Belgium reflected the sentiments of both countries. Nature and history had placed the two countries in such close proximity as to make it impossible for their common interests not to converge.

---

[1] Maeterlinck (1862–1949) was a symbolist poet and playwright from Ghent, who won the Nobel Prize for Literature in 1911. Both a mystic and socialist, his best known works before the war were the plays <u>Princess Maleine</u>, <u>The Blue Bird</u>, and <u>Mary Magdalene</u> and the essay <u>The Life of the Bee</u>. Verhaeren (1855–1916) was also a symbolist poet and French-speaking Fleming, and, like his friend Maeterlinck, lived in France, sympathized with socialism, and saw his work condemned by the Church. He was runner-up for the Nobel Prize in 1911. His best-known book may be <u>Les Flamandes</u>, poems on the paintings of the Flemish primitivists.

Relations with Germany, although not as cordial and extensive, were no less numerous, and they continued to grow year after year. The formidable economic development of the Empire had immediately affected Belgium and particularly Antwerp. This port had become one of the major industrial and trade outlets of the Rhine-Westphalia regions. German shipping companies gradually took over most of the wharves, and it was German firms that conducted the most business there. Germans became more influential than the British. The German colony in Antwerp was admired not only for its wealth, but for the zeal and skills of the expatriates. Belgians were forced to acknowledge German superiority not only in commerce but also in industry. The Belgians learned from the Germans as they had earlier learned from the English. They copied the Germans' procedures, purchased their machinery, and hired their engineers.

The ascendancy of Germany in the intellectual sphere was hardly less profound, though less visible, than the influence it exerted in the world of business. Its universities enjoyed a prestige that matched and even surpassed that of the University of Paris. It became customary for young doctors to go to the Reich to complete their scientific education. The country supplied Belgium with a good number of secondary school teachers, and, little by little, they began influencing Belgian pedagogy.

Germany certainly seemed to be a great nation. Its military power, political clout, growing prosperity, and excellent administration only increased the favorable opinion it enjoyed. This admiration was shared by Socialists, who revered it as the country of Karl Marx. Catholics compared the wide tolerance permitted by its government to the sectarianism of the French government. When William II visited the Pope, his deference made them forget the *Kulturkampf.* The confessional regime of the German schools further increased the clergy's regard for a state so respectful of religion. Liberals themselves, if they were critical of the absolutist character of the Prussian monarchy, were none the less impressed by social legislation that seemed to have found the means of satisfying the proletariat without resorting to demagogy. In short, Germany was the object of universal enthusiasm, though because of its militarism, its reverence for hierarchy, discipline, and force, it was respected rather than loved by Belgians.

A great many parents entrusted their children to the *Deutche Schulen* that the German emigrants had established in Brussels, Antwerp, and Liège.

As for Britain, it was ignored. Contact with it was restricted to banking relations and maritime commerce. Belgians knew well that they could count on the country in case of danger, and that, of all the Powers, it was the one that was most interested in preserving the neutrality and independence of Belgium. However nobody expected to have to turn to it for support. The recent London-based campaign against the Congolese administration had created a certain mistrust among some Belgians

Located at a sensitive point in Europe and in contact with the three dominant Powers of the West, pacifist and free-trade Belgium asked only to live in peace with everyone. The country trusted that its neutrality—as precious from a political as from an economic point of view—would be preserved. Open to the goods and ideas of its neighbors, Belgians believed their country could help facilitate mutual understanding and rapprochement among Europeans. It could be a center for internationalism and cosmopolitanism, but also, given its population and geographic location, it could bind Latin and Germanic Europe. To be Belgian was, in a manner of speaking, to be European, since the country was almost a microcosm of Europe.

Naturally, peace and justice were its ideals; for a small state, a respect for justice was the best safeguard of peace. Of course there were self-interested reasons for its anti-militarism.

No one believed the country's independence would be called into question. The Great Powers had made it the keystone of Europe's equilibrium. The violation of the country's neutrality would unleash a general war, and Belgians felt certain no one would be so irresponsible as to risk such an awful catastrophe. Citizens deluded themselves about developments that had made the world a far more dangerous place. They anticipated the spread of a spirit of cosmopolitanism, and refused to acknowledge that unless peace was formally negotiated among the Powers, it might only be a prelude to war.

Brussels had become a center for international organizations and conventions. The international socialist organization was headquartered there. Universal exhibitions went on continuously. "World" conventions and conferences chose Belgium as a meeting place. Together with Geneva and The Hague, Brussels shared the privilege of being one of those places where individuals worked most diligently for reconciliation and peace.

CHAPTER II

The invasion of the country

§ I. — NEUTRALITY VIOLATED

Absorbed in business and politics, Belgian public opinion was unaffected by the general tension of Europe during the years that preceded the Great War. Belgians didn't believe and didn't wish to believe in the possibility of a conflict. The reassuring statements that representatives of the Great Powers in Brussels repeated on every occasion as to their country's commitment to respect Belgian neutrality helped maintain the illusion. In Parliament, one of the most respected representatives claimed that to doubt the treaties of 1839 would be upheld in perpetuity was to insult the signers. From time to time a newspaper would mention the great strategic projects undertaken by Germany along the border: the parallel railroads running through Eifel and the establishment of Camp Elsenborn in 1894, connected to the main Aachen-Liège line. Such articles were promptly forgotten. The tranquility of the two Chambers was so profound that they did not hesitate to vote for the opening of a railroad from Stavelot to Malmédy, providing a new point of entry for the Germans. The economic insignificance of the line ought to have raised questions about its intended use. News about increases in troop strength in France and Germany and the reinforcement of the British fleet left Belgians unmoved. A tentative initiative by some publicists in favor of a defensive agreement with the Netherlands was of no interest to public opinion. Discussions of the military budget each year elicited the usual pacifist declarations and customary attacks against "militarist folly."

Nevertheless, the government worried about dangers it did not dare disclose to the country. It had barely obtained the millions it needed to build new defensive fortifications around Antwerp in 1906. In that same year, it had allowed General Ducarne to discuss with Colonel Barnardiston possible measures to be taken in the event of a German invasion.[1] In 1912 it had authorized the National Bank to prepare bills of 5 francs to issue in case of war. Finally, in 1912–1913, the ministry succeeded in winning approval for mandatory military service and for reforms reinforcing and modernizing the army, which would be completed at the end of five years.[2] Public opinion saw in this measure merely a new guarantee of peace. It continued to believe that the mission of the Belgian army was "to not fight."

The press was unfazed by the news of the assassination in Sarajevo. In July 1914 newspapers attached much more importance to the sensational trial of Madame Caillaux, then underway in Paris, than to diplomatic events.[3] It took Austria's declaration of war against Serbia (July 28) for the gravity of the situation to be acknowledged. The specter of war was all the more frightening for having been denied for so long. The recall of three classes of reservists by the King the next day (July 29), then, two days later (July 31), the general mobilization, caused sudden panic. Germany's declaration of war against Russia removed all doubt as

---

[1] *Barnardiston was the British military attaché in Brussels, Ducarne the chief of the Belgian General Staff. The talks commenced in January and an understanding was reached in April. After the violation of Belgian neutrality, British troops would be sent first to Dunkirk-Calais, then to Antwerp. Transportation was arranged and information exchanged, including about German war preparations, of which Ducarne was ignorant, Belgium having no military attachés.*

[2] *The new law increased the annual contingent to 33,000 men and decreed that active duty troops would be temporarily raised to 340,000 men.*

[3] *The wife of a leading Radical politician, Henriette Callaiaux had killed the editor of Le Figaro, who had published letters she had written to her husband while he was still married to his first wife.*

to the imminence of a global conflict. But the idea that Belgium could be involved in such a conflict still hardly dawned on anyone. Even after the invasion of the Grand Duchy of Luxembourg by German troops (August 2)

Belgians continued to believe that they would manage to avoid the tempest as they had in 1870. But with Europe in flames, what would be the fate of the country? At the very least Belgium should expect a terrible economic crisis. At that first feverish moment, everyone thought only of himself. One saw crowds storming the markets to buy supplies at random. Banks were overrun by people claiming their deposits or wanting to exchange their banknotes. From July 27 to August 1 the National Bank changed more than 50 million francs in banknotes for silver coins.

On Sunday, August 2, the agitation subsided. It was a gorgeous day. Some calm returned, the anxiety dissipated, and there was a surge of optimism. Belgians had not witnessed war on their own territory for 84 years and had forgotten that their land had been the battlefield of Europe for centuries. The following morning, newspapers abruptly announced that it was to be so once again. The country learned that the night before, the German Minister had hand-delivered to the Belgian Minister of Foreign Affairs an ultimatum demanding that Belgium permit the passage of German troops en route to France. The text was disclosed at the same time as the Government's response. This was a categorical refusal based on Belgium's international obligations, and a declaration that an invasion would be resisted with all its strength. So at the most solemn moment in the country's history, citizens were faced with a decision that had already been made. The men entrusted with caring for the country's interests in times of peace and who had gained positions of power through electoral struggles based on narrow party issues had, with a few sentences, just put at risk the lives and property of all Belgians.

Never, perhaps, had the nation experienced a similar sudden shock. One went to sleep hoping for peace, and one woke up to the certainty of war. The jolt was so powerful and unexpected that it felt surreal. One would have to have witnessed that day and to have been out in the streets with the crowds to understand a state of mind very difficult to analyze, but which, brief as it was, determined the attitude that the nation would adopt until the end of the great ordeal. It is doubtful that—except for a very small number of individuals—people understood the extent of what was going to happen. Many persisted in the idea that the irreparable would never occur, that the enemy—a word that no Belgian had pronounced since 1839—would not cross the border, or at the worst, the Germans would move rapidly through the Ardennes, and that, in any case, the French army would rush to the defense of Belgium, and, with the support of the fortresses of Liège, Namur, and Antwerp and their defenders, they would repel the invasion. The idea that the Belgian Army, with its 117,000 men, could by itself stand up to the world's most formidable military power was absurd.

But the more one became aware of the disproportion of the fight, the more—while trying not to believe it—one felt indignation. Everyone shared this anger. The very terms of the ultimatum exacerbated it. That Germany had believed the nation capable of selling itself for money was insufferable. The more the country had faith in neutrality, tried to maintain it in all circumstances, and basked in tributes to Belgian steadfastness, the more it was determined at all costs to remain faithful to the treaties that were always considered the guarantee of its independence. Allowing their violation would have been to have responded to Europe's confidence by betraying it.

At this tragic moment, what was apparent above all else was that honor was at stake. People felt more insulted than threatened by the German proposition. The fact that the insult was entirely undeserved both intensified the will to resist and united the country. The patriotic sentiments aroused by the ultimatum diverted attention from internal quarrels. People spontaneously began to display the national flag along the streets. The ministry, yesterday, had been only the ministry of a party. Suddenly, it was viewed as everyone's ministry. As Belgians came together, they turned toward the King.

In the whirlwind of the crisis, he emerged from the clouds that seemed to envelope him in times of peace. He appeared as the incarnation of the country. His reply to the German ultimatum filled everyone with pride. It was supported unanimously. The moderation of its language made it all the more impressive. It moved listeners and readers by its calm and, if one may say so, by its honesty. The entire day of August 3 went by in a sort of delirium, filled with rage, anxiety, and resolution. One knew nothing about what was happening at the borders. People lived in a sort of daze, still wanting to doubt the worst, but prepared to face it if it occurred. Only in the evening, bands of young people began wandering around the roads and gathering in front of German shops and breweries, many of which were destroyed.[1]

Meanwhile the government issued emergency measures. Not having prepared for war, it envisioned with real anguish the tasks it now faced, and the fact that they could not be discharged properly because of the lack of time. First of all, it was imperative to keep the country from plunging into a financial crisis. On August 2, decrees imposed a moratorium on bills of exchange and a non-negotiable exchange rate for banknotes. On August 3, the National Bank transferred its gold and silver to Antwerp as a precaution. The exportation of livestock, grains, hay, straw, automobiles, oil, gas, vehicles and horses was temporarily banned as of July 30. On August 2 the prohibition was extended to bread, potatoes, and cereal.

In the mean time, the Chambers were summoned via telegraph to convene in an extraordinary session on August 4. While they were meeting in Brussels, the enemy had already crossed

---

[1] Violence was rare against people and the few incidents that occurred were not serious.

Belgium's border and the first battle was being fought in front of the forts of Liège. Some weeks before, representatives and senators had left the *Palais de la Nation* as partisans; they returned to it as the trustees of public welfare. The session took place in complete harmony with the gravity of the moment and with the cause that Belgium had been called upon to defend: that of honor and justice. The enthusiastic cheers that greeted the King made it clear that the nation entrusted him with its fate and stood behind him. He was dressed in full uniform, and his brief speech was a defense of the rule of law and of the responsibilities the crisis imposed on everyone. The beauty and nobility of his words stirred his listeners.

When he left to mount his horse and rejoin the army, the assembly convened. Without debate, the representatives passed laws that would allow the government to accomplish the task that had devolved on it. For the first time since the birth of national independence, Parliament, so jealous of its prerogatives and so ready to defy the executive power, spontaneously delegated its rights to the leader of the nation. A credit of 200 million francs was granted to the government. The King was authorized for the entire duration of the war to suspend debt collections, limit bank withdrawals, ban exports, take all necessary measures to ensure the population was fed, suppress hoarding, and make funds available to provinces and municipalities. At the same time, the provincial councils and permanent delegations[1] were granted the power to replace those provincial governors who would be forced to leave their posts and also to take over all functions of the government if communications were cut off. Thus, from the first day, Parliament anticipated the progress of the invasion that had just begun. Members did not doubt the catastrophe that would be unleashed on the country, nor, for that matter, the final victory. "People who defend their existence cannot die," said the King. This remained,

---
1 *These were executive bodies elected by the councils that worked with the provincial governor.*

and should remain, the motto of the nation. At the same time, in the Reichstag, the Chancellor of the German Empire pronounced the famous words that so admirably justified the position of the representatives of the Belgian people: "Necessity knows no law; in violating Belgian neutrality, we commit a wrong." The contrast in the language corresponds to the contrasting situations. On the one hand, a Great Power invoked in its behalf the overriding interest of its armed forces and political objectives, and, on the other, a small nation appealed to the rule of law.

Whatever one may believe as to the responsibilities for the war, it is all too clear that Belgium was dragged into the conflict against its wishes. From the opening days, it knew it had done nothing to deserve its fate. And this consciousness energized it and sustained its resistance until the end. It was especially outraged by the idea that Germany could have believed it capable of cooperating with its plans. Belgium's indignation is explained much less by the violation of its neutrality than by the terms of the ultimatum, which were resented as an insufferable outrage. It was not so much out of its duty to Europe but from its obligation to itself that Belgium refused to accept the Germans' demands. The country's military weakness only enhanced its moral strength. Belgians did not want to be treated as subordinate and insignificant. The belief in political liberty, so profoundly rooted in it, made the country impervious to the threat of force. To tell the truth, it was mostly moral reasons that influenced Belgians and made them reject considerations of self-interest. The patriotism they displayed derived from something like offended dignity, from the conviction that a free people ought to endure anything in order to safeguard its independence and its right to live as it chose. The excessive individualism inspired by the Belgian Constitution, the prerogatives that it grants so freely to every citizen, made each oppose the invader. Feelings of race, even feelings of nationality, did not play any role, or at least only a secondary one. Individual Belgians considered the violence inflicted on their country as a personal attack, an assault on rights and liberties they hadn't fully appreciated until now. They had come to believe that their national independence would never be in danger. The long peace that they had enjoyed had diverted their attention from the community as a whole to the interests of family, of class, or of party. War suddenly opened their eyes. They realized that their most precious possessions were dependent on the continued existence of the community to which they belonged. The "*idée nationale*," long regarded as a chauvinistic expression, the subject of belligerent speeches, was suddenly recognized as a profound reality. The crisis into which the country had been dragged necessitated that everyone willingly make sacrifices for the safety of each and every Belgian.

In the evening of August 4, newspapers published reports of the Chambers' session, the King's speech, the powers granted the government, and news of the fighting around Liège. The full extent of the danger was now known. What seemed almost impossible the night before, a war waged on Belgian soil and the guns of the army firing on an enemy, had become reality. The readiness with which one accepted the new reality is a singularly curious fact of collective psychology. In all the other European countries, public opinion had always accepted the eventuality of war. In many of them it was expected as an inevitable catastrophe, or a necessity. Conversely, in Belgium, where the immense majority of the nation had become accustomed to think that they would be spared such a monstrous calamity for good, peace seemed the normal and perpetual status quo. The military reform in 1912–1913, far from raising suspicions, seemed to have brought new confidence—not as to the impossibility of a European conflict, but rather as to the likelihood that it would involve Belgium. Nobody or almost nobody had believed in the warnings occasionally given by clear-sighted politicians or by military men.

Wary of alarming the public, and for diplomatic reasons, the government had never dared call attention to the dangers of the situation. If a politician alluded to it, he was accused of trying to incite voters into accepting ruinous increases in the military budget. Wasn't the inviolability of Belgium's territory solemnly guaranteed by international treaties? Germany's preparations over the last few years undoubtedly disturbed some individuals. But most people persuaded themselves that if in a future war Germany crossed the frontier, it would only be to reach France more quickly by the right bank of the Meuse. It was known vaguely that the French general staff considered this a possibility. The worst that could happen was to have to defend Liège and Namur until the guarantor Powers came to the rescue of the country and relieved the divisions that were protecting the forts. Now all these calculations were overturned. The Belgian army would face a frontal attack. Instead of moving rapidly along the Meuse, the enemy plowed directly into the country, seizing Liège and marching toward the interior. Belgium alone had to bar the route west. Not only did everything come to pass that one would never have thought possible, but it happened in the most catastrophic way.

Though its illusions were so tragically dispelled, the public bore the ordeal without wavering. Undoubtedly the reason for its strength was the great indignation the ultimatum had aroused. All social classes were affected. What would have happened if, five years earlier, the middle class had not consented to its sons serving in the army? What had seemed to be simply a question of justice had ended up becoming, in a moment of peril, an essential condition for the preservation of the country. Actually, the army was for the most part still "an army of the poor." The old classes of militia that had been recalled to active duty included only members of the working class. But no one would want to claim that the legacy of the past still provoked bitter recriminations. The nation was too determined to block the German advance not to fully identify with its soldiers, regardless of their social class. All that had divided Belgians was now forgotten. The banners that the parties formerly displayed in demonstrations and meetings no longer fluttered anywhere. Only the black, yellow, and red flag hung from the façade of town halls, belfries, church bell towers, and windows of private citizens. There was a union of hearts and minds. Bedecked with flags, Belgium awaited the impending catastrophe.

Everywhere volunteers went to the recruitment offices: workers, university students, young people from all social classes and economic backgrounds. Nearly all were from cities and towns. The rural population was not well represented. The outbreak of the war had a deeper impact on the intellectual and industrial classes, which were more sensitive, more nervous, more prone to patriotic idealism and, besides, more directly affected by the sudden cessation of business. They identified more closely with the nation. All civilization is an urban phenomenon. Cities are inevitably the most active and energetic part of a nation. In Belgium, essentially urban, the crisis of 1914 clearly demonstrated that. Of the 20,000 volunteers that were recruited,[1] not everyone was driven by the same reasons. Many would not have dreamt of enlisting if their work hadn't been interrupted. But as always happens in great moral crises, the fervor to volunteer was spread by the example of others.

Alongside the regular army, the government mobilized the Civic Guard. Legally, all men capable of equipping themselves at their own expense belonged to it. In fact, if was organized only in the cities, where it made up a middle-class militia, appointing most of its own officers and having no other military training than some exercises on Sundays. Except for a few "special corps" made of volunteers, its discipline and weaponry were equally inadequate. Its activities were limited to parading in public ceremonies and, during disturbances, maintaining public order as best it could. Clearly, it could not be of value in combat. But it could garrison the cities abandoned by the army, and guard

---

[1] This figure will seem more significant if we consider that the rapidity of the invasion ended voluntary recruitment very early. It only lasted a few days in the provinces of Liège, Namur, Limburg and Luxembourg. It is regrettable that we have no details on the distribution of volunteers among the various social classes.

railways and bridges and works of art. It performed admirably the services it was called upon to provide. The Civic Guardsmen in the countryside (Inactive Civic Guard) were recognizable by their blue blouse and tricolor armband. It was impossible to arm them and they fulfilled police functions exclusively.

The Germans believed and continue to believe that the Belgian government had organized corps of franc-tireurs, that is to say an irregular and illegal force that was to act jointly with the army and Civic Guard. Such accusations are absolutely incorrect, indeed, ridiculous. Here and there some rifle shots may have been fired at marching or bivouacking troops by private citizens or isolated soldiers. One cannot expect civilians to respect the rules of war as scrupulously as the regular army. No one would indict enemy officers for their men's pillaging under the stress of combat. How can military discipline be imposed, even by strong injunctions, on a people who had just been unjustly invaded? The authorities in fact did issue many such injunctions. The ministry, provincial governors, and burgomasters vied with one another in posting proclamations declaring in the most categorical terms the obligation imposed on inhabitants to abstain from any form of aggression against the enemy.

How can it be seriously believed that a government so unprepared for war as to not have to enough rifles to distribute to the volunteers and the Civic Guard could be capable of equipping bands of franc-tireurs?

Is it believable that the Germans could not discover any evidence of an organization, which, had it existed, would clearly have left some traces in the archives or in the official or private correspondence so carefully examined by the invader. Is it conceivable in particular that following their triumphs, the supposed franc-tireurs would not be eager to boast about their noble deeds and claim the reward for their exploits? Their silence is proof that they existed only in those legends that proliferate in every war. Is it possible that German soldiers, surprised by a resistance that they had not expected, may have believed that they'd encountered franc-tireurs when they ran across members of the Civic Guard? Is it possible that they may have attributed to civilians the gunfire directed at them by soldiers on motorbikes or gendarmes posted at the entrance of villages, who had then quickly retreated after shooting? This is not only possible, but certain.[1] Far from dismissing the charges, officers unfortunately shared the misconception. It spread throughout Germany and, from the beginning of the war, it poisoned public opinion. Propagated by newspapers and affirmed as an incontestable truth by the most prominent representatives of the intellectual elite, it served to anaesthetize the scruples that the violation of Belgian neutrality might have aroused in their minds. Almost immediately the spontaneous fable was universally accepted. And like all the fables, it evolved over time. No atrocity was too outrageous not to be believed. Stories portrayed Belgians as an abominable people, assassins and torturers, who poisoned well water, stabbed soldiers in their sleep and cut out the eyes of the wounded on the battlefield. No German in the exuberance of the moment had the level-headedness to dismiss stories that were refuted by their very outrageousness. Hadn't their Emperor confirmed their veracity? And wasn't there proof of it in the burning of villages and the executions? Punishments implied a crime. They couldn't have been the result of an error. German national pride was too heavily invested in the stories to permit doubts. Parents shuddered that their children would be exposed to the treachery and atrocities of a bestial enemy. As I write these lines, I am looking at a letter of a German father who, full of concern, warns his son against the ferocity of the Belgians and recommends that he shoot down all the civilians

---

1 Colonel Schwertfeger, in the *General Gazette of North Germany* dated July 27, 1926 said that, "the events that accompanied the passage of the German army through Belgium during the summer of 1914 have been, without possible contestation, connected to combat with the civilian population of Belgium provoked only by them. The Belgian Interior Ministry, by its prescriptions for the Belgian *Garde civique* must bear the largest part of this responsibility." The Civic Guard, as was discussed, was a regular military force established by the Constitution.

who try to approach him.¹ It is unnecessary to say more. Lacking any proof and contradicted by the facts as well as by common sense, the story of the Belgian franc-tireurs is just one of those war legends whose spontaneous creation shouldn't surprise historians. Legends of this kind unfortunately have a long life. We should expect to see this one to continue for quite some time to stir the feelings of distrust and hatred to which it owes its birth.² ³

§ II. — THE INVASION

Certainly the Belgian army could not resist for very long the assault it was about to face. Its own generals were as convinced of this as foreign military observers. Public opinion believed the army would undoubtedly have to offer only a simulated defense, after which it would concentrate around Antwerp and await events. No campaign had been coordinated with France and Britain, which German aggression had turned into Belgium's allies and defenders. The military reorganization decreed in 1913 had barely begun to take effect. The army's weaponry was defective and incomplete. There was no heavy field artillery, aviation was rudimentary, the armament of the new forts in Antwerp had not been completed, and troop strength was inadequate. The long-range cannons, commissioned from Krupp factories, had not yet been delivered. The army, which had never been in combat, lacked a military tradition. However, it fulfilled to the best of its ability the role that national honor and the respect for treaties had thrust on it: to hold the line of the Meuse as long as possible, then fall back on Antwerp, while continuing to resist, or to fight alongside the French and British forces if they arrived in time.

---

1 It is part of the German collection of the *Archives of War*.
2 For the latest accusations lodged against the Belgian government and the response of the government, see the 1927 *Review of the War*.
3 For recent discussions of the franc-tireur question, see J. Horne and Kramer, A., <u>German Atrocities 1914: A History of Denial</u> (New Haven, 2001), 87–226; J. Lipkes, <u>Rehearsals: The German Army in Belgium, August 1914</u> (Leuven, 2007), 543–574.

We cannot trace here the history of the short campaign conducted by the Belgian Army against an opponent that relentlessly swept it aside. However, it is vital to summarize briefly the phases of the German invasion. Its events had direct repercussions on the country, and it's difficult to understand the attitude of the population during the occupation without offering an overview.

On the morning of August 4, German troops crossed the border by all the routes that linked the province of Liège to the region of Aachen. Except at the bridge at Visé, dominated by Fort de Pontisse, they did not encounter any resistance initially. As they entered the villages and the large industrial city of Verviers, the soldiers distributed a proclamation signed by General Otto Von Emmich. Its readers were amazed to learn that the French had invaded Belgium and that the German Army was marching into Belgium to counter the attack. The telegraph no longer functioned, so the region had been without news since the night before. One didn't know what to think. The uncertainty did not lift until, a few hours later, residents heard the first cannon-shots fired in the vicinity of Liège. Occupied by only 35,000 men, the position could not hold for very long. There were not enough troops to effectively man the gaps between the forts. On August 7 General Erich von Lundendorf seized the city by surprise. The night before, on August 6, General Gérard Leman, facing overwhelming numbers, evacuated Liège with a mobile defense force. The forts, still intact, were ordered to hold off the German advance as long as possible. The shells of the enemy's artillery were still ricocheting off the forts' armored domes. The soldiers believed the structures to be impenetrable. But several days later they were smashed to pieces by the barrages of steel from the Germans' 42 cm. howitzers. On the 15th, General Leman was taken prisoner inside the ruins of Fort de Loncin. The other forts, unable to hold out any longer, were occupied by the enemy.

With the capture of the Liège forts, Belgium was open to invasion. The army had fallen back behind the Gette. The King had taken command of it and his presence assured the good morale of the troops. An offer of peace that arrived on the 10th had been categorically refused. The situation seemed very grim. The French Army, after having penetrated Luxembourg and been defeated on the Semois, began to maneuver its left wing toward Namur and Hainaut. English troops were now landing in Boulogne. But it was clear the Belgian forces could count only on themselves. To stubbornly persist in resisting the German advance would mean the certain loss of the army. After having courageously defended Haelen (August 12), it withdrew toward Antwerp when it appeared that in would be enveloped from the south, while its center was simultaneously breached (August 20). At first the enemy limited himself to observing the retreat. The German objective was to surround the French corps massed behind the Sambre, from where the English extended the Allied line into the region of Mons. At the same time, the enemy advanced rapidly through the Meuse valley and assaulted the Namur forts. The German Army then crossed Brabant and entered Brussels on August 20. The fate of Namur was the same as that of Liège. Here the disproportion between the attacking and defending forces was even greater. On August 25 the forts were unable to continue the fight. A risky retreat allowed the garrison to reach the French border. Transported to Le Havre, it sailed to Ostend, which it reached on September 2nd and 3rd. On the 5th, it rejoined the rest of the army in Antwerp.

Meanwhile, the battle of Hainaut seemed to ensure the success of the gigantic turning movement planned by the German High Command. The French under General Charles Lanrezac and the English under Field Marshall Sir John French were pushed back to the South. Day by day the conquerors widened the space between the Allies and the small Belgian Army. On September 8 the first fighting on the Marne restored the situation. The Belgians contributed by conducting sorties out of Antwerp in order to disrupt the flow of German reinforcements headed toward the front.

Stopped at the Marne, the Germans now tried to turn the French to their left while the French attempted to envelope the Germans' right wing. Through a series of parallel movements, the two opponents extended the front day by day toward the sea. The moment seemed to have arrived for the Germans to eliminate the threat Antwerp posed to their communications. These forts, attacked on September 27 from the east and south, could not offer a more effective defense than those of Namur and Liège. Here, too, the howitzers destroyed the forts designed by Henri Brialmont, who had not taken into account advances in artillery. On October 2 the most powerful of all, that of Waelhem, was flattened. As before, to prolong the fight was to risk catastrophe. It was vital above all to avoid the envelopment and capture of the army. On October 7 the King gave the order to evacuate Antwerp by the left bank of the Scheldt. Covered by a corps of French hastily dispatched to the east of Ghent, the retreat succeeded despite the difficulties imposed by the narrowness of the gap between the enemy and the Dutch border. Except for 35,000 men who were forced to take refuge in Holland, where they were detained until the end of the war, most of the forces managed to reach Ostend. When the Germans entered Antwerp after the capitulation of the inner ring of forts, the city had been completely evacuated by its exhausted defenders. The army was now nothing but a ragged mob trudging along the roads beside the coast toward the Yser. They received the order to stop there and to hold the left of the French line, from Dixmunde to Nieuwpoort. Against all expectations, they recovered and once again faced the enemy. The opening of the locks of Nieuwpoort (October 28–31) flooded the plain between their line and Germans' and saved them at the very moment they faced annihilation. From then on they continued to occupy that part of the front, defending it until the victorious offensive of September 28, 1918.

The army's campaign had been one long and bloody retreat. Deprived of the assistance of its allies, who they joined only at the end of operations, the Belgian Army had to defend alone the neutrality that Europe had guaranteed the country. If it had yielded ground, it had safeguarded what was more essential: the right of the nation to independence. Belgium was occupied, but it was not conquered. Had Belgium disappeared from Europe, it would have meant that Europe itself had been annihilated by Germany.

In a country with such a high population density as Belgium, military operations were bound to have catastrophic consequences for civilians. But the massacres and destruction that took place greatly exceeded in number and gravity what could have been expected. Until the taking of Antwerp, destruction was, so to speak, the order of business. Many incidents took place behind the lines, and could not be attributed to the excitement of troops or to military necessity. Their principal cause, if not their only cause, was the German Army's obsession with franc-tireurs.

One can only explain the conduct of troops so admirably disciplined as a case of auto-suggestion.[1] The unexpected resistance the Germans met with must also have contributed to making them lose their self-control. If the Belgian army dared to face them, didn't it follow that it could count on the complicity of the population? The appearance of the countryside they initially crossed en route to Liège, bisected by thick hedgerows, with sunken roads and scattered, isolated houses, must have seemed perfect for ambushes. Both the occupations and pastimes of the residents only reinforced German suspicions. The little workshops in so many of the villages of the Vesdre valley where rifle barrels were built and the frequent presence of dovecotes—a natural consequence of the locals' passion for carrier pigeons—appeared to them as clear proof of the existence of a vast organization whose purpose was to supply arms to the franc-tireurs and

---

1 *This was not the view of most Belgian intellectuals, who believed the behavior of the army had deeper roots in Prussian* Kultur. *As mentioned, Pirenne follows the thesis of Fernand van Langenhove, who attributed the killings to a collective psychosis.*

provide information on troop movements.[1] If we add to that the usage of a foreign language and the practice of a religion despised by the Protestant soldiers of the regiments from Hanover and Prussia, who seemed to have been particularly numerous among the front line corps, one can explain the horrors that marked the first weeks of the invasion.

During the first days, it may have happened, and it no doubt did happen, that a "civilian," inspired by rage or despair, may have fired his hunting rifle at soldiers from the top of a granary or from behind a hedge. But a shot discharged accidentally, the blow-out of an automobile tire, a peasant running away from a sentry, may also have provoked the panic that resulted in the execution of random men, women, and children.

And once an alleged franc-tireur had been seized, the severity of the punishment often greatly exceeded the importance of the crime. Innocents had to pay for the guilty. In all villages accused of having sheltered a franc-tireur, hostages were rounded up, homes were set on fire, and several inhabitants executed. Proclamations by German officers threatened with death anyone who stuck his head out of a window or left a light on after sundown. Such cruel orders were clearly intended to extinguish immediately the least desire for resistance on the part of a population abandoned by the retreating army and at the mercy of the conqueror.

However, far from diminishing, German terrorism increased as the invasion progressed. From the middle of August all civilians were suspects. All villages were considered culpable where the rear-guard of the Belgian Army had fired on advancing forces, or where a bridge had been destroyed, railroad tracks raised, or telegraph lines cut. When German troops were under fire, they

---

[1] This incredible misapprehension testifies to the degree to which German troops were obsessed by franc-tireurs. To get an idea of this state of mind, read the account of an expedition in the province of Liège by an officer, P. O. Höcker, *An der Spitze meiner Kompagnie*, p. 30 (Berlin, 1924). His mission was to purge the land of franc-tireurs. He didn't see a single one. But he was nonetheless convinced that they were everywhere. He regarded each burnt down house he encountered as a home from which soldiers had been fired at.

forced the inhabitants to march in front of them, using their bodies as a protective shield. Burgomasters and, especially, priests in rural areas were always suspected of having incited the population. A summary judgment in the field was sufficient to sentence them to death. It is estimated that at least 43 priests were executed by the army in the dioceses of Liège, Tournai, Namur, and Mechelen. German officers lent credence to the most extraordinary and fantastic reports as to the presence and movement of franc-tireurs. On September 7 one German officer informed his superior officer that 2,000 franc-tireurs had marched from Liège to Antwerp![1] In all villages, notices from the Belgian government prohibiting any form of participation in military operations were still posted on the walls, and residents had deposited their weapons at the town halls. Clearly, the psychosis of war triggered the most wildly improbable prejudices. The more the devastation and executions multiplied, the more the contagion spread. The troops passing through villages that had been set ablaze had no doubt that their comrades had been assaulted there. The signs of punishment served as proof. If villages had been torched, it surely meant the inhabitants had fired on troops. Soldiers were anxious and exasperated to find themselves in the midst of people whom they believed capable of the worst treacheries. And one cannot be surprised if, as the German troops advanced, their nervousness increased and the consequences become more dire. The final catastrophes caused by this state of mind exceeded all those that had taken place earlier. In Andenne (August 20–21) they killed 211, in Tamines (August 22–23) 384, in Dinant (August 23) 665, including a number of women and even two-year-old children!

It was later rumored in Germany that the activities of the francs-tireurs were a result of "race hatred." Their deeds were attributed

---

[1] German collection of the *Archives of War*. The rumor was naturally false, as proven by the word *erledigt*, nothing to add, inscribed in the document. It may be of interest to recall that the nuncio of Brussels, Monsignor Taici wrote to the pope on December 6, 1914 that there were no franc-tireurs in Belgium. See Beyens in the *Revue des Deux-Mondes*, 1926, p. 866.

to the rage of the Latin population of Wallonia against its German conqueror. In reality, the Flemish part of the country was as cruelly "chastised" as the Walloon part. The tragedies of Aarschot (August 19) and Leuven (August 26) in which hundreds of people died and where a large part of each town was set ablaze equaled in horror the atrocities committed in the provinces of Liège, Namur, and Luxemburg. It was only after the seizure of Antwerp that the progress of the invasion ceased to be accompanied by terrorism. There were no more reports of it when the German army crossed through the two Flanders and Hainaut. Once the front was stabilized and Belgium permanently occupied, German troops were no longer troubled by francs-tireurs—whose existence was too obviously a fantasy. But the four weeks following the invasion were sufficient time for the country to be devastated.

In more than 350 towns and villages out of 1,146 in the provinces of Liège, Namur, Limburg, and Luxembourg, residents lost their possessions and their lives. In the country as a whole, more than 5,000 civilians were executed.[1] It's not surprising that the indignation the August 3 ultimatum had aroused against Germany was now followed by a real nation-wide hatred.[2]

The devastation caused by the German troops had yet another outcome: emigration from that part of the nation most affected by the depredations. At the beginning, the arson and executions that accompanied operations around Liège and Namur were hardly known at all in the rest of the country. The advance of the enemy kept the news from spreading and nobody knew what was happening behind enemy lines. On the other hand, the tragedies of Aarschot and Leuven, which took place not far from Brussels and Antwerp, caused collective panic, as those fleeing the devastation

---

[1] M. Olbrechts, using the lists from the *Reports and Documents of the Commission of Inquiry on the Violation of Human Rights*, tables I and II of the first volume, established the figure of 5,517 victims of massacres perpetrated by German troops, of which only 91 were killed after 1914, in E. Mahaim, *La Belgique restaurée*, p. 16.

[2] For details on the executions and arson, see Horne and Kramer, 9–53, and Lipkes, 39–542.

related their experiences. From that moment, the advancing German troops were preceded by a frenzied retreat. Entire villages fled westward. All the towns in the interior witnessed wave after wave of unfortunate refugees, who needed to be provided for in makeshift premises and housed in neighboring villages. Pretty much the entire population of Leuven, as well as that of Mechelen, fled to the west. Before the surrender of Antwerp there was a massive exodus of terrified residents toward the Netherlands. Refugees massed along the coast, seeking sanctuary in England, after it became evident that nothing could prevent the enemy from reaching the Channel. The number of Belgians who sought refuge in the Netherlands was estimated at approximately one million, not including the soldiers who crossed into Dutch territory after the fall of Antwerp. At the end of November 1915, the number of emigrants to England was no less than 250,000. Others headed to France, both after the battle of Hainaut and especially by sea after the German advance into Flanders. On January 1, 1915, they numbered over 115,000. Altogether about 1,400,000 people, that is to say a little less than one-fifth of the total population of the country, fled the terror, a veritable *diaspora*. Undoubtedly a good number of these terror-stricken citizens soon returned to the country. Yet more than half a million among them were forced to stay abroad until the end of the war. We will later return to this emigration, unquestionably one of the most striking social phenomena of the invasion of Belgium.[1]

---

[1] See Chapter XI.

CHAPTER III

General situation of the country during the occupation

§ I. — AN IMPRISONED NATION

Since the 18th century, Belgium has endured military occupation many times. Dragged into all the great international conflicts, it has served as a battlefield or a pawn for Powers sometimes fighting for hegemony and sometimes to restore the balance of power in Europe. The War of the Spanish Succession saw Belgium pass from the control of the English to that of the Dutch, between 1706 and 1713. France occupied the country during the Seven Years War, from 1745 to 1748, and again after the battle of Jemmapes in 1792–1793, and once more, and this time for twenty years, after the battle of Fleurus in 1794. The defeat of Napoleon delivered Belgium to the Allies in 1815. Thus its possession by Germany from August 1914 to November 1918 was hardly a new phenomenon. It was only one more chapter in the long struggle for mastery among the large states of the West. The most recent occupation was different from previous ones only in the strength of the occupier's grip on the country, and by the national reaction that it provoked.

Starting from the day when the fronts of the armies stabilized on the Yser, almost the whole of Belgium came under the control of the invader for over four years. Of its 2,636 towns and villages, only about fifty escaped conquest. The government retained just a thin slice of West Flanders, wedged between the Yser and the French frontier. Belgium also retained control of the town of Bar-le-Duc, formerly under the jurisdiction of the province of Antwerp, but which, being an enclave within the Dutch province of Northern Brabant, escaped the enemy's grasp. The government itself became a refugee. After retreating to Antwerp, it relocated to Le Havre, where the hospitality of the Republic of France assured it temporary asylum. Only the King, established at La Panne among the troops he commanded, remained on the nation's soil. It was impossible to set up the ministries and their offices directly behind the lines, among field hospitals and barracks. Under a legal fiction, the buildings occupied by the government in Le Havre were designated Belgian territory, giving them the privilege of extraterritoriality. Next to invaded Belgium was another Belgium that continued to survive, governed by its national institutions. From a legal point of view, it didn't matter that the state consisted only of a narrow strip of land. The essential point was that it had not disappeared, that its sovereignty had not been overturned, and that its conqueror could not boast of having annihilated it. It did not exist merely because its allies recognized its right to exist: it existed in fact. Its flag continued to fly in Brussels on the King's palace and on the *Palais de la Nation*.[1]

Naturally, circumstances kept the government from functioning normally. It was impossible for the Chambers to convene. They could not pass laws or budgets. However the Constitution was not officially "suspended," but only considered "unexecutable." At this point the King ruled by virtue of the powers delegated to him on August 4, not by law but by legally-binding decrees. These decrees began with a statement affirming that the Constitution would be respected and retained: "In view of Article 26 of the Constitution that confers on the King the exercise of

---
[1] This is the name given in Belgium to the palace occupied by the Parliament.

the legislative power, which passes to him from the Chamber of Representatives and from the Senate; and given the impossibility to convene the legislative chambers, upon the proposal of our Minister...we have adjourned."

The King now represented the nation and exercised the legislative power given to him in the interest of public safety. The ministry answered to him, and all the parties were now represented within it, or, to better put it, all the parties were absorbed and united in it. Alongside the Catholic ministers, who had come to power in the elections of 1912, some opposition leaders were offered ministries. And so Liberals and, for the first time, a Socialist, sat in the Cabinet.[1]

Of the members of Parliament, a small number continued to advise the government in Le Havre. Others, after the session on August 4, returned to their districts. Intermittent relationships were maintained between the former and the latter until the end of the war.

The government at La Havre had little influence on occupied Belgium, comparable to that exercised over a besieged population by the army coming to relieve it. It was obviously impossible for it to govern. It was barely able to pass along directives to the civil servants in the occupied provinces. Most people, and even some authorities, were unaware of the work it was performing on behalf of refugees and deportees, its intervention in the provisioning of the country, and the efforts it made to focus the world's attention on the suffering in Belgium.[2] For the entire duration of the war, the nation put its faith in the King and the army. The rumble of the cannons from the Yser that the west wind brought toward the interior reminded one too movingly of their presence to be able

---

[1] Emile Vandervelde (1866–1938). He served as minister without a portfolio and, after the war, Minister of Justice and then Minister of Foreign Affairs.
[2] On November 14, 1918, as the *échevain* Lemonnier was leaving the Hôtel de Ville in Brussels, Minister Vandervelde arrived to announce the return of the government and said to him, "We would like to congratulate you for everything you have accomplished, but in the end we know little because we faced an iron wall."

to think of anything else. All in all, the government of Le Havre could only help the country from the outside. It was unable to act directly on Belgium. The conqueror assumed its place.[1]

§ II. — THE ATTITUDE OF THE PEOPLE

The people's outlook was basically determined by psychological predispositions. To fully appreciate these, it's important to recognize the contrast which, from the beginning, Belgians drew between themselves and their conquerors, and which continued to the end of the occupation.

This contrast was not based on race. It is too easy to attribute to race the characteristics that differentiate one people from the other. Comparing the Germanic race with the Latin race is engaging in empty rhetoric. It's not race at all, or even a common language, that brings people together; it's shared feelings and beliefs. That is to say, a people differentiates itself from or feels closer to other peoples because of its education, which determines its collective psychology. And the education of Belgians and Germans had made them too different from one another to avoid misunderstandings that the tragic circumstances inevitably exacerbated.

The preponderance of Prussia, increasingly dominating the Reich, had created an opposition, partly intentional and partly unconscious, between itself and the West, to which, of course, both the Walloon and Flemish provinces of Belgium belonged. The social evolution of Prussia, as well as its political constitution, had transformed it into a state of a particular nature, simultaneously very backward and very modern. Serfdom had only been abolished at the beginning of the 19th century; a land-owning

---

[1] The situation of the ministry in Le Havre was very delicate. It did not want to give offense, as it was itself in a safe place, by inciting Belgians under German occupation to resistance. In this regard its politics could be called the politics of the lesser evil. On its activity, refer in the Belgian series of this work to the contribution of F. Van Langenhove, *L'Action du government belge en matière économique pendant la guerre*.

aristocracy, which preserved the memory of feudal traditions, supplied the civil servants and officers of the monarchic state, which it served both out of self-interest and a sense of honor. Public administration and the army were distinguished equally for their discipline, love of duty, and devotion to the crown. A belief in their superiority aroused in Prussians both an aversion to and a disdain for political liberty and democracy. They had confidence only in the use of force; they viewed it as the primary condition of power. Germany had, after all, been unified by the sword of the Hohenzollern, a unity for which the poets and philosophers of "Little Germany" had so long pined. In achieving this goal, Prussia imposed itself on Germany. Its positivist spirit, discipline, traditions of absolutism, and reactionary principles were interpreted in the universities as the essential traits of a truly Germanic civilization. The belief in the superiority of the German race over all other races and its mission to impose German supremacy on them for their own good spread with a surprising speed that matched the astonishing progress of commerce and industry. Both the intellectual elite and the active and prosperous middle class submitted themselves voluntarily to the service of a state whose victories testified to the virtues of force. As impatient as they may have been regarding the preeminence of the Junkers and of officers, the Liberal and Socialist opposition couldn't help but be influenced by the same spirit of reverence for the state. The government had implanted it in the nation's schools, barracks, and administration, and it was only enhanced by the growing wealth of Germany and by the prestige it enjoyed among foreigners.

The constitution of the Reich contributed even more strongly to propagate the dogma of the all-powerful state. Sovereignty did not reside in the nation. It rested in the *Staat*, a mystical being that existed independently outside and above it. This was embodied in the *Kaiser*, who lent it the prestige of his dynasty and who, in turn, was the object of loyalty, national pride, military faithfulness, gratefulness, and veneration. In former times it had been customary to identify individualism as the fundamental attribute of the Germans. Today, they are glorified for their spirit of discipline and organization, and their voluntary subordination to the state. The Pan-Germans welcomed the Prussianization of Germany without acknowledging that Prussia, a new country that had gradually conquered the Slavs, had contributed only marginally to the German culture they praised as the highest and purest. The theory of races was revived. Dazzled by the military success of the Hohenzollern and the diplomatic success of Bismarck, Germany considered Berlin's government the preordained instrument of its national genius. Intoxicated by its victories, it forgot the hostility that had long been directed at Prussia. Catholics themselves no longer remembered *Kulturkampf*. Despite their confessional differences, and conflicting customs, beliefs, and cultures, Germans shared the same faith in power. This collective political consciousness, dormant during the long centuries when Germany had no national existence, was united in the worship of the state. It viewed the authority that was imposed on it as a spontaneous manifestation of its own nature. It was not only the bourgeoisie of the Rhine who gave way before the Prussian Junker. Militarism became the highest form of civic spirit and force became the most majestic manifestation of the law. The originality and superiority of *Deutschtum* appeared all the more evident the more completely it rejected the pacific, liberal, and internationalist ideology of the decadent democracies of the West.

So Germans could neither understand nor accept the nature of a people so completely unlike them as were the Belgians. The weakness of their small nation was already a reason to disdain them. How could Belgium claim the right to an existence it was incapable of defending? Its refusal to permit the German Army to pass through the country seemed an absurd outrage. In opposing Germany, wasn't Belgium opposing the necessary and inevitable triumph of Germanism? And what did its so-called Belgian nationality consist of? Lacking unity of race and language, it was only a bastard creation of European diplomacy. The name "Belgium" was just a label given to some territories that the interests of the Great Powers had provisionally neutralized in 1839 in order to avoid a general war. The country existed only by virtue of the tolerance of Europe. Belgium ought to consider itself fortunate to have led so long a life as a parasite, enriching itself in peace, thanks to the dubious security arrangements that had created it. The liberalism of its institutions represented only a backward and detestable form of an antiquated political concept. The reigning ideology had only succeeded in discrediting the monarchy, unleashing a selfish rivalry between parties, and allowing a greedy and petty middle class to exploit the people. It had corrupted the people itself by abandoning it to all the disorder of licentiousness and anarchy.

The Belgian state was as execrable as the Belgian nation. It had proven incapable of fulfilling its task. It had left the masses deprived of *Kultur* and abandoned them to the ranting of politicians or the fanaticism of an ignorant clergy. One could hardly be surprised at the atrocities committed by the franc-tireurs. These represented only the manifestations of the ingrained indiscipline of an arrogant and brutal population, incited to crime by the rage of defeat and which brazenly gave its impotent passion the name of patriotism.[1]

In October 1914 this aversion for Belgium was revived by the discovery of a report of conversations between General Ducarne and British Colonel Bernardiston.[2] The Germans saw this as evidence of treacherous behavior toward their country. It was

---

1 Here I am only reporting a state of mind revealed, in so characteristic a way, in the manifesto of German intellectuals of October 1914. It is abundantly proven by all the German newspapers of the time, as well as by numerous brochures published in the Reich from 1914 to 1918 on the "Belgian question."
2 As noted, this was a series of discussions in early 1906 between the British military attaché and the Chief of the General Staff as to the possibility of joint military operations in the event of a German invasion. No agreement was concluded.

interpreted as a flagrant violation of the neutrality the Germans themselves had always scrupulously observed. A long-lasting press campaign was launched to prove Belgium guilty of concluding secret understandings with Germany's enemies, particularly France. The multiple links forged by history, geographical location, and commerce between Belgium and France seemed to be the proof of a sort of systematic encirclement of the Reich accomplished with the complicity of official authorities. In the heat of their polemics, the Germans didn't bother noting that this situation went back to the Middle Ages and that French influence was as traditional in Belgium as British influence was in the United States of America.

To German public opinion, the war seemed to be a conflict of the Germanic peoples and the Latin peoples. Belgium had united with the latter. To demonstrate the perversity of this, German scholars reminded the public that the country was originally part of the Holy Roman Empire and had belonged to the House of Hapsburg. Any way one looked at Belgium, there were reasons to condemn it. Its people, constitution, government, outlook, and sympathies condemned it equally. No matter how hard the Belgians' fate would turn out to be, they deserved it. Whatever was going to happen, it was unacceptable that Belgians retain their independence, of which it they had made such bad use for themselves and others. If, once the war was over, Belgium did not disappear from the map of Europe, it should at least become a protectorate of Germany. Until then, it would serve as a pawn in diplomatic negotiations and provide a base for military operations.

To the antipathy of their conquerors, Belgians responded with hatred, and the Germans' disdain was met with contempt. Under the trauma of the invasion, all that Belgians had formerly admired about Germany was forgotten. A country responsible for such monstrous injustice was capable of anything. Their certainty of not having any responsibility for the catastrophe that struck them made Belgians feel an even deeper indignation at the executions and arson that had marked the progress of the invasion. Even the normal consequences of war seemed unbearably brutal. The requisitions and restrictions the military authorities imposed brought constant suffering and insult. As Belgians lost the unlimited freedom they enjoyed, it became all the more precious, and they were suddenly stirred by a patriotism that had slumbered during the long years of peace. The nation needed this crisis to appreciate the blessings of independence, just as illness makes one appreciate the blessings of good health. In their present misfortune, Belgians recalled the happy years they'd experienced. People felt less bitter about the political warfare and social conflicts. These were remembered only as the manifestations of freedom. And the memories Belgians preserved intensified their hatred of the enemy.

When they compared themselves to the Germans, they detested them all the more. German discipline, worship of the state, and monarchic sentiment were seen as evidence of servility. The Belgians proudly juxtaposed them to the institutions they themselves had created. One gloried in belonging to a nation that conferred on every individual the dignity of citizenship. To the idea of a bureaucratic and authoritarian state, Belgians opposed the conception of the state as the manifestation of national sovereignty. German militarism seemed a monstrous aberration and the clear proof of brutality. The strutting of their soldiers on parade, their passive obedience, their submissive attitude toward their officers aroused mockery or rage. At the passing of their regiments, Belgians asked themselves how many grandsons of serfs marched among them. Crushed by force, the people drew on their conviction that they were superior to their victors and found thereby the courage to endure their suffering. Belgians identified their cause with the cause of law and justice. They were victims because of they'd honored a pledge.

Even the disproportion of the fight was a matter of pride. They did not count on an impossible victory, and they were not demoralized by the setbacks of their army. The popularity of the Belgian dynasty grew as it identified itself with the nation by sharing its suffering. The King became a legendary hero and the Queen a saint nursing the injured and dying in the field hospitals. The little news that one received left it to the imagination to embellish them with an aureole of glory and goodness—which actually corresponded to reality.[1] Belgians began to name their newborns Albert and Elisabeth. The portrait of the sovereigns, which was illegal to display in public, was in every home.

At first it was believed that the war would be very short. In the beginning everyone eagerly awaited the arrival of the French to rescue the national army. The enigmatic reports of the government buoyed one's hopes. People gave credence to the most unbelievable rumors. Until the end of the war, Belgians didn't stop believing their fortune would turn. The German notices, filled with announcements of victories, failed to weaken the resolve to resist until the end. Although in the darkest hour there were some "defeatists," and a small group of "activists" renounced the national cause, one was surprised by how the great majority of Belgians hadn't the least desire to give up resistance. The final triumph was never in doubt. In fact, in 1915 a committee was formed in Brussels to prepare for a world's fair!

This attitude was all the more surprising in that everything discouraged it. From December 1914, Belgium found itself isolated from the outside world. It was truly imprisoned. Along the entire length of the northern border ran a barbed-wire fence with high-voltage current. Along the coast and the border with France, the German armies presented an obstacle even more impenetrable. To cross into Germany, a passport was required.

---

[1] *Reality was, of course, more complex. Unbeknownst to his subjects, and even to his own ministers, King Albert, convinced that the Germans would win the war, opened negotiations with Berlin in September 1915. Intermediaries met in Zurich in November and in January and February of 1915. But Albert feared the loss of the Congo if Belgium were to ally with Germany, as Berlin required. Nonetheless, another round of negotiations was begun in the fall of 1916, and talks were again resumed early in 1918. These also proved fruitless. The "activists" weren't the only defeatists in Belgium.*

In a country so cut off, it was a great risk to slip in French or English newspapers, sometimes several weeks old. Belgians shared them with one other, passing them under their coats. Some Dutch newspapers, however, like the *Nieuwe Rotterdamsche Courant,* were tolerated by the censors, although the Germans often confiscated those issues whose contents did not seem to be sufficiently neutral. With very few exceptions, Belgian newspapers did not want to subject themselves to the control of the enemy, and so ceased to appear. Their place was taken by the gazettes bribed or protected by the *Kommandanturen*: in Liège, *Echo de Liège,* in Brussels, *Bruxellois, Quotidien, Messenger de Bruxelles, Information,* etc. Under the pretense of enlightening public opinion and restoring a sense of reality, they made quite skilled efforts to suppress it. They represented a Belgian victory as an impossibility, and, invoking national interest, preached the acceptance of the inevitable and a rapprochement with Germany. People read the German-sponsored papers to get local news, for want of anything better. However, the only sentiment they elicited was disgust.

The efforts of the German authorities to break the spirit of the people were not successful either. They plastered the walls with notices announcing death sentences, deportation, or imprisonment for spies, who every day in some part of the country faced military tribunals. The authorities widely publicized the deadly accidents that occasionally resulted from bombs dropped by Belgian, French, or British aviators. They published proof of the "disloyalty" of the Belgian government. And they blamed the blockade organized by Britain for the paralysis of industry and the shortage of food. However, no one was influenced by their declarations. Quite the opposite! Instead of spreading fear, they incited resistance. Belgians venerated as heroes the spies executed by firing squads, and their torture inspired emulators in all social classes, from the highest aristocracy to the poorest laborers. The number of executions provides the best proof of this contagion of patriotism. There were over three hundred, it's estimated, by the end of the occupation. As for the people sentenced to imprisonment or deportation, their number was infinitely higher, but it can't be calculated with any precision.[1] In fact, the occupying power felt itself confronted by a permanent conspiracy of the entire nation

To discover the guilty, it made the failure to denounce criminals into a crime. Family members were encouraged to denounce one another, though in cases where spouses and children had failed to accuse their husbands or fathers, attenuating circumstances were sometimes admitted.[2] A series of measures aimed at submitting the population to a sort of secular inquisition. Censorship extended not only to correspondence but also to all "print products, all reproductions of writings or images, and musical compositions, with text or commentary, produced by mechanical or chemical procedures, and intended for distribution."

From the beginning of the occupation, outdoor gatherings had been banned, as well as public or private political meetings. Exceptions were made for gatherings of a "religious, social, scientific, professional, or artistic" nature. This tolerance, however, lasted only a short time. On May 25, 1916 a decree required that even these be authorized ahead of time. After this date, Belgians could freely get together only to attend services at church. All patriotic demonstrations were expressly forbidden. It was also illegal to display in public "Belgian symbols in a provocative way" or to display even "in a non-provocative way" the insignia of other countries at war with Germany or its allies (June 26, 1915). To prevent school teachers from instilling patriotic sentiments in their students, German authorities were given "the right to enter all the classrooms in every school in Belgium and to

---

[1] M. Ollbrechts, *doc. cit.*, p. 16. The number of the deported who died during their deportation has been estimated at 2,614.
[2] See in the Belgian series of this work, the work of J. Pirenne and M. Vauthier, *La Législation et l'administration allemandes en Belgique*, p. 199, 202.

oversee the instruction and all activities of school life in order to prevent intrigues and plots directed against Germany." Even students' books and notebooks were inspected, so rigorous was the surveillance. The discovery of an irreverent phrase was sufficient to send the child guilty of "Germanophobia" to prison.[1] On the other hand, individuals who expressed Germanophile sentiments was protected against those who attempted to harm them by the threat of two years in prison and a 10,000 marks fine.[2]

The interdictions of the conqueror were circumvented by the Belgians' penchant for jokes and puzzles. Since displaying the Belgian flag was banned, on the national holidays women dressed themselves in the flag's colors, while men sported a green leaf in their buttonhole as a sign of hope, and shops and restaurants remained closed. These demonstrations, where mockery allied with patriotism, inevitably elicited a decree prohibiting "organized demonstrations taking place in which special emblems were displayed or colors worn, or the closing of shops and restaurants," etc.[3]

The relentlessness of the military authorities against the least and most innocuous displays of patriotism was counterproductive. On July 21, 1916, the national holiday, a German patrol in a suburb of Lierre saw a Belgian flag that had been hoisted to the top of a large tree during the night. Portraits of the King and Queen surrounded by ad hoc poems were tied to the trunk. Residents were immediately confined to their homes, starting from 9 PM. A thorough investigation was carried out. On August 15, 1916, desperate to find the perpetrators of this crime, "who would clearly be known by the population," the governor of the province condemned the municipality to pay a fine of 20,000

---

[1] A. Berlaere, a girl of 16, was arrested for having transcribed in her notebook naive Flemish poems in which was discovered an irreverent verse about the Kaiser. See the dossier of this issue in the German collection of the *Archives of War*.
[2] J. Pirenne and M. Vauthier, op.cit., p. 26
[3] *Ibid*

marks. The garrison was reinforced and soldiers were lodged with some of the most well off members of the middle class, six of whom were imprisoned at the police station. The charge was "attempted murder" (*Moordversuch*), by virtue of the fact that the branches of the tree having been sawed, the soldiers ordered to remove the flag could do so only "at the risk of their lives."[1]

The *Meldeämt* was one of the most difficult institutions to bear. This was the office that kept track of all men born between 1880 and 1898, that is to say those in the age range eligible for military service, as well as former members of the Civic Guard[2], Belgians who had served in the army, some civil or military prisoners convicted by military tribunals and sent back to their homes until the end of their sentence, and nationals of both sexes of the countries at war with Germany, along with all others who were considered dangerous or suspect. These individuals were required to appear in person at the *Meldeamt* nearest their residence at least once a month. All travel, all temporary or permanent changes of residence, had to be authorized or the individual would be subject to a fine, imprisonment, or even deportation to a prison camp. These restrictions on their freedom of movement were bitterly resented by the Belgian population, who until then had been the most mobile people in the world. Affordable transportation and the institution of laborers' trains brought dozens of thousands of travelers to the industrial regions every day. Penned in and branded, so to speak, one felt humiliation and anger.

In fact, the *Meldeämten* did not manage to achieve their main goal, which was to prevent young men from joining the Belgian Army. Thousands of them made their way through the briars and marshes of the Campine and reached Holland, from where they went on to the recruitment offices set up in Britain and France. Many were gunned down by border guards or electrocuted as

---
1 See the dossier on this event in the German collections of the *Archives of War*.
2 The Civic Guard was dissolved in the month of September 1914. Some of its members served in the army or moved abroad. Others rejoined their families in the interior of the country.

they tried to cross the barbed wire fence that ran along the border. Others were captured en route and deported. The number of those who managed to escape is estimated at around 30,000.

The *Meldeämter* also deprived the Belgians of that most fundamental right: the inviolability of one's home. All suspects—and the most trivial denunciation made one a suspect—were subject to visits by the secret police, the seizure of their papers or correspondence, and to an inquest. To be considered undesirable by the military administration was sufficient grounds for deportation not only without a trial, but also without the least explanation. A person sent to the *Kommandatur* was never sure if he would return home. It frequently happened that he learned he was to be sent immediately to Germany. Often he was not allowed to put his affairs in order or even to say goodbye to his family before he left.[1]

The most terrible suffering Belgians endured was not knowing the fate of their soldiers. The enemy placed a watertight wall between the nation and its army. For over four years, families with sons at the front lived in perpetual anxiety. The uncertainty only ceased when it was replaced by a still crueler certainty, when they learned through the Red Cross that their son, whom they hadn't seen for so long, had died, or that he lay wounded in a field hospital. Only those soldiers who were in prison camps in Germany could correspond with their parents. One tried to interpret the silence of the others as proof they were alive. Occasionally a soldier would reveal that he was still alive by publishing an announcement in the *Rotterdamasche Courant*. An organization called *Word of the Soldier (Le Mot du Soldat)* assumed the dangerous task of serving as an intermediary between the troops at the front and the rest of the country. The police hunted down its members, imprisoning or deporting those it caught, but never succeeded in disrupting its activities. Until the end of the war, the organization

---

[1] The author speaks here from personal experience. His testimony can be replicated by hundreds of others.

rallied the country's morale and buoyed its hopes.

The will to "hold on" manifested by Belgium's population is even more astonishing if one considers their distress. The suffering resulting from the closing of industries, unemployment, and the shortages of food and of fuel for heat and light increased year after year. Here again, and especially here, the spirit of solidarity manifested itself in a striking way. Next to the *Comité National*, many charitable groups worked to fight poverty, and they multiplied as poverty increased.[1]

The collective conspiracy against the occupier was matched by a no less widespread alliance of Belgians against their common misfortune. Good citizens understood right away the duty the situation imposed on them. Charity became a form of patriotism.

Common misfortune and shared hopes bound Belgians together and made them forget the warfare between the parties and the social and linguistic conflicts that had so exasperated them in peacetime. Although the Flemish question would later become a catalyst for disagreement, Catholics, Liberals, and Socialists established a tacit understanding that united them in an indivisible bloc. Attempts by fanatical partisans to exploit the situation by attacking the party that had exercised power since 1884 were generally ignored. The leading figures in all the parties put their differences aside. The three major parties did not disappear completely. The discipline that made members amenable to the influence of their chiefs inspired them to support the directives of the new Order of National Union created by the leadership. One witnessed between 1914 and 1918 something like the union of the parties that had had been responsible for the revolution of 1830. The truce among the parties almost recalled the medieval Peace of God. The fact that newspapers refused to publish and political meetings were banned also no doubt helped prevent a revival of partisan polemics. Many whose combativeness or need

---

[1] On their activity, see Chapter VI.

for action had led them to get involved in political work found an outlet in espionage or charitable activities.

By extraordinary good fortune, from the beginning of the occupation some men who had been influential only within Church or party circles became spokesmen for and symbols of national independence. The proclamations of the burgomaster of Brussels, Adolphe Max, had all the greater impact because of the traditional Belgian reverence for municipal autonomy. The example of the capital's magistrate forged a path for his colleagues. His deportation on September 26, 1914, instead of silencing the others, made them redouble their efforts. He became a national hero, joining the long line of martyrs for liberty: the Arteveldes, the Egmonts, the Agneessens, the Laruelles, whose deeds live on in the hearts of the people. Among the numerous mistakes that the German administration made due to their lack of understanding of the Belgian character, nothing was quite so disastrous as exiling the burgomaster of Brussels. One must go back to the time of the duke of Alba to find an army that operated with such disregard for the psychological impact of its actions.

Among those on whom Burgomaster Max left a lasting impression was Cardinal Désiré-Joseph Mercier. In the general silence, his voice rose all the more eloquently. One knew the cardinal to be a neo-Thomist philosopher, an eminent prelate, and one of Pope Leo XIII's most distinguished colleagues, but, apart from the clergy and the leaders of the Catholic party, his powerful personality had not yet been revealed to the public. In times of peace, his position as head of the Belgian Church made him incapable of influencing Liberals and Socialists. War transformed him into the incarnation of the national sentiment, uniting all the parties. His pastoral letter of January 1, 1915, posted outside the door of every church, was intended for all Belgians. Declaring that the invader "is not a legitimate authority and that from now on in the inner recesses of our conscience we do not owe him esteem, attachment, or respect," his words made it imperative for Catholics to persevere in their resistance and, at the same time, legitimated perseverance for everybody. Belgium, said the Cardinal, was no more a German province than Galicia was a Russian province. If one had to submit to the situation and "to not believe that courage consists in bravado, or bravery in disruptive behavior," the rights of conscience imposed endurance until the final triumph of justice. It was for justice that Belgium suffered, he said. And this suffering will pass. However, "the crown of life for our souls and the glory for the Nation will never pass." His words both consoled and inspired. The responsibility of the man who made this declaration and the eminence of his position insured that this was no reckless provocation. In the presence of the enemy, Cardinal Mercier professed his faith as Luther had professed his before Charles V at the Diet of Worms.[1]

His protests continued to buoy the confidence and energy of the Belgian people. The attempts of the General Government to silence the prelate were met with his categorical refusals. It became clear that it would be impossible to pressure or persuade him and that he would not be responsive to the enemy's benevolent gestures, which he only used to strengthen his position. He was too highly placed for the Germans to lay a hand on him. Exiling him was not an option. The scandal would have reverberated too loudly in Rome and throughout the world, which was paying close attention to this duel between the Catholic priest and the German military.[2] The Germans had to limit themselves to prohibiting the reading of his pastorals, threatening those parish priests charged with reading them, and forbidding the printing and distributing them. All these efforts were in vain. As

---

[1] To appreciate the Cardinal's attitude, one should consult especially F. Mayence, *La Correspondance de Son Em. le cardinal Mercier avec the gouvernment général allemand durant l'occupation* (Brussles, 1919)

[2] On the various attempts made in Rome by the German government to remove Cardinal Mercier from Belgium, see W. Kisky, *Kardinal Mercier und wir* (Horchland, May 1926, p. 156–171). The book's unreserved admiration for the Cardinal and his conduct is even more significant when one considers that the author was a German official in Belgium during the occupation.

soon as they were written, his pastorals irrigated the country as water seeps into the earth. The Cardinal's words were absorbed by the entire country through thousands of invisible channels. Believers and unbelievers alike were influenced by him. The soul of Cardinal Mercier was, in a sense, the soul of the nation. The royal palace was empty; everyone looked instead to the archbishop's palace in Mechelen. The Cardinal became Belgium's leading personality much as, in fourth-century Rome, after it had been abandoned by the emperors, the pope became the leading personage in the Eternal City.

The absence of the King and Queen, however, was only a physical absence. Their memory lived on within the hearts of the Belgian people. They behaved exactly as one would have hoped! With admirable tact, they assumed the role required of them. One could visualize them far off, he in the midst of the troops, she in the field hospitals. They both suffered alongside their people. Their small house in La Panne was exposed, as was everyone else's, to bombs dropped from airplanes. Their simple and sincere desire to serve the nation made them seem all the more its leaders. One had grown accustomed to the dynasty; now one came to love it. And this love manifested itself in a flowering of naive and touching legends that were the poetry of those terrible years.

The underground press also played a very large role in the moral resistance of the nation. It began with the news reports that, from the beginning of the occupation, were secretly transmitted from individual to individual, copied by hand or typed on pieces of paper: translations of articles from the *Times*, excerpts from French newspapers, analyses of the speeches of politicians from the Allied countries, propaganda brochures, ad-hoc verses or writings, echoes of all sorts coming from the outside and which, passing through the grapevine, were naturally transformed into legends. Despite the danger, the idea of increasing the distribution of this information through the press was bound to come sooner or later. Newspapers had become such a pressing need in modern life that one could hardly bear having no other reading material than the enemy's papers, or those in pay of the Germans. Any periodical that provided news and commentary corresponding to the outlook of most Belgians was bound to succeed. Beginning in February 1915, *Libre Belgique* took upon itself the responsibility of supplying exactly that. It was almost incomprehensible how this paper never ceased to appear, though hunted down by the Germans until the retreat of their armies in 1918. It certainly would not have been able to do so were it not for the courage of its writers, publishers, and distributors, and the complicity of the public. As soon as the enemy discovered one of the hideouts where the paper was printed, confiscated its copies, convicted and deported some of its staff, the paper reappeared, even more mocking and aggressive, regaling readers with the story of its own adventure and thumbing its nose at the police more than ever. It boasted that it was printed "inside a car," so successfully did it evade the authorities. Legends began to surface about it. One heard that every issue was mysteriously placed on the desk of the Governor General. In any case, each copy was passed from hand to hand. The danger of reading it made it more enticing. It encouraged its readers not only by its articles, but by the very fact that it existed and endured. It distracted Belgians from their daily anxieties, made people laugh, and gave them something to talk about. Undoubtedly, it was a continual "act of bravado." But it was a bravado so courageous, and so in tune with public opinion, that the Cardinal himself read it, along with the clergy, who made up a good percentage of its writers, and who went to jail along with the journalists and illustrious scholars who contributed.[1] Its example stimulated imitators: *La Patrie*, *L'Ame belge*, *De Vlaamsche Leeuw*, and, toward the end of the occupation, *Le Flambeau* and *L'Autre Cloche*, to which university professors in

---

1 Cf. Fidelis (A. Van De Kerkhove), *L'Histoire merveilleuse de la Libre Belgique*, 2nd edition (Brussels, 1919).

particular contributed.

In the absence of any legal way to act on one's views, those members of Parliament who had remained in the country, along with municipal council representatives, ingeniously used these papers to communicate with the occupying power itself. They did this by addressing the German authorities with statements, requests, and protests. They wrote to the Chancellor of the Empire, the Governor General, and the provincial governors. These documents were written in the two national languages and, recopied by machine, spread with astonishing speed. Whoever received a copy of one quickly reproduced it and passed it under his coat to friends who, in turn, did the same. These writings were soon being passed around in foreign countries, where the propaganda services distributed them around the world. The great number of signatures they contained prevented the enemy from pinning responsibility on one individual and, besides, the official character of these communiqués did not allow the Germans to proceed against their authors.

One read all the more avidly the more completely the country stagnated intellectually. The obligation imposed on scientific and other associations to request authorization to get together put an end to their meetings. The *Palais des Académies*, converted into a German field hospital, was no longer accessible to its members. Academics no longer had access to libraries and archives: among them, those of the three divisions of the Academy of Belgium, the Academy of Medicine, and the History Commission. The state universities of Ghent and Liège, and the free universities of Brussels and Leuven decided not to resume teaching. The library of the latter and many of its lecture halls had been destroyed during the sack of the city in August 1914. Freedom of instruction was manifestly incompatible with a regime of censorship and, in addition, it was distasteful to offer classes to those young people who could not or chose not to join the army, to the detriment of their fellow students who were at the front. Two professors from the

University of Ghent were deported on the pretext that they had inspired their colleagues to arrive at this decision.[1] But the punishment only stiffened the resolve of the other faculty members. Libraries and archives at first remained accessible to all researchers. But many of these facilities, in Liège for instance, had closed their doors, as they were occupied by the military. With the requisition of material and equipment, many university laboratories were unable to continue to carry out scientific research, and were condemned to the same stagnation as industry. The impossibility of obtaining books and reviews from countries at war with Germany was another obstacle to research. And so professors and scholars were reduced to unemployment, just like laborers. Although some of them could complete at home the work they had begun, or correct drafts of books or articles that were in press before the war, no new publications appeared. Editors and publishers objected to the requirement that they obtain permission from the censor: they preferred to suspend publication of periodicals and reviews. If it happened that some publisher had an issue printed, the journal was camouflaged with a cover indicting it had appeared before 1914. In short, besides some commercial prospectuses and secretly printed patriotic pamphlets, the bibliography of Belgian works that appeared during the four years of the occupation contains a nearly complete lacuna.

The strike of authors and publishers paralyzed the printing business. Furthermore, the requisitioning of their materials and the seizure of their type soon made print shops unable to operate even if they had wanted to. There was a shortage of textbooks for children. It was necessary for students to sell to their fellow students those textbooks and dictionaries that they no longer used. Bookstores whose stock was exhausted refused to replenish it with German books which would never find buyers. The German bookstores that were established in some large cities had

---

[1] *Pirenne and Paul Fredericq*

no patrons except German officers, soldiers, or the civilian personnel of the occupation.

Idleness and boredom would have been unbearable and demoralizing had charity work and the distribution of food not provided a distraction. It was encouraging as well to receive the respect and sympathy of the outside world. Belgians wanted to prove that they were worthy of such praise. The women who sorted the linen and clothing that arrived from Canada and America felt tears well up in their eyes as they read the naive and touching notes that foreign mothers had written for Belgian mothers. Acknowledgements were embroidered onto the sacks of flour from the United States[1]. One overcame acedia by plunging into work, as one overcame bad news, grief, and misery by clinging to hope. Some re-read the history of the nation, full of catastrophes that had been overcome, and this renewed their courage. Many wrote their memoirs, which they intended to give to their children when they next saw them. There were no more formal social gatherings, but people often got together to talk about victory and peace in the privacy of friends' homes. The sick were sustained by the will to live until the time of victory. According to an account by an American witness, "The Belgian people were living through a suffocating period, but it was at the same time a period of rapture unequalled in the history of the world."

---

1 Several hundred of these sacks were given as gifts to Herbert Hoover and are preserved in the Hoover Presidential Library and Museum in West Branch, Iowa. Some can be viewed online.

CHAPTER IV

Organization of the Occupation

§ I. — ESTABLISHING A SYSTEM

During the first few weeks of the invasion, Belgium found itself, naturally, in a chaotic situation. As the national government's authority receded westward with the German advance, the authority of the conquering armies took its place. But absorbed in military operations, commanders could obviously not regulate relationships between their forces and the inhabitants. As it always does during any conquest, martial law thus substituted itself for the rule of law. This period can quite accurately be compared to the aftermath of the country's invasion by French troops following the battle of Fleurus, in 1794. As happened then, the military leaders, when taking over territory, seized power at the same time.[1] This meant that the population had at first to live under a regime based purely on force. Officers found themselves obliged to command civilians as they would their soldiers. And since they were concerned only with the interests of their troops, it was exclusively these interests that determined their conduct. While their spirit was the same everywhere, orders differed naturally from one locality to the next according to the personality of the officer who issued them and according to circumstances.

---

1 See H. Pirenne, *Histoire de Belgique*, t. VI, p. 57 and following. (Bruxelles, 1926).

Hence, the considerable differences not only in the style and the language of the proclamations, but also in their content. They were very often written hastily on pieces of paper, and almost always in French, the more or less correct usage of the language indicating the level of education of the captain or lieutenant who wrote them when he arrived. Their subject matter concerned only a few topics, always the same. They included orders for requisitions, and for services such as transports and manual labor, stipulations regarding the lodging of soldiers, and, especially, their safety. In the event of attacks against troops, and sometimes even for simple transgressions, the orders decreed capital punishment by shooting or by hanging, as well as the burning of houses or even villages. They aimed to instill in the population a salutary terror. But their application was just as arbitrary as their content. It depended on the sang-froid, humanity, tact, and intelligence of the military leader. As always in similar crises, the end of the legal regime left power to the whims of the men who found themselves temporarily exercising it.

It is pointless to dwell further on conditions that occur everywhere in times of war. The violence, moreover, was only temporary. While it lasted, it jeopardized the safety of both the armies and the inhabitants equally. As soon as the first battles had ended and the Belgian army, confined to Antwerp, had surrendered the country to the invader, the situation stabilized.

On August 26, six days after German troops entered Brussels, an order from the Imperial Cabinet named General Wilhelm Colmar von der Goltz governor of the occupied parts of Belgium (*General Gouverneur für die besetzten Teilen Belgiens*).[1] Alongside him, a chief of civil administration (*Zivilverwaltung*) was established, in the person of Dr. Max von Sandt, former *Regierungspresident* of Aachen. Thus, even before the occupation was completed and the two

---

1 A complete description of the German organization in Belgium is found in L. Von Köhler's book, *Die Deutsche Verwaltung in Belgien* (1927), which was published in the German series of that work.

provinces of Flanders invaded, Belgium was provided an administration that ended the purely military regime circumstances had imposed on it. Here again, the parallel with the conduct of the French Republic in 1794 is striking. It, too, had soon substituted for the military occupation a regular administrative system.

However, there was an essential difference between its attitude towards Belgian institutions and that of Germany. The French Republic, having decided to annex Belgium and to absorb it into its own territory, proceeded to destroy completely all previous institutions and to substitute its own. Nothing remained of the laws nor of the bodies that administered them. The administrative districts themselves disappeared and nine departments replaced the former provinces.[1] Germany, in 1914, couldn't think of proceeding that way. It was impossible for it, in the middle of the war, to reveal the fate it had in mind for Belgium. It was inconceivable, even if it were possible, to transform the country into a German province and to rebuild its institutions according to a new plan. It was necessary to let it persist as a country, and to be content with assuming its government until its definitive status was established by a peace treaty. Belgium would not cease to exist, but it would find itself under German domination, since the national government had been expelled. It had a sovereign only in absentia, but one who still maintained over it his sovereignty, which had only been suspended. As a result, all the Belgian laws remained in effect.

The foreign diplomats remaining in Brussels continued to be accredited by the Belgian King, and it was in his name that courts dispensed justice. The new government could request only that the inhabitants submit to it. It recognized this itself, and the announcement made on September 2 by General von der Goltz stated that he was "not asking of anyone to give up his patriotic feelings." In compliance with international agreements, the

---

1 H. Pirenne, *Histoire de Belgique*, t. VI, p. 72 and following.

task of maintaining order in the country fell to it. If it could not demand loyalty from the people, it counted on their obedience

The new government was a consequence of the occupation just as the occupation itself resulted from the war. Yet according to German understanding, the Emperor being the supreme chief of war (*Oberster Kriegsherr*), the power to replace the Belgian government belonged to him only. That power was delegated to the Governor General. He was the Kaiser's lieutenant in Belgium; he was in no way a subordinate of the Empire's Chancellor or of the Reichstag. He was not a state official, but an agent of the Emperor, and answered only to the All-Highest. Replacing the Belgian state, the Governor assumed all its powers. He took over the legislative power that constitutionally belonged to the king and to the Parliament, so much so that his rulings were as good as laws, like those passed by the Chambers and sanctioned by the king. He could therefore repeal laws through ordinances. As a result of the conquest, his "dictatorship" replaced the previous regime. The guarantees granted to Belgian citizens by the Constitution now depended solely on his whim. In his eyes, the Constitution was, and could only be, just another law. It goes without saying that he didn't have to worry about making his ordinances agree with the principles it proclaims. The institutions it sanctions would therefore be respected only for as long as he would permit. To avoid unnecessary complications, he would no doubt refrain from abrogating them. But he reserved the right to modify them as demanded by his duty as lieutenant to the Chief of War.

The regime under which the nation would live for as long as the occupation lasted would thus be an arbitrary regime. But it would be an arbitrary regime established to maintain order.

For order was more vital even to the victor than to the vanquished. Belgium, crossed by German communication lines, had to remain peaceful for its armies to be safe. This concern naturally forced the government to prevent any attempt at rebellion by the population. It hoped for their trust, but if it was denied this, it would at least abstain from all pointless provocations. It wished only to make the situation more bearable for the country. It couldn't let itself be guided by anger or hostility. There can certainly be no doubt about the sincerity of the government's intention to provide Belgians with the best treatment compatible with a state of war.

Just as it owed its origin solely to the war, so the war determined its behavior. Until the end, the military administration would necessarily have to prevail over the civil administration. It was impossible to give the latter an independence that could compromise the safety or the supplying of the troops. Depending as it did on the Governor General, the immediate subordinate of the Emperor, it had to obey the directives sent it by the Supreme Chief of War. Under von der Goltz, under von Bissing, under von Falkenhausen, the situation would not change in this regard. As the Supreme Army Command increasingly influenced the Emperor's policy, the *Zivilverwaltung* would further subordinate itself to military injunctions.

It's important to note initially that the domain of the civil administration did not extend nearly as far as its name would have one believe. The military retained, naturally, a large part of its authority. Its sphere included anything directly or indirectly concerning the interest of the armies. The military courts concerned themselves not only with spying and infractions against the safety of troops, but they also had the right to judge numerous other infractions of the Governor's orders. In the end, he really didn't direct civil administration in the entire country

Behind the front, the territory of the Fourth Army's *Étapes* (*Etappengebiet*), its military district, extended over the whole of West Flanders to the north of the Yser, the largest part of the East Flanders, western Hainaut, and the southern part of Luxembourg province. In this war zone, the *Zivilverwaltung* was entirely subordinate to the military. The Governor General's ordinances were only enforced if the *Oberkommando* ratified them and published them in its *Verordnungblätter*. Thus, Belgium was not a single jurisdiction. The line separating the district of the *Étapes* from that of the General Government was a real border. The regimes differed so starkly from each other that they appeared to be different countries. Institutions were the same, but they functioned completely differently. In the military zone, the population lived under a state of siege: freedom of movement and the right to express oneself were severely curtailed. Travel between the *Étapes* and the General Government was essentially forbidden. It required a passport, and these became increasingly difficult to obtain. Mail was subject to particularly close surveillance. It took only an order from the military authorities to have any suspicious or undesirable person deported to Germany. The army's interests were the administration's sole concern. It's necessary to recall, then, that when one speaks of the German occupation of Belgium, it didn't assume the same guise everywhere. One third of the territory and of the population lived under a special regime that was much harsher than what the rest of the country was subjected to.

Confined by the borders with the *Étapes* in the west, the Netherlands in the north, Germany in the east, and France in the south, the General Government's territory included the entire provinces of Brabant, Antwerp, Liège, Namur, and Limburg, most of Luxembourg, more than half of that of Hainaut, and the northeast corner of the East Flanders.[1] The French regions of Givet and Fumay, which protrude into the province of Namur, were attached to it. Besides that modification, made for reasons of administrative convenience, nothing was changed of the existing districts during the conquest. And the German government retained existing institutions. However, it greatly transformed their operation. It merely took control over those responsible for social welfare. But it naturally eliminated those that governed

---

[1] The towns of Tielrode, Tamise, Saint-Nicolas, and Nieukerke. The borders of the General Government and the *Étapes* zone were modified during the war.

the country and oversaw its external relations, replacing them with new bodies. These were of course staffed by the Governor General's appointees.

Heading the new organization, the Governor General himself replaced the King and the Parliament, and assumed their powers. Six of the country's ministries were retained: those of the Interior, of Agriculture and Public Works, of Sciences and Art, of Justice, of Finances, of Industry and Labor. Eliminated were the ministries of Foreign Affairs, of Colonies, and of War, which continued under the sovereign Belgian state, re-established in Le Havre, and those of Railroads and Marine, and Posts and Telegraphs, whose functions were taken over by the military authorities. Of the ministries retained by the Governor General, nothing essential was changed of their organization, including their budgets.

German directors were appointed to head offices within the ministries, and the Belgian personnel were from then on subject to their control. In the beginning, the watchword seems to have been not to change their activities at all, or to increase their productivity. The Governor General did not intervene in their work. All he asked of them was to continue to provide the services the population depended on.

Therefore, in the administrative machinery, the wheels of government continued to turn as they had formerly. But alongside these institutions, others were created that worked closely with the Governor and followed his directives. In them everything was German: chiefs and subordinates. They alone enjoyed the trust of the Kaiser's lieutenant. These were the Department of Civil Administration, the Department of Banks, and the Political Department. The second was in charge of controlling finances. The latter appeared as a sort of council of state, consulted on all political questions that arose either out of the country's general situation, or its relations with the ministers of neutral Powers residing in Brussels, those of United States of America, of Spain, of the Netherlands, the Papal Nuncio, and the chargés d'affaires of a few secondary countries. The head of the first new office, the Civil Administration, had an especially important role, as the changes within his domain were more extensive.

In the Belgian administrative system, each province was managed by a governor named by the king, by an elected provincial council which met at least once a year, and by a permanent board of directors elected by the council and which, in consultation with the governor, managed current business.

This regional organization was modified by the occupying power according to the same principles it applied to the central administration. Much like the confiscation of the powers of king and Parliament by the Governor General, a military governor (*Militärgouverneur*) took the place of both the governor and the provincial council. For the provinces as for the country, the new regime appeared to work identically. In both cases, the elected authority disappeared, along with governor appointed by the king, and the military authorities took charge. But also, just as the Governor General was flanked by the chief of the *Zivilverwaltung*, in the provinces a civil governor (*Präsident der Zivilverwaltung, Zivilgouverneur*) was similarly associated with the military governor. By his side, the permanent board of directors continued to function under the jurisdiction of the civilian president just as the ministries in Brussels did under the Governor General. The similarity was striking.

The situation was very much the same in the local districts between which the provinces were subdivided. The district commissioners were replaced by military *Krieschefs*, paired, for day-to-day administration, with *Zivilkommissäre bei den Kreischefs*. As for the towns, their government remained more or less without change. The burgomaster, the *échevins*, and the town council continued to fulfill their functions. Their autonomy, of course, despite their best efforts, was but a memory, and their power was exercised only on sufferance. Any recalcitrant burgomaster was threatened with deportation. The police were placed under the

Kreischefs' control, and forced to collaborate with German military police or troops in maintaining order. New elections for town councils were naturally out of the question. An ordinance from June 16, 1915 extended indefinitely the terms of office of the current office-holders.

Until the end of the occupation, civil justice continued as it was at the time of the invasion. The Belgian government, when it retreated to Le Havre, had ordered magistrates to keep their posts, under the condition that their judgments be rendered in the name of the Belgian people and executed in the name of the King. Even though this meant a constant reminder of national sovereignty, the occupier agreed to this condition. To refuse it would have meant interrupting court activities and plunging the country into anarchy. The Governor General was content to restrict the scope of their jurisdiction. All infractions subject to the German military penal code, as well as all those covered by the Governor General's ordinances, were heard by military courts (*Okkupationsgerichte*).

Two exceptional jurisdictions were created, in direct violation of the justice system derived from the Constitution. The first, instituted by an ordinance on February 3, 1915, handed over to arbitration tribunals mostly composed of German officials the settlement of compensations due to German victims of violent acts committed in August of 1914 under the influence of patriotic excitement. A second tribunal (established February 10, 1915), was charged with making decisions regarding rents that were contested.[1]

The financial system was left intact. Taxes covered the expenses of the internal administration. But new collections for the maintenance of occupying troops were soon introduced. Here, again, as a result of the state of war, a new organization was imposed

---

[1] Regarding these courts and the protests they triggered, see J. Pihennk and M. Vauthier, op. cit., p. 63 and forward.

on the Belgian system by the victor. On December 10, 1914, an ordinance decreed an annual war contribution of 480 million francs, to be paid in monthly installments of 40 million francs by all the provinces collectively. This contribution was intended to provide Belgium's share in the cost of maintaining the German Army and the administration of the occupied territory. The provincial councils were summoned for a special one-day session (December 19, 1914) in order to consent to it.

They agreed, not without protest, and under the condition that prior war contributions imposed on the country be abolished.

The banks arranged the payments, for which they issued interprovincial war bonds refundable after peace came. The German war tax was not only renewed the following year, but increased, starting on November 22, 1916, to 50 million francs per month, and then to 60 million on May 21, 1917. The Minister of War in Berlin then demanded 80 million per month. He gave in only when the Governor General assured him that this would require the use of force and that there would be serious consequences for the Reich. In October 1915, General von Bissing noted the country's exhaustion: Beligum was by then living only on its capital and had lost a sixth of its wealth, and this was bound to influence the conduct of the provincial councils. Even when these were first convened, on November 30, 1915, the councils of Brabant and of Antwerp had refused their consent, forcing the Governor General, on December 14, to authorize the military governors of these two provinces to negotiate contracts that would secure the contributions and, if necessary, to take out a loan for that purpose. The resistance only got worse thereafter. On December 2, 1916, despite the threat of incurring, in case of a refusal, a higher contribution "which would be imposed if need be through force," all of the councils except for that of the East Flanders voted against the new requisitions. This vote could naturally have no effect on the ruling. The provincial governors were compelled to collect the required amounts through loans.[1] A few months later, on March 17, 1917, a decree gave the German presidents of the provinces' civil administrations the right to "substitute themselves for the provincial councils when preparing the accounts of receipts and expenses, establishing the budget, and determining the means by which the expenses are to be met, after having heard from the permanent boards of directors." This resulted in persuading some boards, for example that of Brabant, to cease their functions

The attempt to administer the country according to the national institutions that Germany had allowed to continue therefore failed. It could not have been otherwise. The long duration of the war obviously forced the conqueror to increasingly exploit the country for its own benefit. From then on, continued collaboration with the invader seemed to patriots like treason. Once it served no other purpose than to support Germany, it was impossible to persist in the fiction that the Belgian state continued to exist. The administrative separation—announced on March 21, 1917—was the inevitable conclusion of German exploitation, and put an end to that state.

§ II. — THE SYSTEM IN ACTION

One must recognize that the German administration had to accomplish an extraordinarily difficult task, and that its failure would be fatal. For it to succeed, it would have to have been able to count on the benevolent neutrality of public opinion, and as we saw, it met with hostility right from the start. It also would have had to have been able to understand the state of mind of a country used to the most liberal institutions in the world, and whose government was unlike its own in every respect. Above all, it would have been necessary for Germany, starved as it was by

---

[1] J. De Smet, "*Majoration de la Contribution de guerre belge en décembre 1916.*" Bulletin des Archivés de la Guerre, t. II, p. 105 and following.

the blockade, to refrain from seizing from the countries it occupied—others, as well as Belgium—the additional resources it required to continue the war.

When Marshall von der Goltz was named Governor General, everyone in Berlin was counting on a swift victory on the western front. The German armies still assumed they were only passing through Belgium. This changed after the line of battle stabilized from the Yser to the Vosges. From then on it appeared that the situation would remain unaltered for a long time. It then became necessary to worry about governing the occupied territory. That was essentially General Moritz von Bissing's mission, entrusted to him when he succeeded von der Goltz, in December 1914.

The Belgian people regarded him with a hatred that was, although easily understandable, undeserved. They charged him with the responsibility for every last misery they were enduring and pictured him as their 16th century ancestors had pictured the Duke of Alba. Actually, the old man, the incarnation of the military traditions of the Prussian nobility, held absolutely no prejudices against them. He governed them as he would have governed any people, without worrying about anything other than to serve his master well. Accustomed to discipline, he thought that the population would submit to it without difficulty, and that he would simply have to give orders for them to be carried out, since he was the one in charge. He could not admit that this people, hybrid in his eyes, could harbor nationalist sentiments. What's more, he had a blind faith in "organization" itself, not thinking that it was only possible through the consent of the organized. Given his presuppositions, he could not understand the Belgian people, and he made no effort to understand them. They appeared to him "psychological mystery."[1]

Secluded in his *Trois Fontaines* residence, he avoided any and

---

[1] One can find an accurate portrait of him in K. Bittmann, *Werken und Wirken, Erinnerungen aus Industrie und Staatsdienst*, t. III, p. 116 and following. (Karisruhe, 1924).

all contact with them, interacting only with his entourage or with the ministers from neutral powers residing in Brussels. In the end, he wished to do no more than restore Belgian prosperity and thus demonstrate the benefit his government was conferring, to the ultimate advantage of Germany and of *Kultur*.

Von Bissing's son never tired of singing the praises of his father's administration in the *Süddeutsche Monalshefte*. Some of the essays attempted to introduce Belgian readers to the progress achieved by social legislation in Germany.

It seems certain that the Governor's entourage believed initially in the possibility of exerting some influence over the socialists. They were at first treated with moderation. Karl Liebknecht was allowed to visit the *Maison du Peuple de Bruxelles* and to expound on the benefits workers received from German social legislation.[1] He waxed eloquent about the joys of universal suffrage. Some time later, the Governor authorized the enactment of a Belgian law on the insurance of workers passed on May 8, 1914. The occupation had prevented its provisions from being carried out. School reforms from the same year, delayed for the same reason, were also initiated in the hope of favorably impressing Belgian voters.

These attempts could not succeed. They even backfired. Of course the Socialist Party had been campaigning energetically for universal suffrage and for the enactment of a very extensive program of social reforms. But to attain that goal, it counted only on itself. It could count on itself all the more confidently since its recent efforts had been very successful. There was no question but that the Belgian Parliament had embarked on the road to democratic reforms. It was therefore not very consoling to be granted by the conqueror laws one felt powerful enough to achieve on one's own. Moreover, the trade-union organization of Belgian socialism made it resist Germany's offers. The only way to favorably impress

---

1 See also the interesting account by Bittmann, op. cit., p. 33 and following, of a conference that took place on November 7 1914 with some of the heads of the Socialist Party in Brussels.

it would have been to permit it a semblance of freedom, and this was obviously incompatible with the necessities of the occupation. All of the restrictions the Germans imposed on freedom of assembly and on freedom of speech were just as strongly resented by the worker's associations as by the middle-class associations. Besides, it was rather ironic to be talking about social progress at the very moment when a grave economic crisis forced people to focus exclusively on securing their daily bread, and to talk about universal suffrage when the country's political life was entirely suspended and the military reigned supreme. Also, everyone knew that while Imperial Germany had greatly improved the workers' situation, the government's motives were clearly anti-democratic. To Belgian socialists, the struggle that had just begun was that of democracy against absolutism—which Governor General von Bissing represented. In these conditions, the reconciliation he wished for was obviously impossible and even inconceivable. If the Belgian socialists felt against Germany absolutely no racial hatred, their internationalist and anti-militarist principles made that country appear the most formidable enemy of the working class. Many of their leaders enrolled in the Belgian Army, convinced that by fighting the Kaiser's soldiers, they were not only fighting for their country but also for universal democracy.[1]

Unable to conciliate the socialists, the German government was even less able to take advantage of the sympathy with which it had been regarded by at least part of the Belgian clergy prior to the war. To have alienated it during the very first days of the invasion was a real catastrophe. In an incredible lapse of judgment, the military leaders held the clergy responsible for the population's hostility and lashed out at priests with particular harshness. In a number of villages, they were accused of having fired on troops or having called on others to do so. A great number of

---
[1] See the distinctive words of Henri De Man, in *Rapport sur l'activité de la centrale d'éducation ouvrière de 1914 à 1918*, p. 3 (Bruxelles 1919). Cf. Lkkeu, *Rapport sur l'activité du parti ouvrier pendant la guerre* (Bruxelles, 1918).

them perished, massacred by soldiers or shot after a summary conviction.

In Leuven, the punishments inflicted on members of the teaching community roused great indignation on the part of Catholics. The consideration that was later shown toward the clergy came much too late. Cardinal Mercier's attitude only reinforced the clergy's opposition. From 1914 to 1918, the Church of Belgium was more obstinately hostile towards Germany than it had been towards France from 1794 to 1800. The General Government could expect nothing from it but hatred and defiance. The complete liberty the Church enjoyed meant that it could not be touched through legal means. The only thing to do was to imprison or deport its most dangerous members. And even this was done reluctantly because of the great influence the Church exercised. There can be no doubt it contributed largely to maintaining until the very end a spirit of resistance among Catholics, all the more resolute because religious sentiments merged with patriotic sentiments.

The clergy's opposition might have been useful for Germany if it induced the government to enact anti-clerical measures which would have appealed to the Church's irreconcilable opponents. But the respect the Germans showed for the institution clearly indicated that though they blamed the priests, they did not blame the religion. Their harshness toward the clergy had been directed against individuals, not their ministry. Their victims elicited as much compassion and anger on the part of free thinkers as from Catholics. As early as September 27, 1914, the Grand Master of Belgian freemasonry futilely proposed to the nine Grand Lodges of Germany that a commission of inquiry be established to determine what had happened in Belgium during the invasion.

If the political, social, and religious differences that so deeply troubled the Belgian people before the war could not be exploited by Germany for its own ends, it ought to have been otherwise with the linguistic differences.

Early on, Germany strove to exploit the language division in order to break the bond of resistance that united Flemings and Walloons. Representing itself to the former as the paragon of Germanism, it appealed to the ties of kinship—their common blood and language—and exhorted them to join with Germany and shake off the yoke imposed on them by Romanized Belgium. Indeed, the government was able to secure the collaboration of a small group of "activists." This group's activities, however, took place only at a later date. It will suffice to indicate here the role it would play, and to save further details for later.[1]

One can therefore conclude that Governor von Bissing's efforts to introduce among Belgians, if not sympathy, at least some consideration for Germany, completely failed. He managed only to impress a few visitors from the neutral powers, to whom he displayed evidence of his interest in *Kultur*: working-class provident societies organized in Brussels and in Mons, measures taken to inspect libraries and archives, inventories of works of art. Neutral journalists were invited to note the calmness and apparent resignation of the country. These strangers, only permitted superficial glimpses of the country, were impressed by the liveliness and apparent luxuriousness of Brussels, though this was owing solely to the presence of the large contingent of German officials who resided there

General von Bissing initially entertained the illusion that he might convince the Belgians of Germany's superiority and overcome their hostility, but he soon had to realize that this hostility was implacable. At least he dedicated his efforts, to the best of his ability, to safeguarding the country's resources—in the Reich's interest. In the words of one of his colleagues, Mr. von Lumm, his policy was a *Konservierungspolitik*. With remarkable consistency, he resisted the authority of the Ministry of War and of the General Staff, which would have forced him, with fatal short-sightedness,

---

[1] See chapters VIII and IX.

to exhaust Belgium's resources. He wrote to Berlin, on October 22, 1915, that his goal was "to preserve, not destroy, the country's economy, so that it can contribute to Germany's needs." He understood perfectly well that it was in the interest of the Reich and the Army that he spare to the fullest extent the country's population and industry. Hence his opposition to increasing the war contribution, and later to the exploitation of workers. In fact he energetically opposed the latter measure, for which he would be so bitterly blamed. However, he was too disciplined to resist orders, so he had them rigorously carried out as soon as he was forced to. He was a devoted and clear-sighted servant of German interests. It was not his fault, but that of the circumstances, that he was unable to rally the Belgian people. He had not been sent to Brussels in order to govern them for their own sake, but for the sake of Germany. He did not persist in trying to achieve two incompatible goals. All he could do, and did, was to demand nothing from those he governed apart from that required by his duty as imperial lieutenant.

The assistants who were sent to Germany were almost all officials or specialists, many of whom had proved their worth. The banks' director, Mr. von Lumm, demonstrated, in a particularly difficult role, the qualities of an eminent financier. The director of the political division, Dr. von der Lancken, was a well-educated man, a worthy diplomat, and was as humane as his role permitted. Under them, outstanding officials worked with the zeal, dedication, and ability one would expect of German administrators. The praise they constantly received from the German press was certainly deserved, despite the eulogistic tone. The finest of them had to suffer from realizing that the formidable task they were charged with could not be carried out. That feeling did not prevent them from demonstrating until the very end the traditional meticulousness and punctuality of good *Beamten*. Nothing was improvised. An examination of their archives attests to their exemplary order and behavior.[1] The number of special volumes the administration was provided with and the precision of the information they contained, is astonishing. But then so was the government's ignorance of Belgian sentiments, despite all this. One must admit that, boycotted by the population and having access to no other information than that provided by the police, the country's temporary masters were not in a position to appreciate Belgian feelings nor to anticipate the response to the measures they imposed.

At first, the collaboration of Belgian officials was generally guaranteed. They had learned through communications that the government in Le Havre was able to transmit through the Netherlands that it wanted them to continue to carry out their tasks for as long as they would not be expected to take part in war measures or in acts incompatible with the nation's sovereignty. This assurance eased their conscience, which had at first made them hesitant. Most of them agreed to sign a declaration that promised "not to initiate anything and to omit everything that could harm the German administration in occupied territories." Those who refused were denied their positions and salaries. The others performed loyally in the interest of their compatriots, as they had agreed. It was only when the "administrative separation" showed them that the conqueror wished to annihilate the Belgian state that they disassociated themselves from the General Government.

Their oath of loyalty to the King and of obedience to the Constitution and to the laws of the Belgian people had not been revoked. Honor and conscience demanded that they not collaborate in the destruction of the institutions they served. Almost all those who were responsible for directing the various services handed in their resignations. They were replaced by Germans or by men recruited from the small minority of activists who had joined, as we will see later, the new German policy initiative. Thus

---

[1] Judging from what remained in the country after the evacuation. These documents are kept today in the *Archives de la Guerre*.

it was only until March 1917 that the day-to-day business of the German occupation was managed by Belgians.[1]

The situation for town magistrates was much more difficult and painful than that of the state officials. The latter had only to continue, under German watch, to fulfill their usual duties. The former, however, found themselves grappling, on a daily basis, with the occupier. The requisitions, the lodging of troops, police measures, issues with heating, lighting, the supply of food, water, gas, and electricity, the worrying unemployment problem, the monitoring of schools, all gave rise to constant conflicts. The more Belgian law had extended the autonomy of towns, the greater was the responsibility assumed by the communal magistrates. Since of all elected officials, they alone remained, they found themselves invested with the dangerous privilege of being the sole representatives of authority left in the country. Their duty, personal dignity, and concerns regarding popularity forced them to look out first and foremost for the interests of the towns they represented, and of which, due to the war, they'd become the natural defenders. Their attitude toward the conqueror could not be that of passive resistance. They attempted, by invoking communal law, which had so greatly reduced the state's control of their administration, to evade the orders they received from the local *Kommandanturs*, from the military governors, or from the *Kreischefs*.

In the countryside, it was easy to overcome the defiance of the burgomasters. But in cities, their tenacity was so much greater because public opinion unanimously encouraged them to resist.

It was indeed impossible, as much for the civil chiefs as for the military chiefs, to forego the approval of local magistrates. They were indispensable intermediaries between themselves and the population. It was unthinkable to replace them with brute force. The Germans simply would have been unable to perform

---

1 Awholt, *Die Deutsche Verwaltung in Belgien*, p. 36 (Berlin-Bruxelles, t. d., 1917). The author was an official during the occupation.

tasks that required the knowledge of that complex milieu that is a large city. Everywhere they would have faced resistance and inertia. Perhaps they would have even triggered riots, which would have had the most regrettable consequences and led to even more intense anti-German propaganda abroad. Besides, the deportation of Burgomaster Max had proven that bullying wouldn't work. The only thing that came of it was that his colleagues redoubled their efforts. Like it or not, one had to resign oneself to discussions with the burgomasters, to respect their scruples regarding legality, to abstain from pointlessly offending their sense of autonomy, and to permit them to submit to the town councils the decisions that they were asked to make. And so the Germans had to settle for compromises, arrived at after long negotiations.

In short, the conduct of town administrations derailed and disturbed German officials. They had thought that by replacing the Belgian state, they had assumed control of the population. They hadn't realized that the very liberalism of the state guaranteed that it would endure. The autonomy that had been granted towns allowed them to continue to lead the nation—and the country teemed with urban agglomerations. In the absence of a central government, they filled its role. In the midst of catastrophe, the communal spirit, which was feature of every period of Belgian history, recovered its former vitality. Just as in the old days, the town halls became refuges of national feeling. It was through the patriotic activities of the towns that Belgium's existence as a nation continued to be maintained from 1914 to 1918.

In accordance with the country's motto, its union formed its strength. Stricken by the same misfortune, the municipalities all reacted in the same way, and their local resistances affirmed the unanimity of the nation, because the nation had not made the state the sole master of its destiny.[1]

---

[1] For a concrete idea of the local authorities' resistance to the occupation regime, see L. Gille, A. Ooms et P. Delands Reere, *Cinquante mois d'occupation allemande* (4 vols., Bruxelles, 1919).

CHAPTER V

The Social and Economic Crisis

§ I. — Causes and Progress of the Crisis

The first consequence of the invasion of Belgium was an economic crisis distinguished not only by its severity, but also by particular features imposed by the nature of the country, in addition to measures taken by the occupier.

As it existed in 1914, the country's economy was especially vulnerable. If one imagines Britain being invaded by an enemy, one will have a pretty accurate idea as to what a catastrophe the occupation was for Belgium. Just like Britain, the country could not survive without importing food; its own territory only provided a little more than a quarter of its requirements. Its industry, like that of Britain, was carried on only through a constant influx of raw materials. Therefore, the paralysis of its international trade inevitably triggered the gravest consequences.

The very conditions of the war made the situation even worse. The blockade organized by Germany's enemies had immediate repercussions on Belgium. It was clearly impossible for the Allies to allow the replenishment of the supplies and raw material that would be immediately transferred from Belgian territory into that of the Central Empires. Belgium was consequently condemned to the same economic encirclement as its invader. And this had for it a double consequence and was a double disaster. Germany was forced to exploit the country for its own benefit and to exploit it all the more as its own resources were exhausted. The need to carry on the war obliged the conqueror, for the welfare of its own people, to rely on Belgium not only for the materials, but also for the men that would allow it to continue fighting. It is true that this obligation could have turned out to be an advantage for Belgium. If the country had consented to work for the occupier, to manufacture ammunition, to produce all those substitutes, those *Ezatz*, through which German technology contrived, with so much energy and ingenuity, to delay the effects of the blockade, it could have simultaneously maintained the activity of its industry and even created or developed new branches within it. But what it could have done, it refused to do. To the physical causes that brought about its distress were therefore added moral causes. The sufferings of Belgium were in part deliberately inflicted on itself. It remained obstinate during its misfortune, preferring to cross its arms rather than serve the enemy.

As terrible as the repercussions of war may have been, one must refrain from exaggerating them. They did not ruin the country. The speed of its recovery is proof enough of that. While it was vulnerable, it was also robust. Despite the material ruin, it retained enough vigor to get right back to work as soon as the torment ended, thanks to what it managed to keep of its savings and equipment, and, most important, thanks to the entrepreneurial spirit and the skills of its inhabitants. The communications network, both on land and on water, was so dense that despite great deterioration, enough of it remained to meet the immediate needs of the population. The funds gathered during peace piled up in banks, where they idly awaited the new dawn. While the forced unemployment and deportations subjected the working class to the most arduous trials, they did not totally exhaust its energy. Yet the devastation brought about by the invasion, then by the continued military operations in the Yser valley, were formidable. The estimated cost of restoring destroyed material goods came to something like twenty billion francs. About 100,000 structures, of which 1,300 were public buildings, churches, schools, town halls, etc., were destroyed or severely damaged. Of all cultivated land, over 220,000 acres flooded after being devastated by shells, and stopped producing. A considerable portion of rich woodland, of private and public forests, of trees planted alongside roads, canals, dykes, and polders, disappeared.

The nation lost half its cattle, two thirds of its pigs, half its horses, 35,000 of its sheep and goats, and a million and a half of its fowl. The damage was even greater and in any case more painful in the industrial sector. As a result of requisitions, raw materials, belts, and lubricants were confiscated from all factories. Many plants were hit more severely through the removal of their machinery and the demolition of their assembly shops. Of the 4,700 kilometers of railroad tracks, 1,100 were destroyed, and 400 more were partially put out of use; local railroads lost 1,649 kilometers of track out of 4,300. Fixed and suspension bridges, locks, tunnels, and railway stations suffered from severe deterioration or were ruined, and the telegraph and telephone networks, canals, port facilities, and railway rolling stock also sustained damage, automobiles completely disappeared, the overall number of animal-drawn vehicles was reduced, etc.[1] And fourteen hundred and nineteen works of art disappeared.

Yet in the middle of so many disasters, the nation displayed the same self-confidence that, as early as the 17th century, surprised Louis XIV's quartermasters. The conquerors had admired the optimism the country had shown. Some 250 years later, in the middle of 1917, annuity bonds were still worth 72.5% of their pre-war face value after three years of occupation, more than annuity bonds from any other warring nation. Until the end of the war, despite the destruction of factories, the price of industrial stocks, although they provided no dividends, remained

---

1 The numbers cited here are from M. E. Mahaim's previously cited work.

remarkably high. The working class did not give up on itself any more than capitalists did. Its efforts to safeguard the unions and to establish education institutions to keep the unemployed busy offer sufficient proof.

§ II. — Agriculture

Of the two forms of production, agriculture and industry, the first suffered incomparably less than the second. A mere 4% of all farmland was truly devastated. Outside of the area near the Yser, where the permanence of military operations put an end to all work, destroyed farms, and made the soil sterile, rural life continued everywhere else in the country. Yet yields did suffer from a lack of natural and artificial fertilizers. The latter disappeared after the interruption of foreign imports and the termination of the domestic industries of which they were the byproducts. The former were largely reduced by the removal of cattle, the lack of animal feed, the ban on straw bedding, etc. The national livestock losses were made even worse by the excessive slaughtering that was necessary due to the end of normal imports. The remaining cattle lost weight from the lack of food. With the 1914 numbers as a baseline, the damages to the soil are estimated at over 500 million francs, those to the livestock at nearly 385 million, those to farming equipment at 86 million, and those to the farms proper at about 250 million[1].

While these losses reduced agricultural production, they did not stop it anywhere, and far from reducing its profits, they actually increased them. According to official statistics, from 1910 to 1918 the cereal production fell from 2,322 to 2,274 kilograms of wheat per hectare, and from 1,981 to 1,250 kilograms of rye. But these numbers are obviously inaccurate. Due to the German decrees establishing maximum prices for cereal sales, it was in the

---

[1] E. Mahaim, same work, p. 154

farmer's interest to hide their actual production figures in order to bring in additional profits on the portion sold on the black market. Therefore, wheat production did not go down even as little as was reported. The decrease in potato and beet production was more pronounced. However, fodder production increased. Indeed, it had to compensate for the lack of concentrated feed of foreign origin which had been previously supplied though imports.

While agricultural yields lagged, farmers' profits kept growing. When capital is withheld, its value grows, as well as its returns. This is a normal phenomenon during times of war. The fear of famine necessarily inflates the price of all products of the soil. In Belgium, where the local wheat production was sufficient only to feed the population 84 days per year, this price increase was bound to be felt with particular intensity. The official prices decreed by German authorities were far from accurately reflecting the increase. According to them, the price of wheat rose 15% from 1914 to 1918, and the price of potatoes 300%. In reality, they increased far more, due to black market sales. During the entire occupation, these never ceased, despite regulations.

The well-off urban population replenished their butter, eggs, meat, and cereal in the countryside, either directly or through unauthorized traders. It was easy to take advantage of the city dwellers, since informing on the black marketeers was impossible without also exposing oneself to a fine. Germany itself largely contributed to the prosperity of this officially forbidden trade. Considerable exports, the value of which is impossible to calculate, were shipped east. At night, ad hoc brokers transferred convoys of horses and livestock across the length of the border. In the woods and moors of the provinces of Liége and Luxembourg, actual battles were fought between them and farmers who tried to bar their way.

The farmers were reaping considerable profits. Documents are lacking to provide even an estimate of these. Some farms increased their returns from 20,000 francs in 1914 to 70,000 francs in 1915.[1] The price of butter, vegetables, and milk rose to scandalous heights. So it's no surprise that the country's rural areas enjoyed a prosperity all the more shocking when contrasted with the misery of the urban populations. The new wealth permitted a number of farmers to pay off mortgages and to acquire more land. Deposits made at the *Boerenbond Caisse d'épargne*, which totaled 16,521,520 francs in 1914, climbed to over 22 million in 1915, to 39 in 1916, to 76 in 1917, and to more than 171 million in 1918. The proverbial frugality of farmers gave way to a love of comfort and for the pleasures of a more sophisticated life. The women and young ladies in villages got accustomed to using soap, and to sweets made of rice powder. Unemployment, which plagued the working class, was almost unheard of in the countryside.

"Although there are no numbers verifying this, we can estimate the funds accrued by agriculture during the war to be on the same scale as the cost of the damages caused by soil depletion, lost cattle, destroyed buildings, even the devastation of arable land. The total of these savings most likely even exceeds that of the damages." If we estimate the latter at a billion francs, then to compensate for it, the increase of net farming revenue would only have to reach an average of 250 million francs during the four years of the war. Such an increase, according to specialists, is very likely. All things considered, "it seems that Belgian agriculture emerged from the war with no overall diminution of its assets."[2] And its social situation naturally followed its economic situation. Farmers kept up their numbers and their activities, which weren't affected by unemployment. Therefore, they remained an important reserve for the nation. Except in the Furnes and Ypres districts, where most of the population had to take refuge behind the

---

1 Ibid., p. 159.
2 G. De Leener, in E. Mahaim, *La Belgique restauré*, p. 162–163.

Yser, the vast majority of the farming population did not abandon their land. The panic that had seized them at the beginning of the invasion lasted only briefly. Those who had fled soon returned to their villages when they realized that the military executions had ended and that the Germans weren't forcing men to serve with their troops, as rumor had it for a while.

Demographic data confirm the general impression one gets from examining economic trends. They show that from 1916 to 1918 the reduction of the number of births was much less pronounced in the countryside than in cities and industrial areas. It was observed that in the districts where the proportion of the farming population was less than 15%, births fell on average 49%, that for the thirteen districts where the farming population was between 15% and 30%, they fell only 45%, and that for the remainder where farming prevailed, births fell less than 39% on average.[1]

It is also worth noting that Belgian agriculture benefited from a much larger workforce than any other warring nation. The very rapid invasion of the country prevented the government from drafting young men eligible for military service. Only a small number of them voluntarily crossed the border to join the army. The number of volunteers from cities was incomparably higher. The lucrative work that was available to the male population in the countryside kept them at home.

Also, industrial workers living in rural areas were much less severely affected by plant closures than their counterparts in cities. Many of them found work on farms. The towns also organized community work to employ them. It was only when the German authorities forbad the continuation of such work that unemployment appeared in rural areas. The contingent it provided to the deportations for unemployment reasons was therefore much smaller than that from urban populations.

---

1 R. Olbrechts, *ibid.*, p. 29.

In all, the country's rural areas suffered from the German occupation only to a limited extent. For many of their inhabitants, if only material matters are considered, it was even beneficial. Therefore, unsurprisingly, the relations between soldiers and farmers lacked the hostility that was commonplace in cities. Villages were occupied only by minor military outposts, if that, and their presence was no burden. The fact that they helped maintain public safety made them that much more bearable. A complete lack of news also contributed to the peace of mind of the rural population.

However, remarkably, given the efforts made to suppress them, patriotic sentiments remained. Spy networks always had many agents in the countryside. Famers, risking their own lives, hid and resupplied Belgian, French, or British soldiers who had been unable to rejoin their units after the battles of August and September, 1914. Each town's public authorities and various personnel could always be counted on for supplies: teachers, notaries, station masters, forest administration officials, surveyors, etc.

Indirectly, the relative prosperity of agriculture turned out to be an advantage for real estate owners, particularly numerous among the nobility as well as the upper and middle classes. Their loss of income caused by the end of dividend payments was at least partially compensated for by the appreciation of land values and rents. The latter are estimated to have climbed on average at least 50%. A similar increase is observed for the market prices of land. As a result, those who had money idly sitting in banks were able to make profitable investments. It is naturally impossible to evaluate the resulting profits, but everything indicates that these were considerable. The war thus had the effect of temporarily giving the national economy the agricultural character which had distinguished it until the beginning of the 19th century. The essential and fundamental remained, which is to say that which is based on the soil.

§ III. — Industry[1]

The routes followed by the German armies during the invasion went directly through the most industrialized areas of the country: the Verviers region, the main textile-manufacturing area, as well as the Liége, Charleroi, and Mons basins, where the most diverse forms of metalworking developed around the coal mines. In the midst of the military operations, battles, general panic, and the complete disruption of all means of transportation, work necessarily had to stop. Yet its interruption was only temporary. Once the wave had passed, it revived. The damage to factories and plants had generally been rather superficial. During the first weeks of the invasion, it was mostly in towns or cities without major industries, such as Dinant, Leuven, Aarschot, and Mechelen, that executions and arson had taken place. The battle of Hainaut did not seriously damage factories and coal mines in the area in which it was fought. The installations of the port of Antwerp hardly suffered from the siege and shelling of the city. The regions around Ghent and Kortijk had been occupied without resistance, and their factories and warehouses were largely undamaged. Therefore, the direct effect of the invasion on industrial activities can be considered negligible. From October 1914 to the September 1918 offensive, the war only affected the purely agricultural areas on the right bank of the Yser.

But while the German occupation did not at first inflict very severe material damage on Belgian industry, it struck at the roots of its existence. The resumption of work could only be temporary.

One need only remember that Belgian industry is essentially an exporting industry to understand that it could not survive the ongoing war. As soon as its stocks of raw materials were exhausted, it would be impossible to replenish them. The situation was all

---

1 On this subject, of which this paragraph provides only a brief sketch, refer to: Ch. De Kerchove De Denterqhem, *L'Industrie belge pendant l'occupation allemande 1914–1918*, in the Belgian series of this collection.

the more critical because the country's industry by and large uses raw material of great weight and volume, and therefore depends on a reliable transportation network. Considering that blast furnaces alone consume 60,000 metric tons of ore per month, the consequences of the increasing scarcity are obvious.

Even if Germany had wanted to, it would not have been able to supply the Belgian factories, surrounded as it was by the Allied blockade. And it was unthinkable for Belgium to obtain from the Allies the authorization to import raw materials. Because of the invasion, the country found itself linked to the Reich's economic system, while its existence as a nation and as a state depended on a German defeat. In order to ensure their victory and Belgium's, the country's allies had to include it in the blockade they had established around the Central Empires. In 1915 Belgian industrialists tried, in vain, to secure from Britain the importation of raw materials on the same conditions and with the same guarantees as the *Comité National de ravitaillement* had obtained for food products. But it was impossible to protect such materials from the occupier's requisitions, and this put an end to negotiations. Germany was forced to claim Belgium's resources in order to survive. These were so considerable when war broke out that their depletion was very slow, despite the growing rate at which they were collected. As early as March 1915, the president of the Chamber of Commerce of Antwerp estimated at more than 85 million francs the quantities of wheat, barley corn, flaxseed, cotton, rubber, leather, cocoa, etc. that had been requisitioned. Of these, only 20 million had been paid for at that date. Additionally, goods that hadn't been requisitioned were "blocked" by the ban on owners disposing of them in any manner without authorization, even when these goods had been already been purchased.

Thus, by the mere fact of the occupation and of the blockade, Belgians found themselves denied the advantages which nature, along with their own hard work, had provided them. Despite the rivers, canals, and railroads that offered outlets to the world in all directions, the war forced them, in a sense, to live in a closed society. This country, of which Gui de Dampierre had said as early as the 13th century that it "could not maintain itself unless supplied from elsewhere," found itself cut off from the international markets that had sustained its activity. It experienced again, but with increased intensity due to the degree of its industrial development, the distress it had faced in the Middle Ages when the kings of England stopped exporting wool to Flanders, and in 1648, when the United Provinces forced Belgium to close the Scheldt, and in 1794, during the beginning of the French invasion. Factories producing for a global market were now restricted almost exclusively to the national market. And so outputs kept decreasing. The contraction of the customer base together with the cut-off of raw materials made the 1914–1918 crisis an unprecedented catastrophe.

If all industries were affected, it was not simultaneously or to the same extent. Coal mining was never interrupted during the entire duration of the war. However, its annual yield was considerably reduced. From 22,841,590 tonnes in 1913, it fell in 1918 to 13,821,930 tonnes. Some technical improvements were even introduced. The use of jackhammers, adopted after the law of January 1, 1912, and which had reduced the miner's workday to nine hours, continued to increase during the first years of the occupation. The exploitation of the new Campine coal basin was not halted. Coal extraction began there in October of 1917. It had reached 55,000 tonnes by the end of 1918, which is certainly low but still, given the circumstances, significant.[1]

There were several reasons for the relatively satisfying situation for the coal industry. Heating is, in a northern country, such an inevitable necessity that it was vital to provide for it. However, this consumed only a very small part of the extracted coal. The

---

[1] In 1919, it went to 140,000 tons, in 1920, to 246,000, in 1921, to 323,000, and in 1922, to 480,000.

suffering inflicted upon the population by the cold kept increasing. During the winter of 1917, several schools had to dismiss their students because of a lack of fuel. Local administrations set up stores to distribute miniscule coal rations. Prices naturally increased dramatically as shopkeepers eagerly exploited the misery of the public. Transport difficulties certainly had a lot to do with this shortage, but they were hardly sufficient to entirely account for it. Public opinion blamed the greed of the coal merchants, who were accused of working on behalf of the occupying power and of neglecting the country's needs. Yet the coal mine directors had created a trade office charged with taking every necessary measure to resupply the pubic, working with communal officials. German authorities prevented its functioning. They had established, as early as April 28, 1915, a centralized coal authority (*Kohlenzentrale*) which was at first limited to controlling the general sale and shipping of the products. The "administrative separation," however, required special distribution mechanisms for the Flemish and the Walloons, resulting in complications that worsened what was already a deplorable situation.

The coal not consumed by the nation's households supplied the few factories that remained in operation, but was also exported to the Netherlands. Thanks to these shipments, the Governor General maintained good relations with this country, which naturally benefited German interests. And so most of Belgium's coal was used outside of the country, and if the population suffered as a result, at least the production sites were able to keep working and their installations would remain intact until the return of peace. The German administration continued to provide them with the explosives necessary for their work. In short, its attempts to interfere with the coal business were not very effective. The government generally had to face the resistance of the companies. In March 1918, workers and managers went so far as to threaten to go on a strike rather than consent to measures that conflicted with their patriotism. That would have stopped work for the enormous coal mining population in the Liège, Charleroi, and Mons basins, and when confronted with such a possibility, which would endanger public peace, the *Berg Verwaltung* backed down.

The country's other extractive industries did not enjoy anything like the favors extended to the coal industry. The stone, marble, and slate quarries found themselves without new orders, owing to the end of all construction. Most of the quarries, abandoned by their operators, were subjected to severe damage, either from water infiltration or a lack of maintenance. As to the porphyry quarries, they kept working, but on behalf of the military administration, which used their products at the front and to repair roads. Managers and workers refused to cooperate almost everywhere. As a result, in most cases work continued under German coercion and the mines were compelled to produce intensively, without any regard for the future.

"Glass factories, however, enjoyed an unexpected goodwill."[1] It was in German interests to keep open the market run by the *Union continentale des glaceries*, which included German factories as well as Belgian.

Prior to the systematic removal of equipment by Germany, the damages suffered by the textile industry were mostly due to requisitions for raw materials. These resulted in unemployment appearing very early in both the cloth-manufacturing area of Verviers and the linen and cotton areas of Flanders.

The same thing happened to the steel industry, which was no longer able to secure ore. The importance of its machinery for Germany resulted in systematic removals from 1917 on, which will be discussed later. The refusals of manufacturers to work for the German Army contributed largely to the end of work in establishments of the Liège and Hainaut areas. What remained of the industry's former activity was negligible. The production of steel mills was estimated at 1,409,460 tonnes in 1913. In 1918,

---

1 Mahaim, previously cited work, p. 203.

it was only 2,380 tonnes. That of zinc factories shows a similar decline, falling from 204,220 to 9,245 tonnes during the same period. Naturally, this decrease did not happen overnight. Until the end of 1916, a certain activity was maintained through makeshift means, thanks to existing orders, and especially because manufacturers wanted to keep their workers employed and to avoid the deterioration of their equipment. In November 1916, the Cockerill establishments were still working four days a week. However, in Ghent, in March 1915, the spinning and weaving workshops were operating only one day in five.

The factories that directly or indirectly worked for Germany were naturally spared—such as, for example, the furniture factories of Mechelen which mass-manufactured for export beyond the Rhine. A certain favoritism existed towards establishments whose production served to increase the country's food supply, and were under the direction of the *Comité National*. The factories necessary for the coal mines to operate received the same favors. Finally, those establishments that had been taken over by the enemy naturally continued their activities.

The growing stagnation of industry had an inevitable consequence: the plague of unemployment. It was relatively low in coal mines for reasons mentioned above. Of 145,337 workers employed in 1913 in various locations, 110,110 still worked in 1918. However, while there were 35,300 steel workers in 1913, only 8,117 were employed in 1916; as to the zinc industry, numbers went from 9,324 to 1,613 during the same period, and employment in quarries fell from 34,893 to 6,055. In the textile manufacturing industry, the near-complete end of operations put most of the population in the Verviers and Ghent areas out of work.

Patriotism was responsible for voluntary unemployment, in addition to the involuntary unemployment. In many factories, managers and workers alike chose to stop working rather than to produce for the invader. This was the case, for example, in the Lessines and Quenast quarries, which refused to supply the military administration with loose stones. Some establishments, such as the Saint Léonard flax field in Liège, declined orders ostensibly placed by firms in the Netherlands, but which were really intended for Germany. The train yard staff in Mechelen, Mons, Gentgrugge, and Luttre, stubbornly refused to work, and the harsh measures taken against them did not always succeed in forcing them to do so.

§ IV. — Banks[1]

Belgian's financial history from 1914 to 1918 can only be briefly outlined here. It had little impact on the social and economic situation during this period. It was only after the war that the consequences of the occupier's financial measures would be felt. These consequences were anticipated during the occupation, but there was no way to prevent them.

As soon as the war started, coins disappeared from circulation. The panic caused by the invasion prompted the public to demand refunds for banknotes from the *Banque Nationale*, and no one wanted to part with the gold and silver coins they possessed. On the other hand, the mass withdrawals of deposits forced most of the banks to rediscount a significant portion of their portfolios with the *Banque Nationale*. The Brussels banks had set up a consortium after the war's outbreak, and the 400 million franc credit extended to it by the *Banque* permitted it to weather the crisis. But it was forced to issue more banknotes. From June to December 1914, circulation of these banknotes went from 1.075 billion francs to 1.614 billion. However, by December the *Banque's* coins and notes had been transported by government order to Antwerp (August 3), from where they were later shipped to London (August 26), as well as securities belonging to the state and the *Caisse d'Épargne*. The government's refusal to let these

---

[1] See B.S. Chlepner, in the previously cited book by E. Mahaim, p. 393 and following

re-enter the country created an awkward situation.

In view of the shortage of cash, a great number of towns issued "*bons de caisse*" in order to liquidate their debts, and small denominations of these began circulating. Thus, the country was flooded by currencies that were legal only within the town that had issued them or, when they were considered trustworthy, in the territory of neighboring towns as well. For their part, the Germans talked about forming a new issuing institution in which they would have forced Belgian and German banks to participate. It would have established a stranglehold over the nation's finances. To avoid such a danger, the largest private bank of the country, the *Société Générale*, consented, after incidents which there is no point in entering into here, to issue banknotes on behalf of the *Banque Nationale*. It ensured their repayment with all its assets. Confident that the war would end favorably, it thus took on a huge responsibility without any guaranteed future benefits, since all its issuing operations were done on behalf of and for the benefit of the *Banque Nationale*. Fortunately, capital, although it remained idle, was piling up in banks. At the *Société Générale*, bank accounts went from 213 million in 1914 to 348 million in 1915 and 519 million in 1918. Deposits rose correspondingly from 16 million in 1914, to 143 in 1915 and to more than 151 in 1918. During the same period, many other banks doubled their capital. Royal decrees between August 2 and 4, 1914 imposed a moratorium on liquidating business assets, limiting withdrawals of bank deposits to 1000 francs per fortnight, and this had largely contributed to protecting them from the panic of the first days of the war.

As early as September, German authorities brought the banks under their control by putting them under the supervision of Herr von Lumm, chief of the *Bankabteilung* established by the Governor General. A decree from the 18th of that month forbad them from "carrying out their business during the war in ways that would compromise German interests." Following their refusal to undertake cash operations for the occupier, an agreement on

October 9, 1914 resulted in the *Banque Nationale* opening, under the rubric *Compte courant de l'administration civile des territories occupé*, an account for the financing of treasury operations that were vital to the operation of the Belgian administration. It was promised that these funds could not be seized. Soon after, all of the *Banque*'s agencies outside of the capital, which had closed following the removal of their funds at the beginning of the occupation, resumed their activities, with the exception of these in Roulers and Ostende.

Until the end of the occupation, an unspoken understanding existed between the *Banque Nationale*, the *Société Générale*, and the country's other financial institutions. Their behavior was inspired by the desire to protect their funds as much as possible from the enemy's grasp, to deny Germany all support, and to preserve their resources in order to help the population and to help restore the country after the end of the war. Such a policy demanded as much tact as firmness. Given the conflicting motives of the occupier and the banks, there was continuous tension, and sometimes acrimonious confrontations. The Governor General would have wanted the banks to have pressured manufacturers to work for Germany, instead of helping them resist. The moratorium enacted in August, by preventing the claim of debts and by protecting debtors from foreclosure, gave the business world a safety net and made it easier to escape the grip of the German government. Thus, as early as December 1914, the Governor General had considered lifting it. But facing general protests, he periodically agreed to extend it until the end of 1916, when it was finally revoked. And this actually had the positive effect of preventing perfectly solvent debtors from continuing to evade their creditor's claims. Revoking the moratorium in 1914 would have been a disaster. At the time it was done, it was no longer dangerous.

The flooding of the country by marks, which the German administration forced into legal circulation at the rate of 1.25

francs right from the beginning of the occupation, seriously threatened the country's monetary organization. The *Banque Nationale* did its best to withhold them from circulation. Its refusal to give them up resulted, on August 3, 1916, in the arrest and internment of its director. The stockpile of 189,500,000 marks it was holding was seized and sent to Berlin. The *Société Générale* acted similarly. On the other hand, money was continually sucked out of the country during the course of the war by forced loans and war contributions imposed upon provinces and cities, and by withdrawals from German bank accounts. Nonetheless, it's estimated that at the time of the armistice, there were about 4 million marks in circulation in Belgium.[1] This was one of the main causes of the inflation that Belgium would suffer so much from after the war.

The country had good reason to be grateful to the banks, particularly the *Banque Nationale*, for the services they provided. These consisted mainly in advances made to the *Comité National de secours et d'alimentation* and to its provincial committees, to towns and inter-town cooperative associations, to public administrations, to charities, to loan societies established at the beginning of the war, to municipal credit institutions, to the cooperative societies' *Fédération ourvrière socialiste*, to commerce, and to industry. In addition, the *Banque Nationale* assigned over 200 million francs to the payment of government annuities. It was also able to remove most town coupons, the *bons communaux*, from circulation. As of August 1915, some 320 towns had issued them, and they totaled 57 million francs. And, finally, the *Banque Nationale* allowed, either directly or by helping other banks, the payment of the war taxes imposed upon provinces after 1915. In short, the fortune amassed by the country allowed it to get through an unprecedented catastrophe much better than one might have expected.

---

1 L. Franck, *La Stabilisation monétaire en Belgique*, p. 15, (Paris. 927).

CHAPTER VI[1]

The Commission for Relief in Belgium and the *Comité National de Secours et d'Alimentation*

§ I. — ESTABLISHMENT AND ORGANIZATION

The economic crisis that struck Belgium from the very beginning of the German occupation was sure to immediately trigger a food crisis. Owing to the country's extreme population density and its insufficient agricultural production, it faced a more difficult situation than that of any of the other states afflicted by the war. Two-thirds of Belgium's wheat supply came from imports. But these imports were suddenly discontinued, not only because of the invasion itself, but also due to the naval blockade imposed by the Allies. Taken by surprise, the Belgian government was unable to do anything to supply the nation. The decrees issued at the time of the disaster, which forbade the exportation of food and allowed

---

[1] The following have been consulted: Albert Henry, *Le Ravitaillement de la Belgique pendant l'occupation allemande* (Belgian series of this collection); from the same, *L'Œuvre du Comité National de secours et d'alimentation pendant la guerre* (Bruxelles, 1920); Ch. De Lannoy, *L'Alimentation de la Belgique par le Comité National* (Bruxelles, 1922); E. Mahaim, *Le Secours de chômage en Belgique pendant l'occupation allemande* (Belgian series of this collection); George I. Gay, *The Commission for relief in Belgium. Statistical review of relief operations*, n. d. (from material kept at the Hoover War Library, Stanford University, California), and the volumes constituting the *Rapport général sur le fonctionnement et les opérations du Comité National de secours et d'alimentation* (Bruxelles, 1919–1921). Collinet et Stahl, *le Ravitaillement des Régions envahies de la France pendant l'occupation* (French series of this collection).

the authorities to seize wheat and flour, had little impact and were barely enforced, if at all, due to the general panic and disorder. The swiftness of the invasion thwarted all calculations and forecasts regarding the surplus. Stores were stormed by shoppers and sold their entire stock, German requisitions made off with a large portion of the foodstuffs, and the railroads were commandeered for military transports. So the already insufficient food reserve was monopolized by individuals, seized by the enemy, or stranded in warehouses.

In every warring country, the national food supply was taken over and organized by the government. In Belgium this task fell to the occupier, as the legal government had been driven back to Le Havre. Replacing king and Parliament, disposing of both legislative and executive powers, directing all administrative activity, the enemy was responsible for guaranteeing the material existence of the people upon which it had imposed itself. But how could it fulfill this essential duty? Struggling with severe food shortages of its own, Germany was in no position to provide for the seven million individuals for whom it had become responsible. The overpopulated country it had just conquered seemed doomed to starve. Its soldiers themselves recognized this. One often heard them predicting that while they were destined to die on the battlefield, Belgians were destined to die of hunger.

However, communal administrations did their best to prepare for the impending food scarcity in the large cities. Through makeshift means, and hindered by the disorder of communications and the closing of produce markets, they were able to organize mess halls for the unemployed and the needy. The welfare offices, the countless private charitable institutions the country abounded with, many manufacturers associations, and private individuals fully cooperated with them. In the province of Liège, provisioning committees were created in most towns. The Antwerp municipal council gave 10 million francs to a rescue committee that was founded in early August. Other cities, in the few weeks preceding their occupation, purchased wheat from abroad, established town bakeries, inexpensive butcher shops, and all kinds of charitable services for the poor, children, and military families. In Brussels, as early as the day after the occupation, a committee was formed under the chairmanship of Ernest Solvay, the universally respected industrialist and philanthropist, *Comité Central de secours et d'alimentation*. It was vigorously supported by the burgomaster, Adolphe Max, and by the directors of banks and large industrial and financial corporations in the capital.

Very early on, local administrations in the poorest areas or areas most affected by the invasion called upon this organization's generosity. The towns around the capital also turned to the *Comité*, which was quick to respond. In a time of great anguish, a kind of national unity emerged, as other towns joined the Brussels organization, which soon changed its name to *Comité National de secours et d'alimentation*.

Just as in 1830, when the improvised *Commission Administrative* in Brussels during the revolution against the Netherlands turned after a few days into a provisional government, so in the middle of the struggle against hunger and foreign occupation, the capital channeled the efforts of the entire nation. By virtue of a sort of tacit delegation of authority, it found itself substituting for the exiled government in the matter of provisioning the country.

But despite the zeal of the *Comité's* members, the devotion of its volunteers, and the abundance of the resources put at its disposal, it was too obvious that while it could delay the catastrophe, it could not avert it. In order to succeed, it would be necessary to break the blockade—to obtain permission to import into Belgium the supplies the local population was unable to provide. The man who directed the *Comité* until peace returned, Émile Francqui, understood this immediately. The difficulties were enormous. Because of the occupation, Belgium had become a sort of annex to Germany, and so was inevitably affected by the measures taken against its invader. The lives of Belgians therefore depended on their allies' goodwill. To convince them to depart, for the sake of the Belgian people, from the ruthlessness necessary to win the war, it would be absolutely necessary to assure them that the imported goods would not be used to resupply the occupier. The *Comité National*, which was a purely private association and had no power, was willing to give that assurance, but it was naturally unable to guarantee that it would be observed. It was obviously necessary to provide the Allies with guarantees they could trust completely. The ministers of the neutral Powers accredited by the Belgian King who had remained in Brussels accepted the honorific presidency of the *Comité*, and generously used their good offices to pledge their word to the London Cabinet—which was essential to the project's success. An American engineer, M. K. Shaler, living in Brussels, had just left for London at the *Comité National*'s request to negotiate a purchase of food. He met with Herbert Hoover, who had come before the war to prepare a Panama-Pacific-Exposition project and had remained there as president of a committee that took charge of repatriating Americans trying to leave Europe after the war's outbreak. On October 17, Francqui and Baron Lambert got in contact with him. As compassionate as he was intelligent, Hoover was immediately interested in their efforts. He devised with them a plan, and then oversaw its execution, that would insure until the end of the war the survival of a people whose misfortune and whose steadfastness were captivating the entire world. At the behest of the American Ambassador in Britain, W. H. Page, the government in Washington intervened very effectively with the British Foreign Office and with the various nations allied against Germany. The authorization was given to import into Belgium supplies that would be reserved for the country's consumption, under the condition that these supplies would be conveyed to the Belgian border under the patronage of the ambassadors for Spain and the United States in London, and from the Belgian border to local stores under that of the ministers in Brussels of these same nations. It was guaranteed that no part of these imports was to benefit the occupier.

To organize the imports and oversee their arrival, a committee of Americans was created under the presidency of Hoover. Their first session took place in London on October 22, 1914. Ten days later, the first shipment of 2,300 tonnes of flour, rice, and beans acquired in England reached Brussels. Thus a breach was opened in the blockade through which food for Belgium would pass during the next four years.

Meanwhile, thanks to Hoover's great energy and that of his collaborators, a gigantic organization began work on both sides of the Atlantic. Committees were formed, deals were made, ships were rented, and warehouses were acquired in Rotterdam, from where the imports were to be sent to Belgium. The Commission for Relief's fleet ended up comprising 2,313 vessels, all flying the flag of the country's savior. Despite the danger of navigating through seas full of mines and submarines, the number of accidents was miraculously small. In the four years during which Belgium was resupplied, 17 ships were struck by torpedoes, and 14 went down after hitting mines.[1]

The scale of these imports testifies to the scope of the services provided the country by the Commission for Relief. According to statistics published by George I. Gay, they amounted, over the five years of provisioning, to 5,174,431 tonnes.

From Rotterdam, where deliveries were unloaded, the task of getting them to their destination posed great difficulties. There was no hope of using railroads, as these had been seized by the military administration. Food was transported mostly on canals, a great number of which had been severely damaged. Grain was sent to Leuven and Brussels, where the country's principal mills turned them into flour. Provincial or local warehouses throughout the country received the shipments. For the purpose of

---

1 Gay, previously cited, p. 43

distributing supplies, the provinces were divided into districts. These bore no relationship to those created by the Germans. There were 3 in the province of Antwerp, 23 in Brabant, 26 in East Flanders, 10 in West Flanders[1], 9 in Hainaut, 6 in the province of Liège, 14 in Limburg, 21 in Luxembourg, and 21 in the province of Namur. The urban area of Brussels counted as a special district. Overall, the Commission ensured the subsistence of all 2,598 Belgian towns in the occupied territory.

While this network was the result of initiatives taken by the *Comité National*, its activity was not restricted to Belgium. The population in the occupied territory in Northern France found itself in even greater distress than that of the Belgian provinces, since they were much closer to the combat zones. In March 1915, the Commission decided to include it in its organization. Some 2,133 towns with a population of around 1,800,000 and covering an area (8,100 square miles) almost equivalent to that of Belgium (11,355 square miles) benefited from its generosity.

The extraordinary success of the Commission was due largely to the skill and energy of Herbert Hoover, and to the support he received from the government of the United States of America. Without Hoover and the U.S., the *Comité National* could not have induced the Allied Powers to lift the blockade, and it's clear that it could not have created the formidable organization of imports that was necessary to accomplish its task. Imprisoned within the country and under the control of Germany, with which the Entente powers refused to negotiate, the *Comité* was fortunate enough to find salvation from the outside. Because it was under the patronage of the American ambassadors and ministers in London, Brussels, The Hague, Paris, and Berlin, of the Spanish ambassadors and ministers in London and Brussels, and of the Dutch minister in Brussels, the Commission for Relief was

---

1 Because of military operations along the Yser river, this province was divided in two districts: North and South.

able to assume the responsibilities that the governments at war against Germany required. Officially recognized by the Allies, it had to be recognized as well by Germany. That country was, not surprisingly, very interested in passing along its responsibilities to the Commission. It would no doubt have preferred to oversee the provisioning operations itself, without having to pay for them. But Germany recognized that the Commission could exist only if it were fully independent. So the Governor General and the military leadership promised not to seize the imported goods. They agreed to permit the American agents of the Commission to supervise their distribution. The organization's cars, adorned with the star-spangled banner, were soon to be seen crisscrossing Belgium. Relationships between the Commission's agents and the German authorities were assigned to a *Vermittelungstelle* sitting in Brussels.[1]

The organization's work required considerable resources. Part of these were provided, especially in the beginning, by voluntary donations, sometimes in cash, but most often in kind or services. The spirit of generosity was not confined to America:[2] no few than 2,000 committees to support the Commission were established throughout the world. They appeared in every neutral European country, in Britain, Canada, Australia, New Zealand, India, Ceylon, South Africa, Latin American republics, the Philippines, Hawaii, and many more nations. During the month of November 1914, donations in kind represented 47% of the total value of overseas shipments. They then experienced a gradual decline which, in March 1915, reduced them to 11.5% and then later to a negligible percentage. This was not because interest in the fate of Belgium faded, but because the Commission requested

---

1 *The first fifteen American volunteers were all Rhodes scholars. Belgians were impressed by the breezy informality with which they addressed German officers. A rumor circulated that America had purchased the country.*
2 *Americans donated over $34.5 million (roughly $750 million today) of the $52.3 million the organization raised from individuals and foundations. The U.S. government contributed $387 million more.*

that monetary payments be substituted for these donations. The items obtained through donations were difficult to distribute because they arrived in very small quantities and required considerable sorting. Moreover, they did not always match the needs or habits of the Belgian population. They also took up cargo space that could have otherwise been used for essential foodstuffs. So, as of April 1915, supplies introduced into Belgium came almost exclusively from bulk purchases made by the Commission.

The value of donations in kind or in cash received by the Commission between its inception on October 22, 1914 and September 30, 1920 totaled 6,556,806 pounds sterling, or over 163 million francs. To that must be added the free services of a large part of the Commission's employed staff, the concessions and privileges granted by railroad, navigation, and insurance companies and by maritime or commercial brokers, and the gracious collaboration of many private individuals.

The Belgian government provided the majority of the funds used by the Commission, fulfilling a duty that events had otherwise prevented it from performing. Thanks to credits from its allies, from January 1915 on it provided a monthly allowance of 25 million francs, which increased to 37,500,000 francs two years later. When the United States joined the warring nations in June 1917, it offered the Commission a $15 million per month line of credit (or 77,850,000 francs) to pay for purchases made in the U.S. It is estimated that from November 1, 1914 until December 31, 1918, the CRB exported 3,442,821,645 francs worth of merchandise to Belgium. The total expenditures between these two dates came to 3.497 billion francs.[1]

America's entrance into the war did not prevent a single day of work at the Commission. It naturally meant that the United States minister, Brand Whitlock, had to leave Brussels, taking

---

[1] About $674 million with Pirenne's rate of exchange. The official final report of the CRB gives the total as $807 million (about $17.5 billion today). This provided around 5.2 million tons of food and clothing to Belgium and Northern France.

with him the Americans who had hitherto supervised the distribution of supplies. A new committee was created, called the Hispano-Dutch Committee, under the patronage of the minister for Spain, the Marquis Villalobar, and the minister for the Netherlands, Mr. van Vollenhove, and it continued until the armistice the work so admirably begun.[1]

The Commission for Relief's task consisted essentially in providing Belgium, during the war years, with the food that it otherwise would have imported. Thus what would in peacetime have been exchanged for exports was provided by international goodwill and the subsidies of the Belgian government.

The country as a whole was reduced to the condition of that of its inhabitants: it received without giving anything in return. It accumulated debt, but it survived.

However, it was not enough to have made possible the provisioning of seven million individuals, despite all the obstacles resulting from politics and war. The food arriving in Belgium from ships that had braved mines and submarines now had to be transported to remote towns in a country in which the transportation system had been disrupted by war. This was the task of the *Comité National*. It fulfilled it with as much devotion and skill as the Commission for Relief performed its task. And thus a double organization ensured the survival of Belgian people: one on the outside, the Commission, the other on the inside, the *Comité*, the first buying and importing, the other receiving and distributing; the one comprising Americans and neutrals, the other exclusively Belgians.

As mentioned earlier, the *Comité National* was established before the Commission for Relief. Founded as a result of the initiative of private individuals in the midst of a chaotic invasion, enjoying only a precarious existence under foreign domination,

---

1 See the report titled *Le Comité hispano-néerlandais pour la protection du ravitaillement en Belgique et dans le nord de la France* (Bruxelles, s. d., 1919).

and uncertain of the future and of whether it would be able to continue to receive supplies from outside, it became a robust and permanent organization as soon as that provisioning was guaranteed. It is worth noting that this provisioning was not solely a question of importing food. The goal of the London Cabinet was to limit shipments so as only to compensate for the low national production. Otherwise, the Germans could have used the imported food for their own benefit. As early as December 31, 1914, the German government made a promise to the United States Ambassador in Berlin to abstain from requisitioning food and fodder of any kind, which would otherwise have had to be replaced by the Commission for Relief. On April 14, 1916, a convention was signed to ban all exportation outside of the General Government's territory of food, livestock, and feed, as well as seeds, fertilizers, and farming supplies, or to requisition or buy them for the needs of the occupying army.

Until the end of the war, the *Comité National* had to continue to maintain the legal status of a private non-profit association. It had no legal standing, and no written rules. The *Comité* did not exist independently from the people who comprised it. It was for good reason that it refused to become a legal entity: as a purely private organization, it was less vulnerable to the German authorities. It was able to evade the control that Germany exerted over commercial enterprises. Officially, its bank assets, merchandise, and supplies were solely the property of the Commission for Relief and the ministers who protected it.

Thus it was in a similar situation regarding the goods it managed to that of government officials regarding public finances. And, in fact, the mission it volunteered for was by its nature within the duties of the state, the provinces, and the towns. The services it provided were essentially public services and, practically, if not legally, its role was that of a public authority. Its unpaid volunteers were performing the work that the national government could no longer undertake and that the occupying government refused to do. Still the German authorities regarded it with understandable mistrust. They recognized that the task it accomplished made it a state within the state and gave it a dangerous influence over the population it fed, reinforcing Belgian nationalism.

As a result, national solidarity inconveniently persisted during the occupation. Thus the Governor General strove to restrict as tightly as possible the *Comité*'s freedom. The organization, and all provincial and local committees depending on it, weren't allowed to give instructions directly to towns, to have them organize investigations, to send them surveys or circulars, or to have them prepare lists or statistics, without first consulting with the German civil commissioner. The *Comité* was also forbidden to pressure towns or private individuals in any way into following its instructions. Any measure taken to that effect had to be proposed to the competent authorities, which would permit it when they deemed it useful. The supervisors appointed by the *Comité* were able to note any misconduct on the part of millers, bakers, etc., but they had no further recourse. All they could do was to notify the authorities of their findings.[1]

The *Comité* therefore had no direct influence over the towns it supplied. It was even deprived of the right granted in Belgium to any charitable association to punish violations of its own rules by ending assistance. It's understandable that the occupying power wanted to force it to act only through its own agents. It's clear that it could not grant it a power that would have turned it into a sort of self-sufficient government in the eyes of the people. From the *Comité*'s standpoint, interference by the German authorities in its affairs would have made it appear as an accomplice of the enemy. Thus, it limited itself to relying solely on the goodwill and patriotism of its staff and of the population to ensure its services were discharged and that its directives followed. And its patience paid off.

---

1 See the dispatch from the Governor General von Bissing to the Minister of the United States of America (June 26 1915), Db Lannoy, previously cited work, p. 8.

The Belgian courts also supported it as much as they could, for as long as they continued to administer justice, which was until the end of April 1918. "They recognized that reselling rations obtained in the *Comité*'s stores after presenting one's card was fraud, and that purchasing rations obtained in that way was handling stolen merchandise. They pronounced sentences for forgeries, since forging or misusing the cards skewed statistics on the number of people needing supplies. They considered as fraud the use of cards belonging to third parties and the holding of multiple cards. Through a loose interpretation of the law, they frequently recognized the *Comité National* as a public service, and used that interpretation to punish violations with sentences defined in the Penal Code for the protection of public institutions. The Liége court, in a June 23, 1917 judgment, declared that misappropriations perpetrated at the expense of the *Comité National* by its employees were felonies, not misdemeanors. Several courts decided that its employees were public personnel and accordingly punished those who were guilty of abuse or assault against them."[1]

The more it took to heart its "public" mission, the more the *Comité National* strove to keep its appearance of a "private" organization, thanks to which it was able to escape German interference. It would recruit only agents with no political mandate. To eliminate all suspicion, it systematically avoided active state officials. While a few politicians were allowed into its ranks, they participated only in a private capacity. It always opposed the tendency among some town administrations to consider its local committees as the continuation of the communal provisioning committees organized at the beginning of the invasion, and of wanting as a result to interfere with their operations. The *Comité* understood that in order to succeed, it had to escape both the grasp of the official powers and that of the parties. This was the price to pay for the moral prestige that was so indispensible. It

---

[1] Ibid, p. 9

knew it was being closely monitored and had to resist giving the least appearance of favoritism. The censored press seized every opportunity to criticize its activities and to excite public opinion against it, and it attacked all the more shamelessly as there was no way to respond. So the *Comité* made it a duty to be scrupulously impartial. It asked its committees to reach out to representatives of all three major parties, and suggested that decisions be arrived at unanimously. No doubt it was not always able to inspire, in its innumerable organizations, the spirit of national unity that motivated it. It could only affect its collaborators through persuasion or example. But while there were occasional breaches of the principles it proclaimed, these were infrequent. It goes without saying that in small towns the influence of local politicians was too entrenched to be effectively circumvented. Everywhere else, and especially in large cities, the union of all for the safety of each was the watchword.

Despite being completely without power, the *Comité National* enjoyed an extraordinary authority. Since the German government could not do without its cooperation, it found itself forced to spare it. The *Comité* always enjoyed the protection of the American and Spanish ministers. It called upon them in times of conflict and their intervention with the Germans nearly always helped out. The occupying authorities could not risk antagonizing these representatives of the neutral Powers, nor provoke scandals by attacking members of the *Comité*, offending both its volunteers and international public opinion.

In fact, the *Comité* never ceased to benefit from the sympathy and compassion felt toward Belgium. The presence of American representatives for the Commission for Relief in the country granted it an even more precious guarantee. To crack down on the Commission would have been to persecute the Americans who ran it.

The *Comité* was well aware of the security provided by its protectors and its own usefulness for the German administration.

It was careful not to jeopardize its position by doing anything imprudent. It trusted the German postal system only with correspondence that was non-incriminating. Most of its communication with subordinates was done verbally. Thanks to an agreement made with the neutral ministers, meetings conducted by the Brussels *Comité* and its subcommittees were not subject to German surveillance. Only rarely did the police manage to find out what transpired during the sessions.

§ II. — HOW IT OPERATED AND HOW ITS WORK WAS ACCOMPLISHED

The system adopted for supplying Belgium was determined by the *Comité*'s legal status. Lacking any coercive power, it could not count on the Belgian administration, which was under German control, and still less on the purely German administration superimposed above the latter. To ask for their support would have effectively been doubly perilous: first, permitting the occupier to interfere in its work would make it appear to the population as if the *Comité* were collaborating with the Germans; second, it would compromise the guarantee that the supplies they allowed to be imported would not be at Germany's disposal. Patriotic sentiment and the need to respect the international conventions thus forced it to rely only on itself to accomplish the formidable task it had taken on. Effectively in charge of a public service, it could only carry it out through private means.

From Germany's perspective, the status of the *Comité* was similar to that granted by the state during the Middle Ages to Church domains through the privilege of immunity. The privilege was intended to prevent public officials from interfering with the Church's business. No actual power was granted to it. It enjoyed nothing but the negative, though invaluable, advantage of escaping the depredations of royal agents, at a time when these agents extorted goods and money from the people under the pretense of enforcing laws. Despite the enormous difference in time and context, it is clear that this state of things corresponds rather exactly to the *Comité*'s legal status. The expedient used by the Frankish monarchy to allow the Church to fulfill its mission in the midst of political disorder looks much like the one Germany was forced to adopt to abstain from seizing the Committee's assets, to respect its stores, and to not exert any control over its sessions. It also recognized the right of the neutral ministers to intervene on behalf of the *Comité*. They were its legal protectors. Just as in the 9th century, the organization was thus freed *ab introitu judicum publicorum*. Within its own sphere, the *Comité* enjoyed complete autonomy.

Thanks to that autonomy, it could organize itself as it saw fit and freely choose its staff members. When the Brussels central committee was transformed into a national committee, it followed the same principle in its recruiting. Individuals were appointed solely on the basis of their competence and commitment. They were for the most part businessmen, bankers, industrialists, and administrators, chosen from all three major parties. Politicians were indeed appointed, but not because of the power the electors had conferred on them, but because of their character. As for Belgian officials, those who continued to work under the Germans were excluded. Their obligations toward the occupier would not have allowed them complete independence and they would have found themselves constantly pulled between contradictory duties and responsibilities. Town magistrates were excluded as well. To have done otherwise would have been to have created confusion between charitable services organized by towns under German surveillance, and the services provided exclusively by the *Comité*.

The Brussels committee was the driving force behind a nationwide organization. With too many members to be able to function effectively, it entrusted daily management of its operations to an executive committee under the presidency of Émile Francqui. It was this committee, and particularly its leader, that inspired and guided the great work the *Comité* carried out until the armistice. Because it lacked the capacity to give direct orders to its thousands of agents, it could guide them only through advice and example. Instead of issuing directives, it appealed to their devotion to the cause. They were granted great autonomy. The *Comité* did not try to impose upon them a uniform method, which it could not have forced them to follow and which wouldn't have appropriate for their very different situations and needs. It let the provincial committees, which were formed in the administrative center of each province, take the measures they deemed most appropriate for the interests of the people they served.[1]

Just like the central committee, the provincial committees were composed of eminent local personalities who worked together without any political considerations. Under these committees, were the regional and local committees. For these, also, inclusiveness was the rule. Members were not paid, with the exception of accountants, transporters, salesmen, inventory personnel—those in charge of tasks that were absolutely necessary for receiving and distributing the commodities that arrived in such enormous quantities. Even many of them worked simply as volunteers.

Relations between the many local, regional, and provincial committees and the Brussels committee were conducted through written reports, collective sessions, and the inspection of town committees by the provincial and regional committees. In the beginning, there was, of course, some resistance. On one hand, there was the Belgian tendency to treat every rule as an infringement on freedom, and on the other, the tendency of the municipal administrations to intervene in the local committees' activities. As a consequence, provincial committees, out of scruples or fears of upsetting influential people or friends, did not always work effectively to end abuses. On February 3, 1916, the *Comité*

---

[1] Only the Luxembourg committee sat in Brussels, due to the communication difficulties with that province, but it had representatives there.

National reprimanded the provincial committees for their negligence in not establishing effective mechanisms for inspection and control. It complained that excessive quantities of supplies had been sold by the local committees, not only to private individuals, but also to storekeepers. It reminded the committees that if Britain were to become aware that supplies were being siphoned off to Germany, it might terminate the imports. And it went so far as to threaten to exclude negligent provinces from the distribution of supplies. This was sufficient for oversight, hitherto lax, to be properly established. In fact, the *Comité National* never had to act on its ultimatum. If abuses continued, they were minimal.

The *Comité* continued to multiply its contacts with the provincial committees. Representatives of the latter met with the executive committee twice a month in Brussels. With experience, there was a convergence of views and greater unity of action. Little by little, not only the local committees, but the entire population became more disciplined.

The German authorities respected the agreements protecting the *Comité*'s activities. They abstained from entering its stores, infiltrating its committees, or deliberately hindering its transports. But they didn't simply resign themselves to tolerating the independence of the organization. Because it was run entirely by Belgians, they were naturally suspicious of it. They tried, more than once, by circuitous means, to gain influence over it. These attempts were thwarted by *Comité*'s savviness and the timely intervention of the protecting ministers. In the Reich, the Pan-German press never grew tired of attacking the *Comité*, which, it claimed, enabled the Belgian people live in abundance while the German government was obliged to adopt stringent rationing. But as food became more scarce, it became increasingly impossible to do without the *Comité National*. What would have happened if it had stopped supplying Belgium, leaving its seven million inhabitants in dire straits—and the responsibility of Germany?

When the first Governor General for Belgium, Marshall von der Goltz, decided to leave the country's supplying to the Commission for Relief and the *Comité National*, he had no idea what the future held for these twin institutions. Focused on military operations, he was only thinking of the short term. He hastily seized the opportunity to turn over the burdensome mission to someone else. It did not occur to him to ask for guarantees in return for the ones he was providing. The Commission and the *Comité* worked hard to take advantage of this. Von der Goltz's short administration was enough to let them cover the country with their warehouses and distribution centers. When General von Bissing arrived in Brussels (December 1914), things had already gone too far. He was bound by his predecessor's word. It was too late to recover lost ground and place the organizations under German control.[1]

He at least managed, without breaking the international convention he was bound by, to prevent the *Comité National* from further extending the scope of its activities. The policy he adopted toward it was in short a defensive one. Since he couldn't overturn the understanding, he did his best to limit it. To the rights granted to the *Comité* through the arrangement made between Germany and its enemies, and that was guaranteed by the American, Spanish, and Dutch ministers, he opposed the rights that belonged in times of war to the occupying power in the country it governs. On June 25, 1915, he submitted a plan to the ministers that, according to him, would solve the relationship between the German administration and the *Comité* in order to "guarantee common and useful work, based on mutual trust, for the well-being of the Belgian people." He proposed, among

---

1 H. Waentig, *Belgien*, p.29 (Halle, 1919), says correctly: "*Leider hat die deutsche Verwaltung die Tragweite jener politischen Schöpfung zu spat erkannt. Viel zu spat jedenfalls um die mittlerweile ins reisenhafte ausgewachsene Organisation auf das unserem Interesse dienliche Mass zurückbilden zu können.*" (Unfortunately, the German government recognized too late the importance of this political creation. Much too late, in any case, to be able to take measures in its interest to dismantle what had grown into a full-blown organization.)

other things, that the presidents of the civil administration attend the provincial committees' sessions, that the civil commissioners and the *Kreischefs* attend the regional committees' sessions, that the income and spending forecasts be shared with the presidents of the civil administration, and that these presidents would, in agreement with the committees, set the prices for the foodstuffs. The *Comité National* immediately protested against these innovations which, by removing the independence it had always enjoyed, would have resulted in the Allies withdrawing their authorization. Intervention by the ministers scattered the storm clouds. On July 29, 1915, von Bissing recognized "that the *Comité National* and the Commission for Relief in Belgium will be able to enjoy all of the freedom of action guaranteed to them by the agreements made between the Governor General and the representatives of the neutral Powers."[1] However, the guarantee was renewed by the latter that the *Comité*'s "humanitarian" work would continue to not "harm the rights of the country's occupier, nor its interests."

The question of food produced within Belgium gave rise to new difficulties. As already mentioned, the British government intended to authorize importation only if there was a guarantee that Germany would not seize the country's own food supplies. This guarantee had been given to it as early as October, 1914. In March, 1915, however, von Bissing declared that an exception would be made for certain products such as oats, straw, hay, potatoes, and sugar, which were only imported in very small quantities or not at all. This restriction was energetically fought by the British government. On December 31, 1915, Sir Edward Grey openly complained that Germany continued to purchase supplies produced by Belgian agriculture for its own benefit. He demanded that exportation of these supplies outside of the country be forbidden, "the only exception being that the *Comité National* and

---

1 *Rapport du Comité*, p. 165

the Commission for Relief in Belgium will be allowed to export to Northern France and distribute the supplies available in definite excess of current and future Belgian needs." He added that if his demands were not satisfied, he would not be bound by prior commitments to the Commission for Relief, whose operations had, through no fault of its own, encouraged the Germans to seize the country's resources, and had thus become a replacement system rather than an assistance and support system.[1] In the face of such a threat—and fully aware of the cataclysm that would result if it were acted on—the Reich backed down. After negotiations led by the neutral ministers and Emil Francqui, who received authorization to come to London in January 1916 with the Marquis of Villalobar, the Governor General agreed to prohibit the export of any goods used to feed people or livestock, except for certain products (chicory, vegetables, fruits), whose availability exceeded the needs of the occupied territory's population. He promised to order the military supply corps to stop buying or seizing these goods. He was, however, granted the concession that purchases made by individuals belonging to the army would be permitted, so long as they were not systematic. In short, he surrendered (April 14, 1916).

While from then on domestic foodstuffs were reserved exclusively for the Belgian people, the *Comité National* was unable to secure the right to distribute them. Very early, the German administration had established organizations under the name of *Zentrale* reporting exclusively to it and which were able to seize and regulate the distribution of produce. There were *Zentralen* for wheat (*Erntezentrale*), for sugar, for potatoes, etc. Thus, alongside the *Comité National*, the Governor General maintained control over all domestic produce, permitting the former to distribute only that which was imported. All the *Comité* and the ministers were able to obtain was the creation of a consulting committee,

---

[1] Ibid., p. 85 and following.

with a few representatives from the *Comité*, which was charged with advising the *Zentralen*.

The role of the *Comité* was not entirely limited to supplying food. As its name indicates, it had given itself a double task: nutrition, but also assistance. The latter included the most varied means to help the neediest: soup kitchens, free or reduced-price distribution of bread and other food, fuel, and clothes. The resources for this work were provided by the nutrition department, which donated revenue from the sale of merchandise, as well as donations and subscriptions collected in Belgium and abroad.

New services were soon added to the basic assistance the *Comité* provided. The compassion and patriotism of countless individuals enabled the organization to create special assistance programs, including *Aid and Protection for the Families of Officers and Noncommissioned Officers Deprived of Their Support Because of the War*, *Aid and Protection for the Families Deprived of Support Because of the War*, *Aid and Protection for the Needy Unemployed*[1], *Aid and Protection for Lacemakers*, *The Commission for Childhood Nutrition*, *Aid and Protection for the Belgian Homeless, Refugees, Foreigners, Artists, The Wounded, Injured Doctors and Pharmacists, and Damaged Churches*. Independently of these programs that it had initiated, the Committee also supported *The Cooperative Society for Advances and Loans*, which was created to provide unemployed state officials with a portion of their pay and to give the state's creditors advances on the securities they held; the *Assistance for Worker Housing Societies*, created to enable those who rented or owned workers' housing to make their payments; the *Belgian National League Against Tuberculosis*; the *Union of Belgian Cities and Towns*, which built shelters for those whose homes had been destroyed by the war, and conducted preparatory studies for rebuilding ruined areas; the *Information Agency for War Prisoners and Internees*, the *Canteen for Imprisoned Soldiers* and the *Belgian*

---

1 It ceased its operations on November 1, 1917.

Soldier's Fund, which organized shipments of packages for Belgian prisoners in Germany and send food to needy internees.

The operation of all these programs and the diversity of the services they provided made the *Comité National* a real power. Very early on, the sort of protection it provided the needy (and the war had made half the people needy), worried the Governor General. In negotiations with the neutral ministers during the early months of 1915, he agreed to permit the existing institutions to continue to operate. However, his permission would be required in the future to create new ones. As with the creation of the *Zentralen*, which enabled him to continue to intervene in supplying the country's food, he also attempted to compete with the *Comité* in providing assistance, in this case by influencing the Red Cross. In April 1915, the executive committee of the Belgian Red Cross was dissolved and replaced by a central administration under the Governor General. Every entity having official connections or business relations with the old executive committee was informed that it must now deal exclusively with the new German executives. The object was clearly to enable the Governor General to assume control of the distribution of charity in Belgium. The central administration of the Red Cross in Geneva immediately protested, asking all of its affiliates worldwide to join with it in protesting a measure that stripped the Belgian branch of its autonomy. But the German plan was foiled by a boycott within the country. None of the numerous Belgian charitable associations would work with the Red Cross, now that it had become a German institution and was competing directly with the *Comité*.

This setback naturally sparked a battle between the *Comité*, supported by the public opinion, and the Governor General, disposing of force—a battle waged, politely enough, by official exchanges of letters. All the efforts of von Bissing to extend the scope of his control met stubborn resistance.

On November 23, 1915, the *Comité* was ordered to end the classes it had offered for the indigent unemployed. On July 10,

1916, a similar measure terminated the home economics classes that had been provided by the agricultural section since spring of 1915. Fifteen days later, the *Comité* was advised that it would have to abandon its classes on draining land and eliminating standing water. The initiative it had taken to provide books for popular reading programs, begun in Brussels on July 14, 1915, had met with such success that it inevitably aroused suspicion. In one year, 313 new libraries had been opened and 18,920 volumes had been distributed to the 1,176 existing libraries. On October 11, 1916, the German authorities decreed that this service be discontinued. It had been enormously helpful to a population condemned for the most part to idleness. Whitlock and Villalobar failed to move von Bissing. He was determined to strictly limit the activities of the *Comité* by interpreting very literally the conventions that protected it. And of course he was doing so in Germany's best interest, in the same way that the *Comité* never missed an opportunity to extend its services and thereby its influence over the country.

As was mentioned, this influence was contested continuously by the censored press. The smallest mistake in the distribution or delivery of supplies, the tiniest abuse by one of the *Comité*'s countless agents, was immediately turned into evidence of the incompetence, negligence, or dishonesty of the organization's leaders. And these attacks sometimes affected the thinking of those embittered by misery. People didn't wish to understand or were unable to appreciate just how difficult it was to supply the entire country, given the disorganization of transportation networks. In short, the number of people who were actually familiar with the situation was very small. Many confused the *Comité National* and the Commission for Relief in Belgium and credited the Americans for what they owed to the collaboration between Americans and Belgians. America's prestige harmed Germany. The generosity of the United States seemed to indicate not only its sympathy for Belgians, but its disapproval of the invasion. In any case, the aspersions cast on the *Comité* by German-funded newspapers had very little impact on public opinion. The vast majority of the population appreciated the good intentions of the patriots who provided for them.

The way in which the *Comité National* operated depended above all on the small size of the country. It would have been impossible in a larger nation. To succeed, permanent contacts had to be established between the Brussels committee and the provincial sub-committees, so that instructions from the center would be communicated all the way to the most remote hamlets. The men who directed the joint activities also had to know each other personally and to trust each other in order to maintain an organization without any official authority and while under intense surveillance. Thanks to the country's small size and to the ease of communications, all of the central committee's members had long before the war been in contact with one another and with the most influential members of the provincial committees. Since almost all of them belonged to the business world, they had multiple opportunities to see and get to know each other in the industrial committees, bank boards, and administrative councils they belonged to. There existed among them a sort of camaraderie that admirably facilitated the new role they had assumed. These men, who had once come together for business, now joined together in a task that required exactly the same skills and competencies they had developed during peacetime. They understood clearly the agonizing situation the country faced. They felt it in a very concrete way: they knew the large cities and had toured their factories.

The density of the population also helped make the *Comité* more efficient. The more closely people lived to one another, the easier it was to organize and monitor the distribution of supplies and assistance, once the difficulty of getting them there had been overcome. The canals, roads, and railroads, though damaged and occupied by the military, were so numerous that they were always sufficient for the transportation of food.

But it was the nation itself that enabled the *Comité* to accomplish its task. Without the thousands of volunteers that flocked to it from day one, it would have been powerless.¹ In a sense, the social and political life of the Belgian people saved its material existence. In this country, where work is an absolute necessity, all it took to get assistance was to request it. And the good will of the volunteers was matched by their competence. The political decentralization, the number of private charities, syndicates, cooperatives, insurance companies, etc. had spread throughout the country a love of collaborative activities and a taste for responsibilities. The personal ambition that drove individuals to seek public office and the presidencies of organizations, and to take part in municipal affairs, was now focused on the charitable committees. A surplus of applicants was much more common than a lack thereof. The decentralization of the *Comité*'s services made its task easier rather than harder. People would have defied the organization had it been authoritarian, tightly regulated, hierarchical. But Belgians were eager to offer help to a program that left so much to private initiative. The "self-government"² ingrained in the nation by its history came to its aid in perilous times. Surprised by the results obtained in the midst of difficult circumstances, Germans called the work accomplished by the *Comité* "brilliant" and "ingenious" because their mindset, so different from that of Belgians, didn't permit them to see it as simply a manifestation of the national character.

The establishment of what could be called the "common front" against the occupier by the thousands of *Comité National* volunteers was accomplished rather simply. Every Thursday, the presidents and representatives for the provincial committees would gather in Brussels for an executive committee meeting, under the presidency of Émile Francqui. Once the session had ended,

---

1 Refer to von Köhler, previously cited work, p. 73.
2 *In English in the original.*

they had lunch at the Taverne Royale with politicians, magistrates from large cities, and others. During the conversation, they would reach agreements on the attitude they would adopt in the event of conflict. Since all parts of the country were represented during these gatherings, directives were transmitted without delay. The very next day, they were relayed to the provincial committees, from where they immediately reached the local committees. "The Germans were dumbfounded to meet opposition for similar reasons in every town. They might have expected a given line of reasoning from administrators of large cities, but it was harder to discount the arguments made in remote provinces, from burgomasters of unknown towns."[1]

To appreciate the significance of the *Comité National*'s work, one has to ask what would have happened to the Belgian people if it hadn't existed. From all evidence, nothing could have taken its place. Unable to feed Belgium on its own, Germany could at most have abstained from confiscating domestic supplies for its own use and have allowed the Netherlands and Switzerland to import their excess produce into the occupied territory. But Switzerland could have provided only very few things. The Netherlands, better supplied, would not have been able to meet Belgium's food needs, though a considerable amount of commodities was imported from there until the German authorities forbade these in July 1916 for financial reasons.[2] It is also worth noting that on December 5, 1914, the Dutch government created an official committee charged with assisting not only the many Belgian refugees in the Netherlands, but also these living near the border. Later, that committee extended its activities to the entire occupied territory, where it created sub-committees operating under a central committee established in Brussels. In

---

[1] I borrowed this quote from a note that was kindly provided by Mr. Louis Franck, who, until his deportation to Germany, presided over the lunches at the Taverne Royale.
[2] The goal was to defend the German exchange rate that the exportation of Belgian funds to the Netherlands depreciated. Henry. *Le Ravitaillement de la Belgique*, p. 167.

fact, it mostly distributed bread, 52 million kilograms of which were handed out in 1916.

But these were only palliatives. The fact remains that the survival of the seven million Belgian under German occupation depended mostly on the collaboration of the Commission for Relief with the *Comité National*. Bread being a staple of Belgian food, they dedicated most of their efforts to importing wheat. A daily ration of 250 grams of flour had to be guaranteed to each resident. The domestic wheat seized by Germany was sold to the *Comité National*, which then distributed it under its supervision. It was calculated that, on these grounds, the available amount per capita per day was 108 grams in 1915, 69 grams in 1916, 82 grams in 1917. Belgium's dependence on the German administration for domestic wheat and on the *Comité National* for foreign wheat meant that its distribution to the public was not as efficient as it might have been. A single system would have saved a lot energy, waste, and fraud. But the Governor General did not want to do anything that would increase the influence of the *Comité*. The efforts it took to retain its autonomy under the patronage of the neutral ministers was reason enough for von Bissing not to voluntarily surrender anything to it. So two distinct organizations existed side by side: next to the Committee's stores and offices, other stores and offices operating under German control were administered by the towns. The presence of representatives from the *Comité National* on the advisory committees mentioned above did not and could not create harmony between the two organizations. While cooperating towards the same goal, they felt a degree of mistrust towards one another.

The Commission for Relief and the *Comité National* were not always able, despite their best efforts, to provide the population with the bread ration they intended to. From August to October 1916, 220,000 tonnes of wheat came into Belgium, or an average of 73,000 tonnes per month. But in November, imports fell to 40,000 tonnes, then to 34,000 tonnes in December, 47,000 in January 1917, and 24,000 in February. The intensification of submarine warfare markedly worsened the situation. In March 1917, only 5,745 tonnes of wheat arrived. The bread rations had to be reduced, and corn and barley had to be mixed in with the wheat. The crisis wasn't overcome until July 1918.

Overall, the fact remains that Belgium did not have enough food during the war. The upper classes were able to secure extra food through the black market. And the grain-producing farmers' situation was largely guaranteed, as noted earlier. It was impossible for the German administration to control their output. Generally speaking, this was always underestimated, so much so that farmers were able not only to fulfill their own needs with the surplus, but also reap sizeable profits on the black market. But in the industrial regions and in large cities, people had to endure very harsh privations, which were exacerbated by the shortage of coal for heating in the winter. The unemployed and lower middle class were particularly affected, but they handled their situation with unexpected courage and resignation.

The fears of revolts triggered by the food shortage never came to pass. While there were a few strikes here and there, such as the one that resulted from a lack of potatoes in the Borinage in spring of 1916, they did not last long and were not serious. As inadequate as it was, the daily ration still allowed all those with normal physical endurance to live through these terrible years. Death rates did increase, but apparently never reached the levels of France or Germany. Infant mortality rates even dropped at times. The assistance provided by the *Comité National* and a number of charities for the newborns of the lower classes encouraged hygienic practices that were not sufficiently widespread at the time. In almost all parts of the country, the *Goutte de Lait*, a charity organized by middle-class women, took care of young children and particularly of frail children. In the midst of the adults' misery, young children grew up in more favorable conditions than before the war.

Of all the social classes, the petit-bourgeoisie was the most pathetic victim of the events. Employees, small *rentiers*, and civil servants who were getting pensions or who were unemployed were deprived of resources either by factory closings, or by the non-payment or insufficient payment of their annuities, salaries, or pensions. Here again, the *Comité National* was of invaluable help. In return for the funds lent to it by the Belgian government, it took upon itself to pay the state employees who had been left without a job. Nevertheless, the sufferings of the lower middle class were all that much greater insofar as their sense of personal honor made them reluctant to seek public charity. The *Secours Discret* was instituted to help them. Committees were organized in all large cities that enabled thousands of needy people to survive the crisis without being forced to advertise their distress.

The *Comité National* acted as much on the spirit as it did on the body. Of course it was forbidden to address the public directly, and it never attempted to stray from the neutrality forced on it by the convention that permitted it to exist. But its very existence bolstered the courage and hope of the nation. The *Comité*'s 125,000 workers were 125,000 instruments of energy and "self-help."[1] The assistance Belgians provided each other in a time of common misery gave them a strong sense that their future was secure and reinforced their desire to remain united. All parties spontaneously gathered around the *Comité*. Its weekly meetings were the only assemblies where Belgians were able to freely discuss their situation, so much so that under the cover of charity, it rekindled both patriotic and civic sentiments.

The *Comité* realized only too well that the influence it exercised depended entirely on its independence from the occupying power and sought jealously guard this. The sympathy and support it received from Whitlock, Villalobar, and van Vollenhove, and the compassion and admiration for Belgium throughout the

---

1 *In English in the original.*

world, strengthened the resolve with which it resisted Germany's attempts to interfere with its mission. Its international popularity made it, despite its weakness, a formidable opponent. The Governor General was not mistaken when he dubbed it a state within the state. Indeed, thanks to it, the nation, invaded and dominated by brute force, continued to exist. As Ernest Solvay said on November 26, 1914, the *Comité National* was and remained until the end "a sort of provisional government, paternal and well-meaning," which would disappear only after the occupier departed.

CHAPTER VII

Exploitation of the Country[1]

§ I. — Rational Exploitation and Worker Deportation

The violation of the Belgian neutrality had long been a part of the military plan conceived by the German General Staff. Its objective was to rapidly finish off the western enemy in order to then hit the eastern enemy with full force. The goal was to end the war quickly with two swift strikes, one to the left, then one to the right. All of the strategic calculations to ensure success had been carefully considered. But they were based on an incorrect assumption—that France would be *hors de combat* before Britain would declare war. The OHL counted on that country either remaining neutral, or, at worst, entering the war only after the German armies had seized the Flanders coast, Dunkirk, and Calais. The Empire's outposts on the North Sea and on the Channel would enable it to threaten Britain and thwart its war plans. Belgium was not considered capable of upsetting these schemes. Germany assumed that the country would either resign itself to accepting the ultimatum, or that it would offer a purely nominal resistance which would be no cause for concern. Everything had been admirably planned.

---

[1] We will refer in this chapter to the works of Ch. De Kebchove, D. De Terchem, *L'industrie belge pendant l'occupation allemande*, and of F. Passelecq, *Déportation et travail force des ouvriers et de la population civile de la Belgique occupée*, published in the Belgian series of this collection.

But Britain's declaration of war on August 4, 1914, the time lost besieging Liège and Namur, and the need to keep an eye on the Belgian army in Antwerp, all made the situation take an unexpected turn.[1] Instead of surprising its adversaries, Germany was surprised by them. When the battlefronts stabilized around the Marne and Yser rivers, it became evident that all hopes for a short and triumphant war had been dashed, and that Germany faced the bleak reality of a war of attrition. Victory depended no longer on the movement of armies on the battlefields, but on the endurance of the warring nations. The war would be won by those whose material resources and morale would enable them to hold out the longest.

But the naval blockade organized by Britain put Germany in a situation glaringly inferior to that of its enemies. To break it, the country would have needed at least one outlet to the Channel in the West.[2] Holding the Flanders coast was actually more of a hindrance as long as Dunkirk and Calais remained inaccessible. It could and indeed was used to harass the enemy, to launch submarines against it, and to disrupt its transports of troops and supplies. But it could not give Germany free access to the sea. Unlike its opponents, who still had the entire wealth of the world at their disposal, the Reich found itself confined to that part of Central Europe that the trenches encircled. To its own territory were added, without even doubling it, Belgium, northern France, and parts of Russia and Poland. It was restricted to surviving solely on these. To sustain the conflict, it had no choice but to use all available resources. Such was the price to be paid for its survival. Since circumstances forced it to exploit its own people, it could hardly spare those in the enemy territories it had conquered. Just as Napoleon had imposed a continental blockade

---

1 *The Belgian Army launched two sorties from the city, on August 25 and September 9, in which German positions were attacked and over-run and towns liberated in southern Antwerp province and northern Brabant. In the second, one German division was recalled and a corps halted en route to the Marne. Of course, however important the contributions of the 110,000-man British Army and the 117,000-strong Belgian Army, it was the rapid redeployment of the French Army that thwarted the German war plan.*
2 *It's not clear how this would have enabled Germany to circumvent the Allied blockade.*

on Europe, Germany extended its war economy to all the countries it occupied.[1] Its genius for organization and for technology allowed it to accomplish in four years the spectacular feat of mobilizing all forces, physical and human, to help its military goals. Suffocated by the enemy's blockade, Germany considered that that the inhumanity of the Allies justified the inhumanity it was obliged to employ to defend itself. It was ruthless because the only other option was defeat, and it was no less ruthless with itself than with others.

In these conditions, the exploitation of Belgium was unavoidable. But it seemed all the more atrocious to Belgians because they were completely innocent. The war had been forced upon them, and its devastation was more horrifying because the country had been so wealthy and industrious. But how could it have been spared the fate that weighed so heavily on the German population? Having been conquered, it had to be sacrificed.

It was, to tell the truth, the victim of a tragic mistake made by the German General Staff. It is more or less certain that if those who had planned the campaign, instead of being seduced by the chimera of a short, victorious war, had anticipated the possibility of attrition warfare, they would have decided against invading Belgium—which obliged them to impose on the country an odious regime universally disapproved of.[2] The war's long duration rendered the occupation futile. The country's wealth was plundered, but how much more profitable would it have been had it been allowed to remain neutral and to contribute through trade, as did the Netherlands, Switzerland, and Sweden, resources that would have certainly been more abundant than what was taken by force—with the world watching in indignation![3]

The economic crisis that the invasion triggered in Belgium

---

[1] "We were constrained," said Napoleon, "to use against the common enemy the same weapons it used against us."
[2] *Not invading Belgium would also, at the very least, have delayed Britain's declaration of war.*
[3] *This hypothesis seems dubious. Germany would not have been able to have obtained from a neutral Belgium the raw materials and machinery it requisitioned, the workforce it conscripted, the war taxes it collected, the profits reaped by the* <u>Zentralen</u>, *etc.*

was at first only a natural consequence of the war. Germany certainly did not intentionally provoke it. If the requisitions were enormous, it was because the needs of its armies were also enormous. Imposed by the military authority in the midst of strategic operations, they had no other goal than to supply the troops in the field. They were made in fits and starts, according to current circumstances. The brutal exactions turned the country upside down, but the intention was to provide for the immediate needs for the German offensive. It was not until August 13 that the *Deutsche Kriegsrohstoffabteilung* was created at the Ministry of War in Berlin, the role of which was to make available to the military administration all the raw materials in the countries occupied by Germany, as well as in Germany itself.

Belgium was bound to feel the effects of this formidable organization sooner or later. However, it's worth noting that it was only during 1916 that the country began to be subjected to it. Until then, it seems that the civil and military administrations had not come to an agreement as to the system that would be adopted. The one, impatient and wanting immediate results, wished to submit the country to economic siege without delay. The other, more cautious, and also more solicitous of public opinion in Belgium, preferred a less radical approach. It believed that it was not in Germany's best interest to exhaust the resources of the wealthy territory it had just conquered. It even imagined itself able, for a certain time, to conciliate the Belgians and persuade them to work voluntarily for their conqueror's benefit. It hesitated to fell the tree to gather its fruits. To strong-arm tactics, it preferred a more flexible and conservative approach.

While agreeing with the General Staff that Belgium must be exploited in German interests, it was influenced by its first-hand knowledge of the country's situation.

As early as September 2, 1914, Field Marshall von der Goltz assured the Belgian people that "citizens who want to tend to their business peacefully will have no reason to fear German troops or authorities. As much as possible, commerce ought to start up again, factories will have to resume work, and crops will have to be harvested." The words "as much as possible" obviously refer to restrictions subsequently imposed by the war on economic life, such as taking control of banks (September 18) and banning payments to the enemy (November 3). It cannot have referred to more far-reaching measures. Indeed, the Field Marshall seems to have envisioned the possibility of maintaining Belgium in as advantageous a position as circumstances would permit. The terms of his October 16 letter to the *Comité Central de secours et d'alimentation* further confirms his perspective. He expressed his "strong satisfaction" and "did not hesitate to assure it formally and expressly that the goods it imports would be exempt from requisition by the military authorities." There is no doubt that these words were carefully chosen and that they reveal hope to reduce as much as possible the suffering caused to the country by the violation of its neutrality. Nonetheless, while he was absorbed in military operations, abuses were committed that von der Goltz either ignored or could not prevent. His successor, General von Bissing, complained in June 1915 of the seizing of raw materials which the Field Marshall had allowed.

On October 26, 1914, the Belgian economy first felt the impact of the *Kriegsministerium*. As a result of a decree on that date, a quantity of raw materials was put under supervision of a commissioner established in Brussels. He would be able to hand these over to the German Empire or to third parties, at a price set by a commission named by the war minister in Berlin. Among these raw materials were products essential to industry: copper, lead, zinc, cotton, jute, wool, hemp, and products manufactured from these materials, skins, leathers, rubber, grease, mineral oils, benzene, etc. On November 20 tar, linen, olein, etc. were added to the list. Thus the systematic seizing of all materials that could be used in the war effort was extended to occupied Belgium. The comprehensive plan for rational economic exploitation conceived by Walther

Rathenau was substituted for the ad hoc military requisitions.

This was increasingly imposed under von Bissing's administration (from December 2, 1914). The list of economic decrees from that date forward shows the constant progress of the German expropriation not only of raw materials, but also of the country's equipment. As of February 22, 1915, the exportation of metal-working machines was banned, with the exception of those exported under the Governor General's orders. And these orders were issued frequently, for in June of the following year, von Bissing noted that thousands of machines had been transported from Belgium to Germany to manufacture ammunition.

The fact that military courts handled all violations of the decrees regarding the seizures made them all that much harsher for the Belgian people, and more efficient for Germany. In the end, the army had the last word regarding confiscations made in its interest.

The contribution of 40 million francs per month imposed on Belgium on December 10, 1914 added financial withdrawals to the withdrawals of raw materials and machinery. The ease with which it was collected led the War Minister, as early as 1916, to raise it to 50 and then 60 million per month. It seemed to him that Belgium was rich enough to help support the expenses of the German treasury. It also seemed to him that it ought to "have a proportionately equal part to that of Germany of war expenses."

This policy, which would inevitably and quickly drain Belgium's resources, met with opposition from the Governor General.

On June 19 1915, von Bissing very clearly laid out his ideas before of an industrial commission he had summoned to Brussels. "I think, he said, *dass eine ausgepresste Zitrone keinen Wert hat und dass eine getötete Kuh, keine Milch mehr gibt.*"[1] He wanted to maintain the country "*lebensfähig*"[2] and heal the wounds from

---

1 "A pressed lemon has no more juice and a slaughtered cow gives no more milk," *Rapports et documents d'enquête*, vol 3, t II, p 49.
2 *viable*

the war. On October 22, 1915, he estimated that of the 30 to 40 billion francs of the country's estimated pre-war worth, more than a sixth had been wiped out. He saw very clearly that it was impossible to compare Belgium to Germany. In the latter, a large part of the war's expenses helped maintain industrial activity. In Belgium, in contrast, industry was paralyzed by the removal of raw materials and machines. If factories were still working, they were doing so at a loss. For the time being, the country was consuming its capital. It had already provided, both in requisitions and through the 480 million in war contributions, more than 2 billion francs. Germany's best interest lay not in the destruction of Belgium's economy, but in actually helping the rebirth of commercial and industrial life. Whether the country was destined to be annexed, or whether it was to be attached in any way to the Reich's economic system after the war, it would be more profitable to keep it solvent than exhausted and depleted. In addition, commanders at the front preferred to have behind them territory in a more or less normal situation. Violence in Belgium's cities would play into the hands of the enemy. Undoubtedly, the liquidation of existing stocks had introduced a lot of cash into the country. And the importations by the Commission for Relief in Belgium had brought in goods with a total estimated value of 576 million francs, as of June 30, 1915.

But current opinion in Germany and that of the War Minister did not regard this as any sort of economic revival. It was simply the case that "the enemy countries having contributed to making Belgium solvent, Germany ought to continue to extract great value from it."

Thus the Governor General, wanting to "conserve" as much as possible the productive forces in Belgium, and the War Minister viewing the country as a resource to be exhausted, went head to head. Von Bissing won the first encounter. The war contribution was, for the time being, not raised.

Von Bissing's confidential statements regarding the real

situation of the Belgian economy are in striking contrast with the supposed prosperity that the German newspapers credited it with around the same time. Deprived of their raw materials and stripped of their machinery, industries could only sustain themselves by consenting to work for Germany and thus directly or indirectly support its military power. The one honorable option at this point was passive resistance. As noted, the vast majority of employers and workers alike preferred inaction to collaboration with the occupier. Apart from exceptions that are impossible to estimate, manufacturers closed down their factories rather than letting them serve Germany. This obviously prevented them from restocking raw materials. In many factories, these were removed within the first months. The temporary resumption that occurred after the shock of the invasion could therefore not be sustained. Only coal mines remained active until the country was freed.

It would have been possible to enable industry to survive, at least marginally, by opening for it a door to foreign countries through which it could have received raw materials and exported products. But on February 28, 1915, a decree banned any exports that were not authorized by the War Ministry's commissioner, an authorization that would later be replaced (April 15, 1916) by that of the chief of the civil administration. What remained of the export trade was also hindered by the fact that goods could only be exported below a price set by the German administration, and were taxed when exiting the country.

For its part, Britain wanted to monitor all merchandise exported overseas from the Netherlands, and would permit these only if profits from the sales were deposited in a bank in the United Kingdom. But Germany was opposed to these measures, and Belgian industrialists saw their interests sacrificed to the incompatible interests of the belligerents.[1]

As for imports, it was obvious that the countries at war with Germany could not allow products to enter Belgium that would have increased the volume of goods requisitioned by Germany. However the Governor General, true to the policy of conservation that he advocated against the War Ministry's policy of exhaustion, wished for a modus vivendi that would allow Belgian industry to secure raw materials by using a system similar to the one used by the *Comité National*. At the end of August 1915, von Bissing engaged industrialists to negotiate such an arrangement with the British government. He promised to examine carefully ways to protect the imported merchandise from requisitions. But the plan obviously could not be implemented. Britain had no guarantee that the Governor General would be able to resist the demands of the military administration. In London, it was deemed that enough had been done merely by allowing the Belgian people not to starve to death. To permit the country to resume its industrial activity could unquestionably only work to Germany's advantage. Even assuming the Reich would stop requisitions, it was obvious that the slightest improvement of the economy would be used as a pretext to increase the war contribution demanded from the Belgium. The failure of negotiations at least provided the German press with fresh grievances against "English egotism."

The institution of *Zentralen* and of purchasing companies (*Einkaufgesellschaften*) in the spring of 1915 further complicated and worsened the regime imposed on economic life. All production and distribution was now subject to German control. On April 26, 1915, the *Kohlenzentrale* was created, which was in charge of all coal mines. It established reduced rates for railroad transports and made the purchase of the explosives, oils, and greases necessary for production easier. Thanks to this agency,

---

[1] *The unspoken assumption here is that it was hoped Belgian exports might be transshipped through Dutch ports.*

mining was allowed to continue without interruption, but under supervision. The *Zentrale* set the prices and had complete control over the exportation and domestic distribution of coal. The profits it made from July 1915 to July 1917 came to over 33 million marks. Out of consideration for the neutral nations, the Netherlands, Switzerland, and Scandinavian countries, a considerable portion of coal production was exported.[1] The quantities made available to the Belgian population were insufficient as a result, and gave rise, during the terrible winter of 1917, to a shortage that further disrupted the means of transport.

The central for oils (*Olzentrale*) was created by a June 3, 1915 decree. Those for gas, water, and electricity were added to it on July 26 of the same year, and one for barley on July 20. On November 24, 1915, the *Zuckerverteilungsstelle* was put in charge of managing the distribution of sugar and its byproducts. A *Zentraleinkaufgesellschaft fur Belgien* was charged with gathering and sending to Germany the products that had been seized or requisitioned, as well as food that the agreements with the *Comité National* did not reserve for the Belgian people. Under it were specialized organizations such as the office for the supplying of potatoes (January 17, 1916), a central purchasing company for endive roots (August 13, 1915), a central purchasing company for butter (August 24, 1916), and a central for vegetables (*Obstzentrale*).[2]

All these organizations, while providing considerable benefits for Germany, drained Belgium. What they left to the country was subject to strict rationing. When, for example, the production of potatoes exceeded the country's needs, the administration

---

1 This exportation was done for the most part to the Netherlands, and had in the beginning, as a counterpart, an importation of raw materials from the Netherlands to Belgium. But the creation of the *Nederlandsche Overzeetrust Maalschappij* imposed by Britain on the Dutch government greatly reduced this importation from 1915 on. See on this topic the explanations given by von der Lancken to the Economic Committee in June 1915.

2 The *Zentrale* organization existed only in the General Government. In the *Étapes* territory, the military administration retained the power to regulate at it wished the distribution of commodities.

provided only 300 grams per day per person in 1916, and 200 grams in 1917. One of the clear results of the system was an enormous black market and an increase in all prices. All kinds of abuses were inevitable. The *Zentrales* entrusted to certain firms a monopoly on selling the products they controlled. These companies passed them on to intermediaries who then sold them to retailers, from whom they finally reached the public. Butter, hoarded by an association of merchants working under German surveillance, became a luxury item.[1] Sugar became almost as rare.

In addition, seizures became increasingly demanding. Beginning with the Antwerp warehouses, they were extended in 1915 to private homes. Nothing angered the population more than the visits to their homes by soldiers sent to make requisitions—first copper, and later wool. The more the average Belgian valued the comfort of his home, the more outraged he was to see the Germans confiscate his clocks, hanging lamps, the sparkling saucepans that decorated his living room and kitchen, and to have to surrender the excellent wool from his bedding. People would try in vain to bury the requisitioned items in the yard, to hide them under the floorboards, under the roof tiles, in nooks in the cellar masonry, or behind barrels or bundles of sticks. These precautions only made the home visits longer, more meticulous, and more obnoxious. Soldiers probed the walls, lifted floorboards, opened cupboards, in order to thwart the ingenuity of the residents—violating what citizens regarded as their most sacred right, the sanctity of the home.

When the Governor General levied the first war contribution from the provinces in 1914, it had been agreed that the payment of requisitions past due would be cleared without delay and that in the future they would be paid in cash. This promise was not honored. In December 1916, the Commissioner of the Imperial

---

[1] This organization, called the *Buttervertriebsverband*, united the merchants and butter producer unions. As a result, and to escape the official prices, farmers resorted to hiding a large portion of their butter, saving it for the black market.

Banks estimated the amount of unpaid requisitions at 800 million marks. The amount of money accumulated in the country was considerable. The sale of seized merchandise and the expenses of officers and soldiers brought in a significant amount. But due to unemployment, it just sat in banks. Meanwhile, a number of black market operators, speculators, and exploitive merchants were making scandalous profits. While factories were being closed, theaters and cinemas, paradoxically and shockingly, were open, especially in Brussels, maintaining an outward appearance of luxury which misled foreigners.

In December 1917, at least 140 motion picture theaters remained open in the capital.

But at the same time, public parks and squares were being turned into vegetable gardens and potato fields. Streets that had been deserted, apart from military or *Comité National* automobiles, started being used by bullock carts. Meat disappeared from restaurant menus. Even in the homes of the wealthy, fires were kept going in one room only. Gas was rationed just like food items.

In the midst of this distress, the plague of unemployment grew. It had started with the outbreak of war, and it worried both the Germans and the municipal administrations. It was both a humanitarian duty and a necessity for public welfare to remedy it. In a working population as dense as Belgium's, the lack of employment could give rise to disorder. Riots would no doubt have been ruthlessly suppressed, renewing the horrors that had marked the beginning of the invasion. For their part, patriotic employers worried that their workers, under the pressure of hunger, would agree to work for Germany. The boycott could not be sustained on empty stomachs. In order to maintain their passive resistance against the occupier, the unemployed had to be fed. From Germany's perspective, too, it was necessary to maintain order behind the front lines. Thus, for various reasons, occupier and occupied came together in their desire to act against the dangers of idleness, whether forced or voluntary. Realistically, the goodwill shown by Field Marshal von der Golz toward the Commission for Relief in Belgium and the *Comité National* could essentially be explained by his desire to see them fight effectively against the dangers of unemployment.

All sorts of measures were taken to provide an occupation for the increasingly numerous workers left unemployed by the progressive constriction of industry. E. Mahaim estimates that their number, from the middle of 1915 until the end of the war, was about 650,000 per year on average, or about 54% of industrial workers.[1] Twice that number of people were affected by poverty across all classes of the population.

They were certainly not all equally impoverished. Welfare cheaters got their names on assistance rolls to receive extra supplies, at the expense of the truly poor. But these unavoidable abuses were not significant. The German press often accused Belgian workers of laziness, but these charges were groundless. The zeal Belgian workers displayed during all periods of the region's history did not suddenly vanish because of an invasion. On the contrary, it was clearly in evidence when it could be useful to the country. In France and Britain, Belgian emigrants distinguished themselves by their ardor and enthusiasm in every task assigned them. At home, unemployment was simply a result of the country's economic paralysis and of its inhabitants' unwillingness to work for the occupier.

As long as the factories had raw materials, their personnel continued to work. The coal mines, as mentioned, remained in operation. It was only where it became evident that normal operations benefited the enemy that employers and workers agreed to end them. Such was the case on railroads, in the Brabant and Hainaut quarries, in metalworking factories, etc. But while ethical motives did contribute to unemployment, their influence must not be exaggerated. The occupation was too long, and the hardships that

---
[1] E. Mahaim, *Le Secours de Chômage*, p 140.

accompanied it too cruel, for the passive resistance of the working class to continue indefinitely. This would have required superhuman heroism.

A considerable number of workers agreed to return to factories that had been previously closed or that now produced for the Reich. Others resigned themselves to working in Germany. Nevertheless, the number of those who, either deliberately or due to lack of jobs, remained inactive, continued to increase until the end of the occupation. On November 6, 1916, at a point when worker deportations had already begun, the Commissioner General for Banks estimated that there were about 2 million poor, most of whom were unemployed.[1]

Very early on, municipal administrations turned to the traditional and classic means of relieving unemployment: public works projects. In Ghent, all men who were not employed were put to work digging new channels for the port. Elsewhere, men worked on building new roads, clearing stones from local railroad tracks, draining wetlands, planting trees, and clearing brush. The province of Luxembourg in particular distinguished itself by its intelligent initiative these activities.[2] Efforts were made to take advantage of the crisis to improve the country's economic resources, while avoiding any project that might assist military operations. Rural towns, for example, almost always avoided repairing the major roads and railway lines used by troops.

As for industrialists, for their part they tried to keep open those factories that were not obliged to work for the enemy. As long as the requisitions and seizures left them with some machines and raw materials, they kept their workers employed. The hours were reduced in order to prolong production as much as possible. Several factories even resorted to working at a loss. The

---

[1] "There are currently," he wrote, "2 million Belgians in poverty, among whom many are unemployed,...[and] savings are gradually being consumed, and much more money is withdrawn from than deposited into savings accounts."
[2] E. Mahaim, *Le secours de chômage*, p 85 and following.

unemployed and those with reduced salaries received assistance from the *Comité National*, towns, private charities, and worker associations. Fortnightly distributions were made of food, clothing, and coupons.[1]

The goal of unemployment assistance was not only to relieve the deprivation that affected the unemployed, but also to discourage workers from yielding to the enemy's solicitations and accepting its job offers. Also, the *Comité National* always tried to maintain the appearance of a purely private charitable organization, so that its assistance was voluntary and not something the unemployed could claim as a legal right. This resulted in misunderstandings that German authorities did not fail to exploit. As the Germans began using Belgians to replace their conscripted workers, the government increasingly attempted to interfere with the distributions made by the *Comité*, though without much success.

Assistance to the unemployed, on top of food allowances provided by towns, resulted in some waste and abuse. In August 1917, the *Comité* replaced it with another system.[2] The granting of food and food vouchers was placed under the control of the provincial committees, and was made more responsive to those in need. To be eligible for food relief, one needed only to be poor. Other requirements were eliminated. The importance of the assistance the *Comité* delivered is shown by the numbers. Expenses incurred by unemployment assistance until November 1917 totaled 330 million francs, while 660 million was spent on food relief from November 1917 to June 1919.

The *Ligue nationale du coin de terre*, created in 1896, provided useful services for the unemployed, although it was not specifically intended for them, but for anyone without resources. The organization made small plots of land available to the unemployed for

---

1 The assistance did not come in the form of money, but of coupons valid in *Comité National* stores and in town shops.
2 For details, see E. Mahaim, *Le secours de chômage*, p 176 and following.

cultivation. In 1914, it helped 16,000 families with 800 hectares. In 1915, these numbers jumped to 31,000 families and 1,700 hectares, then to 69,000 families and 3,000 hectares in 1916, and 118,000 families and 5,000 hectares in 1917.

The German administration appeared at first to view with favor the efforts organized to prevent unemployment and to assist those affected by it. It saw in these, with good reason, a guarantee of public order. At least it did nothing to prevent them.[1] But its perspective would soon change.

Early on, recruiters came from Germany to find additional workers in Belgium. They were turned down almost everywhere. In June 1915, an official institution, the *Deutsche Industriebüro*[2] was created to centralize and organize the recruiting. Propaganda posters illustrated for the unemployed the joys of working in German factories: high wages, hygienic working conditions, a comfortable life. The censored press joined the chorus. Letters were published in which men who had agreed to leave for Germany expressed their satisfaction and urged their friends to join them. But the *büro*'s success was incommensurate with its efforts. The number of those who agreed to sign contracts remained small. An almost unshakable repugnance to enroll in the service of the enemy foiled even the most tempting solicitations.[3]

This repugnance was naturally encouraged by the *Comité National*. Its exhortations were all the more persuasive in that they drew on both patriotism and self-interest. Since the unemployed had no official right to assistance, nothing was easier than to cut off relief from those who yielded to the temptation to work for the Germans. For the same patriotic reasons that led

---

[1] The recommendation made "most energetically" by the Governor General to towns in the Brussels area, on November 7, 1914, to "stop freely distributing supplies to men who could be proved to have the opportunity to work but who do not seize it," appeared to aim only at eliminating abuses, and did not reveal any intention to exert pressure on the unemployed.
[2] Refer to K. Bittmann, cited work, t III, p 131 and following.
[3] Von Köhler, previously cited work, p 149, estimates that from June 1915 to March 1916, only 12,000 workers were hired by the *Industriebüro*.

to its founding, the *Comité* would only assist the unemployed if they kept up their passive resistance. For Germany, the war and the conquest had established an economic union between the Reich and Belgium, and the one had to support the other. For the *Comité*, a purely Belgian institution, it was essential to prevent this union and to maintain, for as long as the occupation lasted, the nation's physical and moral integrity. The opposing viewpoints, both inspired by patriotism, were incompatible. Since Belgium's conqueror wanted to impose its war economy upon the country, the only possible response was to do everything possible to thwart its plans. Acting otherwise would have betrayed not only the Belgian people, but also the country's allies.

The town administrations agreed. By hiring the unemployed or helping private associations hire them, they tried to prevent them from being tempted by the *Industriebüro*'s offers. The socialist unions, Christian or liberal worker groups, employers, members of charity offices, volunteers visiting the poor, and influential individuals all worked assiduously toward the same goal. A general conspiracy was organized against the German efforts. It was assisted by the resentment that had accumulated in the hearts of all Belgians. The *Industriebüro*'s machinations were discredited by its obvious status as an official institution. The clumsiness of its methods didn't help. Its promises were too good to be true. Many of those who had been deported had spent some time in a concentration camp before being repatriated and were able to refute claims about the affluence Germans supposedly enjoyed. For the vast majority of unemployed, the choice between continuing their resistance and collaboration was not difficult to make. In view of the problematic advantages, it was better to live on Belgian assistance and fold one's arms than to face public disapproval and exile far from loved ones.

The Governor General didn't stand a chance against the opposition, and this soon become evident to him. The *Comité National* remained beyond his control, as did the municipal administrations. The only way to counter the propaganda that was harming German military interests was to act directly on the unemployed themselves, by giving them the choice of either resuming work or being deprived of assistance. No doubt would this would force men who had remained unmoved by persuasion and posters to finally turn to the *Industriebüro*. This procedure certainly conformed to international law. Its goal was simply to provide a workforce for Germany industry. There was no question of requiring Belgians to perform military work. Therefore, as far as the Governor General was concerned, there would be no objection to the decree he announced on August 15, 1915.

It stipulated that if anyone receiving public or private assistance refused, without sufficient reason, to accept a job corresponding to his abilities, he would be jailed for at least fourteen days and up to six months. Those assisting the unemployed who refused to work would be subject to a fine of up to 12,500 francs and up to a year in prison. The leaders of towns or associations guilty of these activities would be held responsible, and the funds intended for assistance would be confiscated and given to the Red Cross. The decree was intended to force workers to accept the German offers of employment, provided that the Belgians, in compliance with the Hague Conventions, were not obliged to perform military work. The Governor General certainly expected results. He even initially left the enforcement of infractions to the Belgian criminal courts. A few months later, on November 23, the *Comité National* was forbidden to offer courses for the unemployed. Clearly, he wished to deprive them of the psychological support their compatriots were providing.

The inefficiency of this first intervention led the Governor General to adopt stronger measures. On May 2, 1916, he decreed that "proposals for jobs that directly or indirectly had as a goal the providing of paid work to the unemployed must first be presented to the burgomaster of the town in which the work is to be done. This official is required to pass the proposal along to the civil commissioner for the district. The latter will consult with the civil administration president for the province, who will decide if the job is permissible." Sentences for violations of this ordinance could be up to three years in prison and a 20,000 marks fine. Finally, only German military courts were permitted to adjudicate these cases.

Thus, after unsuccessfully condemning people who refused to work, the government now made unemployment mandatory for those whom local authorities were trying to provide with work. Clearly, the hope of seeing Belgians voluntarily accept the occupier's offers had given way to a policy of forcing them to do so. By locking them out of the building sites organized specifically for them, the government forced unemployed workers to accept offers from the Germans or be punished for choosing not to. The fact that those charged would face a military tribunal guaranteed that the penalties would be rigorously enforced. Fifteen days later, on May 15, 1916, a new decree went even further, instituting mandatory work. It gave governors, military commanders, and district leaders the authority to forcibly transport recalcitrant men to sites where they would be obliged to work.

The May 1916 decrees were not the Governor General's initiative. To alleviate the shortage of workers in Germany, the High Command pressed him to deport 400,000 Belgian workers to the Reich. In the eyes of the military authorities, Belgium had to contribute to the war no less than Germany. It was unacceptable that its working population should remain intact, while that of Germany was so radically diminished by military conscription. The surplus on one side had to compensate for the deficit on the other. Since Belgian industry was almost entirely idle while German industry had an ever-increasing need for workers, what could be more convenient than drawing on the masses of unemployed Belgians? But this radical proposal from the military horrified von Bissing. At the risk of being accused once again of treating Belgians "like spoiled children," he pointed out the disadvantages of the High Command's proposal, not only for Belgium, but especially for Germany itself. Being on the scene, he had a much clearer perspective, and this bold initiative of the High Command frightened him. One can't help but compare his attitude to that of Fouché and Talleyrand when Napoleon, blinded by visions of dominating Europe, lost sight of reality.

Von Bissing argued that the measure would outrage Belgians, arouse the indignation of neutrals, and be difficult to execute and unlikely to succeed. In the end, would the Belgians who were forced to work actually work? What good would it do to stir up Europe against Germany, to provide new fodder to the campaign carried out against it all over the world, if those deported, torn from their families, simply crossed their arms? His recent decrees, he said, would yield good results through more legal means. Those who refused to work could be deported to Germany, but as a penalty. Instead of a general deportation, individual deportation would solve Germany's shortage of workers. In secret circulars from May 15 and August 4, 1916, Von Bissing had already laid out the details for the organization of these penal deportations.

But this method seemed not to be working out, and von Bissing's arguments failed to move the High Command. For the latter, victory depended on Germany's productive capacity.[1] It had come to the point where the resistance of the Belgian people was more important in deciding the outcome of the war than the resistance of the country's army. It would be criminal not to take advantage of the thousands of hands made idle by unemployment in Belgium. A tragic situation called for a dramatic solution. Like the violation of Belgium's neutrality in 1914, the mass deportation of Belgian workers was, or at least seemed to be, a matter of life or death. In the eyes of the German High Command, it was a necessary consequence of the Allies' encirclement. The generals might have said, as Napoleon did when the continental blockade

---

[1] Von Köhler, previously cited work, p 151.

was declared in 1807: "We are taking measures that are repugnant to our hearts, and it is costing us to make the interests of private individuals subject to their countries' quarrels, and to return, after so many years of civilization, to principles that characterized an early, barbaric age. But we have been forced for the good of our people and of our allies to use against our common enemy the same weapons it is using against us."

On Thursday September 28, 1916, the fatal decision was made to deport the Belgian workforce en masse. The actual decree was dated October 3, and the directive that put the General Government in charge of its execution, October 26.[1]

On September 25, General von Bissing had threatened to give up his "difficult task" if his advice was not heeded. He certainly hoped that the Emperor would support him. But as the Supreme War Chief decided in favor of Hindenburg, he had no choice but to accept defeat. Reluctantly, but with the discipline of an old soldier, the Governor General carried out his orders.

The obligation it imposed on him was particularly arduous. To succeed, he would have had to be able to rely on the collaboration of the *Comité National* and the municipal administrations, which alone had lists of the unemployed. But he knew it was hopeless to count on their cooperation. They flatly refused to provide the requested information. By October 27, the fifteen towns of the greater Brussels metropolitan area had declared that they would have nothing to do with a measure aimed at forcing Belgians to work against their country. They did not want to commit what they regarded as a felony. Local authorities everywhere else adopted the same position. Town halls were surrounded by troops and burgomasters were arrested, but all in vain. They did not give

---

1 For everything that follows, see Passelecq, previously cited work. Von Köhler, previously cited work, p 148 and following, exposes the measures from a German point of view and without addressing the consequences for the Belgian population

in.[1] The staffs of the municipalities backed their leaders. The assistance lists, which had become proscription lists, were concealed from the Germans, who had to settle for taxpayer rolls and voter registration lists.

In the *Étapes* zone, however, things were done more energetically. In Bruges, as early as October 8, the city's military governor demanded that 400 workers be turned over. The burgomaster, who refused to obey this order, was dismissed, the unemployment committee's secretary was jailed, and the military authorities took the list of unemployed workers by force. The following day, since the 400 men on this list had not shown up, the Germans substituted an equal number of individuals taken at random, and made them come to the *Meldeamt*. A few days later, 2,000 workers were requisitioned in Dendermond, 1,000 in Aalst, and 300 in Ninove. In Tournai, since the local authorities had refused, just as in Bruges, to hand over the list of unemployed, the town was sentenced to a 200,000 marks fine, and an *échevin* and three communal councilors were deported to Germany, while men were taken at random on the streets, in markets, and on roads. Before the end of the month, in the entire *Étapes* territory as well as in Flanders, Hainaut, and southern Luxembourg, the deportation was running at full capacity.

Within the General Government, the first human exportations came a little later, on October 26. Von Bissing would obviously have liked to organize them with as much restraint as the circumstances permitted. But the refusal of Belgian authorities to denounce the unemployed meant that this would not be possible. In general, every individual over seventeen was summonsed. A physical examination eliminated those deemed not sufficiently strong. The rest were immediately deported or held at the disposal of the military authorities. The men were transported by

---

[1] These arrests were not continued. Authorities who refused to collaborate were later sentenced to paying fines.

rail, very often in livestock cars. Families were often prevented from accompanying their fathers, husbands, and sons to the station. Along with the truly unemployed, the trains carried middle-class citizens, students, and factory workers. People were randomly picked out of a crowd, the only concern being to satisfy the demands of the German High Command. Those taken away by mistake were told they could file a complaint later.

After all, they had only their own compatriots to blame, whose stubbornness in refusing to hand over the unemployed forced everyone to suffer. But Germany's mistakes were mostly harmful to itself. They increased the general outrage. Nothing indicates that they made anyone demand of the local authorities that they turn over the information they were concealing.

The measures prescribed by the Governor General for the execution of his orders were only partially followed. The authorities in Berlin grew impatient. Officers in charge of gathering and transporting men were told to execute their instructions without restraint. There was senseless violence, deplorable scenes, despicable acts of intimidation. But this very violence intensified the resolution not to give in. Only rarely did the terrorist tactics coerce individuals into signing contracts.

Public opinion unanimously supported this resistance, which often rose to heroism. The deportation had barely started when an outcry of protest was raised against it. After two years of occupation, it came at just the right moment to reinforce national solidarity, which had progressively weakened under the weight of misery and discouragement. The Germans had struck a blow at both the personal liberty and the dignity of Belgian workers. Of all the measures adopted in Belgium, the deportation indisputably did the most irreparable harm. It dug an "abyss of hate" between the two peoples. It was even more repugnant than the massacres during the invasion. These could be seen as the inevitable consequence of war. The deportation, however, was regarded as an abominable act of tyranny, as a restoration of slavery, and as an outrageous subjugation of a defenseless people to the rule of force.

On October 19, Cardinal Mercier begged the Governor General, "in the name of the sanctity of the home and the freedom of labor of Belgian citizens, in the name of the inviolability of families, in the name of morality," to end the deportation and to return to their homes those who had been torn from them. He reminded von Bissing of the promise made in the Bishop's Palace at Mechelen by Field Marshal von der Goltz that the freedom of Belgian citizens would be respected. This promise had enabled him to calm the fears of families. And by having himself trusted the Governor General's word, he now risked being blamed for disappointing the trust he had inspired in others. To these reproaches were soon added, on October 30, those by representatives of the socialist and independent unions, followed by the deputies and senators of Mons on November 2; the deputies, senators, and leading citizens of Antwerp, the bishops and the Grand Master of the Grand-Orient Masons of Belgium, addressed to the German Grand Lodges on November 7; several government ministers, senators, and deputies, and the permanent delegation of the province of Brabant on November 9; the *échevinal* college of Brussels, and the deputies and senators of Luxembourg on November 17; the magistracy, the Academy of Professors from Brussels, Liège, and Leuven universities, many professional groups, courts, and industrial associations. Every organization protested the breach of international law and the inhumanity and injustice of the measures. Flemish and Walloons, Catholics and Freemasons, conservatives and socialists, each using their own language, reflecting their differences in faith or opinion, voiced their outrage. "A clamor without historical precedent, in which curses united with prayers" assailed the Governor General. Lawyers invoked the law against him, priests, religious principles, the unions, "the great voice of the working class of the entire civilized world."

Von Bissing's situation was all the more embarrassing in that he himself disapproved of what he had been forced to do and had foreseen the indignation that the edict would trigger and the political difficulties that would follow. He answered Cardinal Mercier and journalists from neutral countries with the same arguments he had once opposed: it was good for the Belgian working class to no longer stagnate in idleness; the men would receive high salaries in Germany and would not be forced to participate in war industries. Von Bissing was not deluded regarding the effect of these declarations. He was quite aware that they would only increase the general disapproval. This he feared less than that of the ministers from neutral countries, who regularly passed along protests they'd received. The Vatican, Spain, and the United States all made representations to the Foreign Office in Berlin. Even small countries did not refrain from intervening. The Swiss expressed their feelings quite plainly. On December 2, the Dutch government handed over a note that was all the more embarrassing in that it reminded Germany that it had advised Belgians who had taken refuge on their territory to return to their homeland, following the solemn assurance given by General von Hoene, the commandant in Antwerp, that they had no reason to fear for their freedom. It was also very disagreeable to observe the diplomats in Brussels watching the trains with conscripted workers heading toward the German border.

Meanwhile, in the *Étapes* zone, thousands of men were being sent to the front lines, enrolled in the *Zivil Arbeiter Betaillone*, and forced to construct barracks and to perform military work under Allied fire.[1] There was no way to hide the spectacle of the unfortunate individuals who had returned from the front, and who could be seen miserably wandering the streets, or stop the letters sent to families to announce the death of relatives who had died in concentration camps.[2]

---
1 Most laborers from the *Étapes* zone were immediately put to work constructing the Hindenburg Line (the Siegfriedstellung), to which the Germans retired in February and March of 1917.
2 The number of these deaths is estimated at 2,614. Mahaim, *La Belgique restaurée*, p 16.

The Governor General secretly wished for an intervention to deliver him from the the opprobrium of the entire world. But Germany had committed itself too deeply to withdraw. Von Bissing, however, still hoped for an appropriate occasion to yield to the outcry. What the Reich refused to grant to Belgian protests, perhaps it would grant to their pleas. The chief of the German civil administration advised the Spanish Minister, the Marquis de Villalobar, to ask Cardinal Mercier to draft a letter, which was then signed by the most prominent Belgian leaders who could be contacted. Baron von der Lancken then brought this to Berlin on February 14, 1917. The letter was addressed directly to the Emperor. Without hiding from him "that it is at the cost of our national self-esteem to appear to be requesting as a good deed what we, in normal times, would claim as a right," it appealed to his humanity. Three weeks later, on March 9, the signatories were verbally informed that "His Majesty would have the Governor and the competent authorities carefully examine the requests expressed in the address he had received. His Majesty reserves his final decision until the end of this examination. However, in the meantime, His Majesty has issued instructions so that those who were wrongly brought to Germany as being unemployed would be immediately allowed to return to Belgium if they had not already done so, and that the deportations of unemployed Belgians to Germany would cease until further notice." Political considerations had unquestionably trumped the demands of the military. Without withdrawing the measure, the Emperor suspended its application. And it was likely that this suspension would be permanent. To resume deportations after stopping them would indeed have provoked an even more glaring scandal than the one that was coming to an end.[1]

---

[1] In Germany, the *Gewerkschaften* (unions), from whom the deportation projects had been hidden, tried in vain to have them halted. This was the reason given by the socialists for rejecting the Reichstag budget for the first time since the beginning of the war. P. Umbreit and Ch. Lorenz, *Der Krieg un die Arbeitsverhältnisse*, p 123, Berlin, 1928 (German series of this work).

However, the Imperial decision was only partially executed. While it was intended for all of Belgium, it took effect only within the General Government, which is significant evidence of the subordination of the Emperor himself to the German High Command. In the *Étapes* zone, where the military was all-powerful, not only did the requisitions of men proceed without interruption, but attempts were no longer made to hide their use for military purposes. In Flanders, Hainaut, and Luxembourg, thousands of Belgians continued to be taken from their families and transported to the frontlines. It even seems that plans to extend this seizure to women were considered. At least a census of the female population aged 15 to 60 was carried out.[1]

The strictness of censorship and of denials from the official press managed to keep the German people in ignorance of this violation of the Imperial promise. Over time, the requisitions turned in to full roundups, indiscriminately taking workers, employees, shop-keepers, and farmers. Those who resisted or tried to flee were detained in "discipline camps." The forced labor – unloading shells or materiel, building railroads, digging trenches – was sometimes carried out so close to the battlefields that the deported had to be provided with gas marks. In short, military recruitment and discipline were forcibly extended to the civil population. Everyone was threatened. One has to have lived in the *Étapes* zone to appreciate the regime of terror that prevailed in 1917 and 1918. The constant anxiety that reigned there certainly explains the apparent progress of "activism." To escape the labor requisitions, there was no other way than to become an outspoken Germanophile. The only hope for those who refused to disown their beliefs was the mercy of an officer or the compassion of a military doctor willing to issue a certificate of illness.

The military authorities shifted the stigma of their conduct

---

1 *Women in rural areas had been conscripted for labor in Northern France since 1915. In the spring of 1916, this was extended to cities. The most notorious episode was a raid in Lille beginning at 3 a.m. on April 16, in which 25,000 young women were seized at gunpoint and marched into the countryside.*

onto the towns. The men were led to believe that they had been designated by their burgomasters. They were even told that these officials opposed their return because they were no longer able to feed them. Officially the deported were considered free workers. They all collected a salary and many of them even agreed, under duress, to sign work contracts. Whether they signed or not, they all had the same task. They were no longer merely serving the German economy; they were serving Germany's war.

Within the General Government, however, von Bissing wasted no time in obeying the Imperial order. He stopped all deportations. The return of Belgians who had been sent to Germany in error, though, did not depend on him. All in all, the number of deported Belgians in the part of the country under his direct administration came to about sixty thousand. A similar number of men were drafted in the *Étapes* zone between October 1916 and August 1918. The requisitions only ended there when German troops retreated in 1918. They lasted twenty-two months, compared to only five within the General Government. And they were not evenly spread throughout the latter. They were fully implemented only in the provinces of Antwerp, Brabant, and Luxembourg. A few towns were spared, for unknown reasons, in the provinces of Hainaut, Namur, and Limburg. Liège province was the least affected.

One can therefore conclude that the High Command's scheme did not succeed in the end. Instead of the 400,000 deportees it demanded, it only got at most 120,000. Only 60,000 of these helped compensate for the Reich's shortage of workers. The others, as mentioned, were almost all employed on the fronts in France. It would be interesting to know how effective the deportees were in helping German industry. One can assume that their contributions were negligible and that their presence resulted in more inconveniences than advantages. Nearly all seized every opportunity to flee. They had to be pursued, captured, brought back to work, and then they escaped again. The author can confirm from having seen with his own eyes that they only accomplished their tasks with incredible ill-will and apathy. In the concentration camps where employers looked for new recruits, they picked Belgians last. They were, they said, bad workers, unwilling to obey. In their exile, they kept up the passive resistance they had begun back home.

While the deportation was inefficient for Germany, it had most regrettable consequences in Belgium. Not only did it give rise to feelings of deep hatred, which would last well beyond the end of the war, but it also considerably affected public health. The mortality rate was very high among the deported: it is estimated to have been twenty per thousand. Thousands of workers came home depressed and disabled. Their inability to work lasted very long; it was sometimes even permanent. A mixed German-Belgian arbitration tribunal conducting a trial in January 1925 heard pathetic testimony.[1]

It's important to note that while the deportations failed to fulfill their purpose, they still indirectly profited German industry. The fear they inspired drew many men to the *Industriebüro* offices. They voluntarily signed contracts in order to avoid being requisitioned. The fact that they were allowed to bring their wives and children along helped persuade many of them to sign up. Others were guaranteed that their families would receive assistance while they were gone. The profits made by the *Zentrales* were assigned to cover the resulting expenses.

In October 1916, General von Bissing estimated that there were about 30,000 of these voluntary workers. The number kept increasing thereafter. In April 1917, one third of the coal miners in La Louvière had signed up. The high salaries they collected in Germany lured many to follow in their footsteps every day. The volunteer workers were almost always lodged with locals, and spared the stay in concentration camps. The friendliness

---

[1] See the documents from this trial in the War Archives.

of their German hosts surprised them after the harshness of the occupation. They were freer in enemy territory than in their own country. Their letters and accounts were all the more seductive as the misery in Belgium kept getting worse. Under such pressure, many even decided to accept jobs in Belgian factories that had been taken over by the Germans. Little by little, the resistance that had been provoked by force gave way in response to more subtle and adroit methods. Paradoxically, the recovery of Belgian industry seemed more likely at the end of 1916 than at the beginning of the occupation. But at that point, restoring it was no longer an option. Its equipment was to be exported to German factories or destroyed in order to be made into ammunition. As men had been previously, machines were to be deported, beginning in February 1917.

§ II. — Exploitation *à outrance*

The clash between the opposing views of the civil and military administrations regarding Belgian industry would inevitably end with the triumph of the latter. The Governor General's long-standing wish to protect the country's manufacturing activities was not going to be realized. No doubt von Bissing was quite correct to claim that Belgium would be more useful to Germany if it were prosperous than if it were ruined. The more it produced, the more it could feed the war's insatiable demands. Unfortunately, it was impossible to prevent the death of this "cash cow."[1] It perished for lack of nourishment. The immense stockpile of raw materials that the country had accumulated was quickly depleted by requisitions, seizures, and purchases. The failure of negotiations with Britain to restore it through imports meant that supplies would inevitably be exhausted. What was arriving through the Netherlands, in increasingly small quantities, could at best

---

1 See von Bissing's message transcribed above, p 172.

merely prolong the agony of Belgian industry. By June 1915, it became clear that cotton spinning had been dealt a fatal blow. The same was true of the wool, linen, jute, and hemp industries. By the same date, almost all blast furnaces had been extinguished. Cement industry workers were unemployed as well as those in the machine-building industry.

German industrialists feared that they would again have to compete against Belgian industry after the war, and this pushed them to lobby the Governor General to prevent the revival of industries, such as the cement industry, which could have survived through Dutch imports. Glassmaking, however, was maintained, as much in the army's interests as to prevent Britain and America from exclusively taking over the market. Thus, even for industries for which the country could produce the raw materials, their future depended on the interests of the conqueror.

This interest was not that of the conquered. While Belgian manufacturers did their best to maintain production, albeit at a lower level, it was under the condition that their output would not be used for the war. Almost all preferred to close down their factories rather than to serve the occupier. Many others, for lack of work, kept their employees busy enlarging or improving their installations, counting on a happy end to the war and a period of renewed prosperity after victory.

The economic conference summoned in Brussels by General von Bissing on June 19, 1915, had to have shown him that his projects were unrealizable. The growth of unemployment during the following months further convinced him of the futility of his illusions. Thus it became increasingly impossible for him to defend his "conservative" methods against the military authorities' "exhaustion" policy. Since Belgian industry could not survive, it would have been dishonest to spare it any longer. There was nothing left to do but to use it to help Germany fight for its existence. The economic solidarity between Belgium and Germany that the war brought about thus ended in the complete exploitation of the one by the other.

If Belgians had accepted the occupation, if they had voluntarily adhered to the Rathenau plan, if they had consented to turn their factories into ammunition workshops, to use their laboratories to produce gas, explosives, or *Ersatz*, it would obviously have been possible for them not only to keep their equipment and personnel occupied, but also to achieve the same technical progress that took place in Germany. Because they refused to do these things, the only question was how to invest the capital they insisted on leaving unproductive.

Berlin was increasingly determined to put the closed factories and inactive machines at the disposal of Germany industry, just as it had deported the unemployed to the Reich. On February 17, 1917, a decree was issued stating that from March 1st "various industrial establishments, particularly factories, would be able to continue working only pending consent from the chief of civil administration." It was also forbidden to construct new industrial buildings, or to modify existing ones. The only exceptions to this measure were the coal mines, coke ovens, gas, water, or electricity plants working exclusively for the public, mines and phosphate factories, all mills, and local railroads and tramways.

All industry thus fell under German control. Similarly to the way in which the *Zentrales* took over the distribution and marketing of agricultural products, the civil administration's commerce and industry section extended its power to all manufacturing activities. Only very small industries remained outside of its control. Workshops with fewer than twelve employees, or using motors weaker than 5 horsepower and consuming fewer than 5 tonnes of coal were not obliged to obtain the authorization imposed on all others. The decree not only affected current industry, but its future as well, as it forbad extending and improving works.

The goal of the decree was probably not to trigger a new wave of unemployment in order to provide additional recruits for the deportations. General von Bissing was hostile to the latter and he undoubtedly knew that they would soon cease. The reason for the decree, therefore, was simply to keep industry entirely under the control of the military authorities. The edict of February 17 represented the capitulation of the Governor General to the High Command. It marked the moment when it became clear that it would be impossible to preserve Belgium's industrial activity any longer.[1] The harshness of the punishments for violating the decree (two years in prison and a 100,000-mark fine) and the fact that violators would appear before military courts testified to the importance of the decree.

From March 1, 1917, Belgian industry thus became nothing more than a branch of Germany industry. What would remain of it would depend on Germany's military needs. Factories had earlier been sequestered or requisitioned under orders from the military authorities, and exploited by the latter. But what had thus far been only sporadic became regular, general, and permanent. As early as March 13, ministers, senators, and deputies who remained in the country protested to General von Bissing. They naturally received no reply.

A certain number of industrialists, wanting to keep their workers employed and to save their supplies, were willing to seek the authorization imposed by the decree. But many others closed their factories.

Thousands of machines of all kinds had already been requisitioned by the *Kommandanturen*. In the beginning, the removals were done with such haste and lack of foresight that they had provoked complaints to the Governor General. However, the disorder soon gave way to organization. The requisition services were placed under the direction of the *Stabsoffizier der Pioniere* for electric machines and the *Stabsoffizier der Fussartillerie* for

---

[1] Bittmann, previously cited work, t III, p 81, said exactly "*so war den die Aera, in der der Gedanke der Wiederbelebung des belgischen Wirtschaftslebens vorhern schend gewesen war, endgültig abgeschlossen.*" (And so ended the era in which the idea of reviving the Belgian economy was the dominant idea.)

other machines. The lists of machines were sent by them to the *Waffen und Munitionenbeschaffungsamt* (Wumba) or to the *Rohmaterialbeschaffungsamt* (Rohma), both under the auspices of the War Ministry in Berlin. The first was an intermediary in charge of providing for Germany's industrial needs and satisfying the Quartermaster General's demands for machinery for the armed services. The second was in charge of having machines which could not be used turned into scrap metal, as well as metal from workshops and idle industrial installations.

In France, the dismantling and destruction of machines and factory buildings started at the beginning of 1917. This was extended to Belgium in the middle of the same year. The destruction was merciless and systematic. The targeted factories were listed by the civil administration's commerce and industry section. After being sent to the proper German services, the list would come back with their observations. The fate reserved for the condemned factories was decided only after a thorough examination. The military administration reserved a few of them to use as warehouses, barracks, or airplane hangars, either where they were or in some other location, in which case they would be dismantled, transported piece by piece, and rebuilt there. Rhoma received all of the machinery and equipment that were to be destroyed, and Wumba organized the transportation to Germany of machines that had been spared. A consortium of German firms, the *Abbaugruppe*, was responsible for dismantling the factories, rebuilding them in Germany, or reducing them to scrap. Their profits were considerable. As of December 31, 1917, they came to 1,443,000 marks, for a total of 18,937 tonnes of demolitions, both in Belgium and Northern France.

And so the implacable logic of the war of attrition had this final consequence. Having devoured the entire stockpile of raw materials in Belgium, all Germany could do was to either take or destroy the equipment. To continue the fight, it had no choice but to sacrifice the country to its insatiable need for ammunition.

Belgium had become nothing more than a machinery and scrap metal store, to be drawn from until empty. Germany had come to the point where it had to choose between victory at all cost, or a final catastrophe. All-out submarine warfare and the destruction of Belgian's economy are explained by the same causes[1] and are only two aspects of the resolution of a cornered military power to assume unflinchingly the most dreadful responsibilities. All that was left for Belgium was to passively endure its fate. It had become an instrument of war. No longer was it necessary for Germany to bother with humane or judicial considerations. It is worth noting that three weeks after the execution of the February 17 decree, the proclamation of administrative separation (March 21, 1917), effectively put an end to the Belgian state. Its material destruction preceded its political destruction by only a few days.[2]

It was thus the military authorities who were solely responsible for the destruction of Belgium's industry, and for the deportation of its workers. The High Command had planned these measures long before, and they would have been applied much earlier had it been up to them. The Governor General delayed their execution for as long as he could. But his resistance could be effective only for as long as it was backed by the Emperor.

When Wilhelm gave in to Hindenburg and Ludendorf, von Bissing no longer had any choice but to accept defeat and execute the order he had done everything to prevent. He did not have to witness the ruin of his policy for very long. On April 19, 1917, he unexpectedly died in the castle of Trois-Fontaines. His successor, General Ludwig von Falkenhausen, passively executed the orders of the Quartermaster General.

The destruction of Belgium's industry was welcomed by an influential group of German industrialists. Provided with discounted machinery, they were able to spare their own equipment

---

[1] They are more or less contemporary. All-out submarine warfare was renewed on January 31, 1917.
[2] See Chapter VIII, p 207.

and reserve it for the post-war period. And they would no longer have to worry about Belgian competition. Thus, the war offered them the means to eliminate for many years a formidable competitor. Wumba was assailed with their requests and its agents answered them so hastily, and so many machines were shipped, that many of them had yet to be used by their recipients when the war ended. It can be said that while the order to destroy Belgium's industry was motivated by the necessities of war, the way in which it was done was largely influenced by purely economic calculations.

And the way in which the task was accomplished led to much waste. Time was short, and there were few knowledgeable personnel to insure that machines were dismantled with proper care. Very often, soldiers and especially prisoners of war, Russian for the most part, were given with the task. Equipment was brutally broken and destroyed. The emptying of the workshops was conducted like looting. The compensations paid to the owners were calculated by the Imperial commission charged with removing the machines and demolishing the metallic frameworks. Since it only took into account the value of the metal, these compensations were obviously infinitely lower than the real value of the removed goods.

The metalworking industry naturally suffered the most. Indeed, it provided most of the machines that were exported to make ammunition, and its iron buildings offered a splendid supply of raw material for shells. In the textile factories, only copper pads and transmission shafts were taken. However, of the country's 37 blast furnaces, 26 were demolished. Most rolling-mills were also destroyed: 10 out of 11 at the John Cockerill Company, 8 out of 12 at Ougrée Marihaye. Almost all travelling cranes, electric motors, locomotives and train cars, boilers, and sledgehammers were taken or demolished on the spot. When the country was liberated, the metalworking establishments of Liège and Charleroi were scenes of utter devastation.

The political authorities still worried about the future. In October 1917, the Governor General summoned his various department managers to discuss the question. Assuming that Belgium would somehow remain Germany's subordinate, they considered ways to establish between the countries a provisional modus vivendi. Everyone agreed that it would be impossible to revive industrial activity immediately. It had been so profoundly affected that it would need at least two years to recover. They considered it inevitable that Germany would pay Belgium for damages. Some estimated these at 8.5 billion francs, others at 5 billion. A longer war would completely exhaust the country. Some 50,000 tonnes of metal were exported from it each month, so much so that the moment it would run out could be predicted. If hostilities were to go on for another year and a half, all that would be left in the country would be what its soil contained: coal and phosphates.

Considering that these assessments were made one year before the armistice, and that during the next twelve months the destruction of Belgium's industry relentlessly continued, one can get an idea of the condition of a nation which, in 1914, had been the most industrialized in Europe. The devastation was complete. The damages that occurred at the beginning of the war in the beginning were insignificant when compared with the devastation that was methodically inflicted from the middle of 1917. The demolition of the communication network by the German Army during its retreat in 1918 further added to the toll. While intervention from the neutral powers prevented the execution of an order to blow up mine shafts,[1] many bridges, locks, and railways were destroyed by the troops. When the armistice was signed, machines that had been recently dismantled were still awaiting removal. Attempts were made to convey them to the Netherlands, or to sell them to Belgian industrialists. Thus, the demolition continued until

---

[1] *specifically, a request by President Woodrow Wilson, at the instigation of Herbert Hoover.*

the very end. The *Abbaugruppe* showed a curious and desperate persistence to continue its activities, even as military setbacks and revolution back home left no doubt regarding the pointlessness of their efforts.

Clearly, the organization was no longer working with military interests in mind. Its only objective was to pillage on behalf of German industry. What had been a desperate war measure had turned into a kind of piracy.

CHAPTER VIII

Administrative separation[1]

§ I. — Until March 21, 1917

From 1914 to 1918, the German government's conduct toward Belgium went through various phases which correspond to the war's twists and turns. During the first of these phases, between the invasion of the country and the stabilization of the front on the Yser River, Belgium was treated as a strategic territory. There was as yet no vision as to its ultimate fate. Its first governor, Field Marshal von der Goltz, was purely a military man. He saw the occupation as only a temporary measure imposed by the German Army. His announcement of September 3, 1914, revealed nothing about what was to come. It even seemed to anticipate that the nation's independence would be restored, as soon as circumstances would allow.[2]

But the nomination of his replacement, General von Bissing (December 1914), marked the beginning of a new period. At this point, there was no longer any doubt that the failure of the offensive against France would delay the conflict's resolution for an undefined and probably lengthy period of time. And, at

---

[1] For this chapter and the two following, we have consulted in particular *Les Archives du Conseil de Flandre*, published by the *Ligue Nationale pour l'Unité belge*, (Bruxelles, 1928)
[2] "I ask no one to give up his patriotic sentiments, but I expect a reasonable submission to the authority of the Governor General and an absolute obedience of his orders."

that moment, the "Belgian question" emerged. Obliged to retain the country it had intended only to cross, Germany could not limit itself to exploiting its resources: it needed to make Belgium serve its war objectives. It was determined to make good use of the political advantage provided by such a valuable "security" (*Faustpfand*). The silence observed by the German government over the fate it reserved for Belgium makes this clear. No one, not in the Reich, not among the Allies or the neutral nations, had any doubt that a direct or disguised annexation was in the works. The decision had been made not to permit Belgium to regain its sovereignty when peace came, because it had misused its independence by cooperating with the Empire's enemies. Its temporary occupation would be followed by a permanent subordination, of which only the specifics remained uncertain. At bottom, both political and military authorities agreed that this would be the price of a German victory.[1]

The Belgian state, however, did not disappear. At this point, there was no indication of any intention to break it up and annex some of its provinces. It would eventually be absorbed as a whole into the Imperial Confederation as a *Reichsland* or a vassal state. Everything we know about General von Bissing's administration until the end of 1916 clearly reveals these intentions. His "conservative" policy indisputably reflects his desire to save Belgium, not only for Germany's immediate interests, but also for the future. He probably wanted to assimilate it. Since he could not, he limited himself, as we shall later see, at least to create a movement of public opinion favorable to his intentions.[2]

However in early 1917, the military situation, as well as the political situation (the rejection of the German peace proposal

---

[1] This surmise is borne out by the famous program of September 9, 1914 drafted by the German Chancellor. Liège and Verviers, a strip along the border, and possibly Antwerp, with a corridor to Liège, were to be annexed. The rest of Belgium was to become a "vassal state," with the country's ports at the disposal of the German military, and the country "economically a German province." (F. Fischer, Germany's <u>Aims in the First World War</u> (New York, 1967), 104.)

[2] See the document known as general von Bissing's will.

by the Allies on December 12, 1916;[1] all-out submarine warfare, the diplomatic break with America), made the realization of von Bissing's plans impossible and forced the "Belgian question" into its final phase. In order to carry on the war in the face of increasingly depleted resources and waning morale as a result of the naval blockade, Germany risked everything. The High Command, which the civil government could no longer resist, wanted to force victory by a terrific jolt of energy. At the same time as it decided to exploit Belgium's remaining resources without scruples, it also decided to break it up as a political entity. No longer counting on dictating the terms of the peace to its enemies, it at least wanted to make it impossible to restore Belgium when the time for negotiations would come. It divided the country into two sections, hoping that this would prevent its reconstruction, and with the intention to more easily retain its influence and its military bases, which it considered vital for its future security. The decree announcing the administrative separation of Flanders and Wallonia (March 21, 1917) marked the beginning of this policy. Von Bissing lived only long enough to see it proclaimed. It took place, up to the final catastrophe, under the direction of his replacement, General Ludwig von Falkenhausen.

Thus, the Belgian question evolved in response to the war that had given rise to it. An annexation policy followed an occupation policy, and finally became a policy of destruction. This sequence of events was paralleled by the German government's attitude toward the Flemish question.

Until war broke out, the government had never displayed any interest in the subject. It had never shown the least sympathy

---

[1] *The proposal was phrased in deliberately vague terms, but the Chancellor and High Command agreed that among the "guarantees" that would be required of Belgium before it was evacuated would be its economic attachment to Germany, control of the railroads and Campine coal fields, annexation of Liège and the dismantling of the other forts, and the right of passage in wartime. The Germans only disclosed their conditions on January 29, 1917, announcing at the same time the resumption of unrestricted submarine warfare in three days. The proposal had been a concession to the Chancellor and others opposed to unleashing the u-boats.*

with or provided the slightest support to the Pan-Germans who, in the name of a common race, advocated the return of the Low Countries to the Fatherland. These individuals were more focused on the Netherlands than Belgium. However, their demands had never troubled anyone. They were considered the innocent reveries of romantic patriots or harmless professors. The few attempts at fraternization between Flemish and Germans, first undertaken in the distant days of Hoffman von Fallersleben,[1] never had any results.[2]

The launching in Brussels of the journal *Germania* in 1898, intended to steer the Flemish movement towards Pan-Germanism, was a complete failure. Obviously, while Belgians were concerned about the language issue, they intended to resolve it among themselves, without involving foreigners. The leaders of the Flemish-speaking movement in the beginning of the 20th century were even more indifferent to Pan-Germanic appeals than their counterparts had been in 1848. There was never an understanding between them and Germany, and not even much sympathy. If they looked beyond Belgium's borders, it was exclusively to the Netherlands. The *Algemeen Nederlandsch Verbond* did its best to encourage cooperation between the Dutch in the Netherlands and the Dutch in Belgium, but had no political agenda.

The attitude of German émigrés in Belgium toward them would have discouraged the *flamingants*,[3] had they had considered it. These immigrants showed a profound indifference towards Flemish demands. In their relationship with the population, they

---

[1] August Hoffman von Fallersleben (1798–1874), poet and scholar, author of <u>Deutschland über Alles (Das Lied der Deutschen)</u>, expressing the hope of liberals for the unification of German-speaking territories. The line in the first stanza, "from the Meuse to Memel," proposes that eastern Belgium and the Netherlands be included in the new Reich. (It's worth recalling that <u>über Alles</u> originally meant that unification should be placed "above all other goals," rather than that Germany should triumph "over all other nations.")
[2] Otokar Fischer, *Belgie a Německo. La Belgique et l'Allemagne.* (Prague, 1927.)
[3] The French term goes back to the Middle Ages and originally referred to that part of Flanders where Flemish was spoken. By the middle of the nineteenth century, it had come to mean a Fleming who was proud of his or her language and culture, and wished to see Dutch recognized as the official language of the northern provinces, as it had been between 1815 and 1830.

behaved as *"fransquillons,"* speaking only French, patronizing only French-language theaters, using French exclusively for both business and personal relationships. The Flemish language was barely represented in the curriculum of the *Deutsche Schulen* of Brussels and Antwerp.

So it comes as no surprise that during the first few weeks of the conquest, German officers and officials alike were not in the least concerned about the Flemish question. For the most part, they were entirely unaware of its existence. While most if not all of them knew French to some degree, absolutely none of them knew Dutch. The first declarations made to the population were written only in French, or if they were bilingual, the second language was German. For Belgium's official Franco-Flemish bilingualism, the occupier substituted initially a Franco-German bilingualism. Instead of flattering those who spoke Flemish, it offended them.[1] It seemed that they were considered a negligible minority, and that Belgium was returning to old practice of regarding French as the sole official language.

Such a paradoxical situation obviously could not last. It was inevitable that the new German administration would adhere to the laws regarding the usage of the national languages, and that it would adopt Belgium's bilingualism. From August 25, 1914, Flemish was not only used on posters and in decrees, but from October 6, it was even put ahead of German, French coming third. A small detail of course, but a significant one, and indicating a new direction with major consequences.

The reasons for the increasing importance of the Flemish question were plain to see. While Germans were generally taken with the theory that race is the main factor in social activity, its most fervent believers were members of the military caste. They were brought up to think of themselves as the representatives of

---

1 I've systematically used the term *flamingants* to refer to followers of the Flemish movement. There were too many Flemish people who were hostile or indifferent to the *flamingants'* demands to claim that the latter's views were those of the entire people.

Deutschtum[1] par excellence. It was superior, they claimed, to any other "national engineering," and they believed that it was not only their right but their duty to instill an appreciation of it in all Germanic populations. And the Flemish population was indubitably Germanic. Their fate throughout history, and more specifically their "oppression" by the Belgian government, had long bastardized them by subjecting them to the yoke of the Latin world. The time had come for them to recall their origins. It would probably suffice simply to spread the good word to them and to offer a fraternal hand. Since the fate of the Germanic peoples depended on the war, the fate of the Flemish was also at stake. If they understood this, they would no doubt join Germany, which, in fighting for itself, was consequently fighting for them.

And to these racial considerations were added, to justify them further, military considerations. It was evident that the safety and comfort of the troops would be further guaranteed if the locals were more sympathetic toward them. So military interest as well as political prudence dictated that hostility be replaced with trust. It was therefore the military authorities, as much on principle as by necessity, who first advocated winning the support of the *flamingants* and thereby gaining the support of the entire people, whose linguistic rights, it claimed, should immediately be recognized. Proof is that it was in the *Étapes* zone that the new orientation first appeared. Also, this territory contained most of the Flemish population.[2]

In order to succeed, some circumspection was required. It was too obvious that before presenting Germany to the masses as a liberator, it would take some time before the still vivid memories would fade of the executions and arson in Leuven and Aarschot, the siege of Antwerp, and the first battles on the Yser. It was important to first test the ground. The *Kommandantur* of Ghent

---

1 *German culture*
2 It contained, indeed, both West and East Flanders almost in their entirety, and approximately two thirds of Belgians whose first language was Flemish.

worried about this as soon as the city was taken (October 1914).

A Protestant pastor originally from Holland, who combined religious passion with zealous Pan-Germanism, immediately offered his services.[1] Had they been better informed, the military authorities would no doubt have refused to be associated with such a man, who had just outraged the believers of his church by publicly praying there for the victory of the German armies. He immediately got in touch with a few excited or bitter young people, bookish admirers of German *Kultur*, and as convinced as he was of its irresistible strength and of its ultimate triumph. For them as for him, the war would end with a reorganization of Europe. Belgium was doomed to disappear. Victorious Germany would tear Flanders from the hybrid that oppressed it. Emancipated, it would be welcomed within the great community of Germanic nations, either reunited to the Netherlands, turned into an independent duchy, or connected in some way to the Empire, whose glory and prosperity it would share.

The reports of victories published by the German High Command encouraged these childish dreams in the minds of a few fanatics affected by war psychosis. The *Kommandantur* was not deluded regarding the number of these cranks, which was minuscule, nor regarding their influence, which was null, nor regarding their value, which was even less. But the military authorities wanted to win the support of at least a few of the notable figures of the *flamingant* party. They knew from the way their advances were greeted that they should not expect anything from them, and so were obliged to support, for lack of a better alternative, the followers they were reduced to. Secret funds were provided to them. On February 21, 1915, they published in Ghent the first "activist" newspaper of the occupation period: the *Vlaamsche Post*. The censor did not allow the printing of a protest that was immediately written by the leaders of the main Flemish

---

[1] *Derk Jan Domela Nieuwenhuis-Nyegaard (1870–1955)*

groups of the city. This nonetheless reached the public, hidden among the classifieds in the socialist newspaper, *Vooruit*. A notorious *flamingant*, who vigorously fought against the promoters of the *Vlaamsche Post*, was fined, jailed upon refusing to pay, and then deported to Germany.

Some carelessness[1] had in the meantime strengthened the positions of the small group from Ghent and eliminated the last of their qualms, if they had any. Meanwhile, the many refugees who had fled into the Netherlands during the siege of Antwerp began publishing newspapers there. Free to say anything, they inevitably revived old quarrels with the bitterness and violence exiles are famous for. The refugees' newspapers published in Amsterdam, in London, and later in Le Havre, went so far as to accuse some *flamingants* of making pacts with the enemy and of being largely responsible for Antwerp's surrender. According to them, the Flemish question was over. It could no longer be asked in a Belgium allied with France. "The future of Belgium," one of them said, "will be Latin or it will not exist."

This excessive language, carefully collected and commented on by the German press, angered those who didn't have the common sense to dismiss it. Censorship prevented the leaders of the Flemish party from expressing their thoughts. For their defense, they could count only on their émigré supporters. Almost all confirmed their loyalty to their invaded homeland. Without abandoning any of their demands, they declared that the linguistic conflict was a purely Belgian question, that it was in no way directed against the Walloons, and that the solution could only be found within the context of the national state once peace was made and independence recovered. But the controversy got worse as it grew longer. Extremist tendencies started to arise within the exile press. The *Vlaamsche Stem*, in the Netherlands, was rapidly

---

1 *The king failed to reply to a telegram of support from the leading flamingant refugees in the Netherlands written in Dutch. When it was written in French and resubmitted, his chilly response was considered insulting.*

moving towards separatism, calling for an autonomous Flanders, and increasingly attacking the Le Havre government. Imitators of the *Vlaamsche Post* sprung up in Belgium itself: the *Antwerpsche Tyndingen* and *Vlaamsche Nieuws* in Antwerp, and the *Gazet von Brussel* in Brussels. Though less extreme than their older brother, they still expatiated on the emancipation of Flemish Belgium, Germany's inevitable victory, the decline of France, and England's mercantile selfishness. Violent attacks on Cardinal Mercier depicted him as an anti-Flemish Walloon. To the French-language censored press was now added a Flemish-language censored press, which was eagerly assisted by the former.

One of the issues that had stirred public opinion just before the war was the creation of a Flemish university, or rather of the transformation of the University of Ghent into a Flemish-speaking university. For many years this reform had been called for by *flamingant* political associations. After long debates, there was general agreement on a formula negotiated by the Chamber of Representatives. The invasion had postponed further discussion. The promoters of the idea, respecting the truce the parties had decided to observe, resolved to stop discussing the proposal until the end of the war. This was one of the reasons the German-subsidized newspapers immediately made it one of their basic demands. They urged the German government to give the Flemish the satisfaction that the Belgian government had always refused them. And it goes without saying that their propaganda was far too beneficial to the occupying power for it not to expressly support it.

In 1915, a press campaign was started in Germany about the Flemish question. At every opportunity, brochures and newspapers exposed the "oppression" imposed on Germanic Belgians by their Walloon compatriots. The artificial nature of the Belgian state and the Reich's duty to help its racial brothers were repeatedly stressed. History was utilized: readers were reminded that the Netherlands, formed during the 16th century by Charles V, were part of the Holy Roman Empire. The *Vlaamsche Post*'s and others' claims were presented as the authentic voice of Flemish opinion and of its confidence in Germany. In April 1915, Chancellor Theodor Bethmann Hollweg himself entered the fray. He confirmed, in front of the Reichstag, the government's sympathy for the Flemish demands and promised to provide support.

In Belgium, the military authorities leaked to *flamingants* the good news that a Flemish university would soon be established. On December 2, 1915, the Governor General ordered that the funds necessary to achieve this goal be added to the budget. He would have wanted, it seems, to have carried out the initiative calmly and to avoid controversy. He ordered that the all the universities resume operations. None complied, refusing either to work under censorship or to make education available to the young people remaining in the country while their peers were fighting on the Yser. This refusal eliminated any possibility of gradually transforming University of Ghent into a Flemish-language university, either by duplicating classes, or through cooperation from the professors.

It was hoped initially that this consent would be gained. On February 16, 1916, faculty members were asked to state whether they were able to teach in Flemish and, if they could, whether they would consent to do so. Determined to prevent the enemy from interfering with the running of the university, all but five of them answered that they could or would not teach in Flemish. The fact that two of them[1] were deported to Germany only served to strengthen their colleagues' determination. All that was left was to do was to proceed without their support by issuing a decree. On March 15, 1916, it was announced that the University's classes were to be taught in Flemish, starting with the new school year in October.[2]

---

1 Pirenne and Paul Fredrique.
2 For what follows, see Th. Heyse, *L'Université flamande*, Ghent (1918 – 1919).

This decision was met with great enthusiasm by the press that had originally agitated for it. In the name of the Flemish people, it was profoundly grateful. The sister nation had justified the hopes it had created. It confirmed the decline of the Belgian state, which was clearly only a henchman for France, hereditary enemy of Flanders. A redeeming Germanism had finally triumphed over Latinity, as it had triumphed in 1302 on the battlefield of Kortijk.[1] Thanks to Germany, Flanders was freed from the tyranny of Rome. "Los van Havre" became the watchword.[2] The future of Flanders could be secured only by Berlin.

This pathetic line adopted by a minuscule minority of hotheads was immediately countered by protests signed by some of the most eminent figures from the *flamingant* party. Without abandoning any of their demands, and claiming to be strong supporters of the establishment of a Flemish university, they objected to receiving it from the occupying power. "We are a race," they said, "who in the past has always insisted on dealing with its own issues on its own soil by its own means… Both Flemish and *flamingants* agree that the Belgian nation must remain independent. In this respect, there is not the least difference between the views of the Flemish and those of the Walloons." The protest was immediately distributed clandestinely by the thousands, and the Governor General responded with an open letter, in which he claimed his right as "holder of supreme power over the country" to act in the best interest of the Flemish people. He refused to consider the signatories of the protest as spokespersons for the Flemish, and concluded with a threat to crack down "with particular strictness against any action aiming to prevent either professors or students from cooperating with the new project."

---

1 a reference to the "Battle of the Golden Spurs" between Flemish urban militia defending the autonomy of Flanders against their French overlord Phillip IV, one of the first battles in which a disciplined middle-class infantry defeated an aristocratic cavalry.
2 echoing "Los von Rom"—away from Rome—the battle cry of the Pan-Germanic movement in Austria. This also originated in a language question—a decree requiring civil servants in Bohemia and Moravia to be able to speak Czech.

This threat was superfluous. On their own accord, the Ghent professors refused to collaborate with the enemy. Only seven of them, five of whom were Belgian, agreed to continue teaching. To fill the vacancies, the *Studienkommission zur Vorbereitung unterrichtstechnischer Fragen an der Universität Gent* was forced to make do with what came along: dentists, engineers, doctors, middle school teachers seeking a more lucrative job, along with a few Dutch Germanophiles and some Germans. As it was organized, the new University was but an expedient, an improvisation, a publicity stunt. Even in peacetime it would have been impossible to recruit overnight a full staff with the appropriate minimum qualifications. In the circumstances of the time, establishing an institution of higher education was a real challenge. Public opinion opposed it. While meetings were banned, the few supporters of cooperation with Germany were free to organize public gatherings. These took place in empty rooms. Supporters were allowed to march and sing the *Vlaamsche Leeuw*.[1] The Governor General ordered the police to allow them access to premises from which they had been banned.

The pathetic failure of this agitation clearly showed that the Ghent Germano-Flemish University did not meet with the approval of the people. It was nothing more than an instrument of German policy. The opening ceremony, on October 21, 1916, presided by General von Bissing, sealed Germany's alliance with the "activists." There were barely any students. Including visiting scholars, there were 110 the first year, 417 the second. And most of them only went because they were tempted by generous scholarships, food allowances, and immunity from deportation. As for the professors, they were offered guarantees in case the Belgian government, after its return, attempted to take their chair away or strip them of their academic rights.

---

1 *The Flemish Lion*, national anthem of Flanders, written in 1847 by Hippoliet Van Peen to music by Karel Miry.

Thus the "stillborn"[1] university was obviously linked to the German occupation. No one could doubt that it could only remain under one condition: that of Germany's victory. The Belgian government had declared as early as October 14 that civil servants who agreed to join it would permanently lose their position, and that the diplomas issued by the new university would have no legal value in Belgium.

These measures left no room for doubt. The *flamingants* who clung to their illusions would have to choose between Belgium and Germany. Among them, only those blinded by linguistic fanaticism disowned their native country. But disowning it meant they would have to associate with the invader. From then on, they could no longer insist that they were only supporting the linguistic rights of the Flemish population. While the vast majority of the people they claimed to want to liberate remained loyal to the nation, they were forced, through their own weakness and through the disapproval they faced, to side with the enemy.

Through a delusion that was part of a war psychosis, they convinced themselves that the support Germany offered them was altruistic. They believed the professions of love from the Pan-Germanic press. They abandoned themselves to the illusion of racial theory and kept repeating that the terrible conflict that was turning Europe upside-down was that of Germanism against Latinity. Of course they did not wish to see Flanders absorbed into Germany. For most of them, the ideal was and remained until the end an autonomous Flemish state. In their naïveté, these dilettante politicians failed to understand that their weakness left them no other option than to become pawns in the hands of the German High Command. They trusted the promises that were used to lure them, much as van der Noot had trusted the promises

---

[1] Here I cite the expression I heard used by a German officer who was a member of the military judiciary in Flanders.

made by Prussia during the Brabant revolution.¹ ² In both cases, it was the same self-importance, the same lack of political savvy, the same provincialism, the same atrophy of both heart and brain. Their behavior is even more pathetic than it is shameful. Seen from afar, it seems almost farcical, in light of the glaring contrast between their plans and the means at their disposal to carry them out. A minuscule group among a population which disowned them in horror, they were forced to rely on support from the enemy to attack their opponents. In order to be consistent, they ought to have been willing to risk their lives for the Reich. The fact that they never took up arms is sufficient to condemn their initiative. While Czechs and Poles were joining the armies of Germany's enemies in droves, not one of the activists served in Germany's own army. They were satisfied, as one of their leaders admitted on August 28, 1917, with letting it fight for them.

What explains their behavior is their belief in Germany's invincibility. They thought they were betting on the winner. Had they predicted the eventual defeat of their protectors, and even if they had accepted the possibility of peace without compensations or annexations such as the Reichstag called for on July 19, 1917, they would have prudently remained neutral. They only broke with Belgium because they thought it had been dealt a death-blow and was doomed to disappear from the map of Europe. Having based their plans on Germany's triumph, they had to hope it would be decisive. From then on, their enemy was Belgium. They sought to build an independent Flanders on its ruins, without wanting to admit that an all-powerful Germany would not fail to annex Flanders, which provided Germany with a strategic position on the North Sea and would ensure its hegemony in Europe.

---

1 H. Pirenne, *Histoire de Belgique*, t V, 2ⁿᵈ Edition, p 485 and following.
2 Hendrik van der Noot (1731–1827) led the revolt against Austrian rule that resulted in the year-long United States of Belgium, of which he was Prime Minister. He counted on the support of foreign powers, particularly Prussia, Austria's enemy. However, after Berlin and Vienna signed the Convention of Reichenbach (July 1790), the Prussians abandoned him, and Austrian troops took over the country.

Incapable of any foresight, these individuals proudly called themselves activists, when nothing could be more passive than their attitude toward their masters.

§ II. — The Flanders Council

The linguistic policy that General von Bissing adopted was initially in compliance with Belgian laws. On February 25, 1916, he issued a decree putting into effect the law voted on June 15, 1914, about the use of languages in primary education.[1] On March 22, the May 22, 1878 law forcing state officials to correspond in Flemish with towns and individuals in Flemish provinces was strictly enforced and soon (September 2) even made applicable to the Flemish localities in Liège and Hainaut provinces, as well as several towns in the Brussels metropolitan area.

The transformation of the University of Ghent into a Flemish-language university marks the moment from which the occupying power was no longer content with simply applying Belgian laws, but instead assumed the right to itself legislate in linguistic matters. It claimed the right in virtue of authority having been transferred from the Belgian to the German government. It wished "to carefully take into account the various perspectives that result when people speaking different languages live together in the same state." It justified its intervention out of its concern for "fairness and for the well-being of the Flemish people." And it was clear that, now embarked on this path, it was not about to stop.

If one equates a people's identity with its language, nothing is easier than to pursue this belief to its ultimate conclusion, which is the state's dissolution. And it would be unfair not to recognize that in the eyes of General von Bissing, this dissolution would

---

[1] According to article 20 of this law, the common language to be used in education had to be the child's native language.

serve both Germany's war goals and the principle to which he claimed to adhere. To him, the Flemish question was obviously much like the Czech question in Bohemia, or the Polish question in Poznań. Unaware of the historical conditions that had peacefully introduced over centuries the usage of French in Flanders and that defined the relationship between Flemish and Walloons, he viewed the situation as the result of a racial struggle, when it was only the consequence of a long political association, of a secular community of the interests, and the traditional prestige exerted by French civilization on a country neighboring France which had always been receptive to its influence. What was very ancient and very complex appeared to him as very new and very clear. He assumed that the Belgian state was controlled by Walloons much as the Austrian state was controlled by Germans and that the Walloons had deliberately decided to Latinize and exploit the Flemish population for the benefit of the "dominant" race. He could not realize that the conflict he was determined to resolve was linguistic and not national, that the use of different languages did not imply any hatred between those who used them, and that French, far from being a language imposed by conquest or domination, was a language voluntarily adopted for centuries and had became a native language.[1] And finally, he could not realize that the Flemish people, since they spoke a Germanic dialect, could be opposed to the *Deutschtum* which, according to him, was

---

[1] While true for the upper classes, this repeated claim is otherwise not entirely accurate. Charles Rogier, one of Belgium's founding fathers, its first Minister of the Interior and twice Prime Minister, confessed, "the efforts of our government have to be directed towards the annihilation of the Flemish language," and declared that "the first principle of good administration rests on the exclusive use of one language, and it is obvious in Belgium that this language must be French." Schools in Flanders were required to provide instruction in French and more than half were abolished. Municipal councils that supported the union with the Netherlands were deposed and other coercive measures taken against those opposing the new Francophone regime, whose leaders originally sought a union with France.

to be imposed on them for their benefit as well as Germany's.[1] The hostility they showed toward his government, he felt, was explained by the inevitable harshness of the conquest. There was no doubt that it was destined to dissipate as the Flemish became accustomed to German rule and that, with a little assistance, they would soon be favorably disposed toward Germany under the all-powerful influence of a commonality of race.

The small group of activists confirmed his position. Did they not also hold the Belgian state responsible for the "oppression" of the Flemish people and oppose the "Latinity" of this state to the fundamentally Germanic nature of their people? It would have been foolish to neglect their support. No doubt were they still only a minority. One of their leaders estimated that 90% of Flemish people were hostile to them and that most of the rest were indifferent. But their program was more important than these numbers. It was sufficient only that they speak up for the measures they demanded. In the great silence imposed on the majority, their voices, echoing the German press, reverberated loudly.

The Governor General's good will encouraged them to persevere in their efforts. Their activity increased relentlessly. They held more propaganda meetings, published new brochures, and their language became increasingly violent. In the Netherlands, within the Belgian colony, their associates launched a press campaign in which the *Toorts* and the *Vlaamsche Stem* were the most ardent participants. The indignation they aroused could not harm them as there was no way to speak out against them. Theirs were the only voices heard by neutral countries and Walloons, and it was impossible to know to what extent they spoke for the entire

---

[1] The Germans who were in Belgium were able to appreciate the situation, and noted quite to the contrary that Flemish customs had nothing to do with the *Germanentum*. See Bittmann, previously cited work, t III, p 75. In 1915, I witnessed an officer's surprise at the lack of anything German about the city of Ghent. He had expected that the Austrian regime had exerted in Belgium during the 18th century the same influence as in Bohemia!

Flemish population, as they claimed. While they all called for the dissolution of the Belgian community, they did not agree on their goals. The most radical ones demanded the establishment of a Kingdom of Flanders within the German confederation. Others were expecting peace to provide an international solution to the Flemish question, one which would put an end to "nationalist Belgian power." Still others advocated some sort of home rule and limited themselves to demanding, either within Belgium or outside of it, an autonomous administration.

All activists accepted Germany's participation, be it out of principle or out of necessity. Many of them differed from the "passivist" *flamingants* only by their refusal to consider the Flemish question as a Belgian question, that is, a question that could be resolved only when the country again enjoyed independence.

Their conviction of Germany's eventual triumph put them at its mercy. Whether they liked it or not, Germany would decide their fate as it pleased. The wisest among them knew this. They comforted themselves by assuming that Germany's interests were identical to those of Flanders. "We know full well," the *Gazet van Brussel* wrote with censorship approval, "that the Germans do not determine their policies in order to please the Flemish. If they are fighting the frenchifying of Flanders, it's only to lessen France's all-to-great influence over our country, but this happens to be advantageous to Flanders as well as Germany."

One must acknowledge that, apart from insignificant exceptions, the activists' ideal was purely Flemish. Pushing to its extreme the Flemish motto "*de taal is gansch het volk*" (the language makes the people), imbued with a belief in the identity of language and nationality, fanatic supporters of an exclusivism that was contrary to both the traditions and the interests of their own people, they hoped to establish a strictly Flemish civilization by virtue only of its language. Everything else would follow. The national dialect, rekindling the energies of a people who had supposedly been debased by bilingualism, would lead to prosperity and bliss. Their chauvinism made them dream of a wonderful future. Under the influence of a war psychosis, they increasingly saw France as having viciously persecuted Flanders over the centuries, and thought that its defeat would allow Flanders to blossom.

Germany's victory would not only emancipate Flanders, but also increase its territory. The most hot-headed activists called for the return of Dunkirk and Cassel, which had been annexed by Louis XIV. Their outlook was increasingly influenced by the Pan-Germanists. But they forgot that they did not dispose of the force the latter boasted, and that the army occupying their country was not Flemish but German.

They naturally received encouragement from Germany, which contributed to their boldness. Where the Flemish question was once a matter of indifference, it was now considered very passionately. All of its aspects were discussed, and it figured largely in the country's war literature. Editors inundated the market with historical works emphasizing the artificial nature and baneful effect of the Belgian state; scholars discovered multiple links, hitherto unsuspected, that connected Flanders to Germany in the past; other writers demonstrated that the future of the port of Antwerp depended on its relationship with the Reich; new editions of the works of Flemish poets and novelists were published. In Belgium, a lavishly illustrated journal was founded, the *Belfried*, intended to acquaint Germans with the Flanders their armies had just conquered. The press kept publishing articles filled with compassion for and protests of devotion to a sister nation which had been oppressed for so long by a government in the pay of the hereditary enemy of Germany.

In March 1917, the *Deutsch-flämische Gesellschaften* were founded in Dusseldorff and Berlin, under the honorary presidency of von Bissing and Grand Admiral von Tirpitz. They offered to dedicate themselves, "without any political agenda," to the interests the Flemish and German people shared by virtue of their racial and linguistic ties. But if Germany's sympathies toward its Belgian "brothers" were conspicuously flaunted, the military authorities were unable to spare them from the necessary measures for their common victory. They had to take part in the worker deportations of October 1916. On the very day the new University of Ghent was opened, a group of workers was seen in the streets being escorted to the train station by soldiers, along with the cortege of officers and officials who had been invited to the ceremony. But what satisfaction was given to the demands of the Flemish race! In Bruges, under orders from the *Kommandantur*, all of the French-language signs disappeared from storefronts; the street names were now only displayed in Flemish; tram operators in Brussels were forced to announce stops in both languages.

The time came when the activists felt the need to organize. Nothing could be easier, as the occupying power allowed them to retain the freedom of speech and assembly it denied their compatriots. The more they realized that they were only a tiny minority, the more they convinced themselves that they would never be able to impose themselves on the people if not by using force. They also realized that the Governor General would be pleased to be able to recognize them as the representatives for the Flemish nation and to invoke their support. Their official recognition by him would also enable them to steer his policies in the right direction, they believed, avoiding the sacrifice of Flemish to German interests. Besides, nothing would be more advantageous than to get a jump on the peace treaty by making Flemish independence a fait accompli, providing it a legal government to replace the Belgian state. There would then be no way to reinstate the latter. Germany had so far not yet declared the fate it had in store for Flanders. But having already given the *flamingants* the right to speak in the name of the Flemish people, Germany, they felt, would be obliged sooner or later to confer on them political power.

These ideas had already been expressed by the activist press for quite some time. In August 1915, a group from Ghent demanded the creation of a General Council for the Flemish people

(*Algemeen Vlaamschen Raad*),[1] with which the Central Powers could deal after the victory. But it was obviously impossible to hold an election in order to establish such a council. This would have resoundingly revealed the people's continuing faith in the country they shared with the Walloons. The activists themselves admitted that "Belgium lives in the people's heart and spirit." The situation was embarrassing. It was resolved through a subterfuge. Just as the country's annexation to the French Republic was voted on in 1794 by a handful of Jacobins under the protection of the sans-culottes' bayonets,[2] so a meeting of stooges in Brussels, under the protection of German police, instituted by acclamation, on February 4, 1917, the Council of Flanders, the *Raad van Vlaanderen*, which, as a result of popular indignation, soon became known as the *Veraad van Vlaanderen*.[3]

The Flemish people thus found itself endowed with a parliament despite its wishes. But its consent didn't matter. The comedy of February 4th had been prepared with assistance from the Governor General.[4] The Empire's Chancellor recognized these results without delay. On March 3, 1917, he received in Brussels a delegation from the Flanders Council. After reminding it of "the ancient political, economic, and cultural ties that united Germany and Flanders," he declared that "his Majesty the Emperor, whom I made aware of your desire to engage with the Imperial government, made known his willingness to satisfy the legitimate wishes you have expressed, to the extent allowed by the state of war and military requirements." He announced "the imminent execution of measures that had been decided upon earlier in discussions between myself and the Governor

---

[1] The title was taken from an institution created by Philip the Good, 3rd Duke of Burgundy, in the 15th century to supersede the <u>parlement</u> of Paris as the highest judicial authority in Flanders, ending six centuries of vassalage to France.
[2] H. Pirenne, *Histoire de la Belgique*, t VI, p 42 and following.
[3] *Betrayal of Flanders*
[4] The political program that the Flanders Council claimed to adhere to on February 4 had been written in the Brussels *Kommanantur*.

General, which would allow the Flemish people to pursue freely its own cultural and economic development. These measures, which defend human rights, will be deliberately pursued so as to achieve a complete administrative separation during the occupation. We will work together with the Flemish Council. The German Empire, during peace negotiations, and also after peace, will do its best to ensure and promote the free development of the Flemish race."

The highest political authority within the Empire thus accepted the collaboration of individuals elected during a party meeting and considered them as the representatives of the Flemish people. By providing them with support, he seemed to even give them hope of letting them participate in the peace negotiations which would definitively sanction Flemish independence on the ruins of Belgian independence. The sincerity of these promises was made clear when, three weeks later, on March 21, 1917, the Governor General decreed the administrative separation of Belgium into two regions: Flanders and Wallonia.

For the first time in history, the linguistic border became a political border. The simplistic dogma that determined nationality by language had been imposed on the people, without any consideration for its desires or interests. "The people always wants what's best, but it doesn't always know what this is," said the representatives sent by the French Republic on a mission to Belgium at the end of the 18th century. The linguistic Jacobins of 1917 had no reason to envy the political Jacobins of 1794. Although a full century apart, they both showed the same narrow-mindedness, the same fanaticism in the service of the conqueror. No doubt General von Bissing had as great a faith in racial theory as the Committee of Public Safety did in the Declaration of the Rights of Man. But in both cases, this faith was all the stronger in so far as it supported the annexation of Belgium.

The decree instituting administrative separation divided Belgium in two territories, the first including the Flemish provinces of Antwerp, Limburg, and West and East Flanders, as well as the parts of the province of Brabant corresponding to the Leuven and Brussels districts. The Nivelles district was detached from it, to be reunited with the Walloon provinces of Hainaut, Liège, Luxembourg, and Namur. The first group was to be directed from Brussels, the other from Namur. The country's capital, which during the French occupation had been reduced to a mere prefecture, was this time reduced to a regional administrative center. As for Namur, a second-rate city, there was no particular reason to make it the administrative center for Wallonia, except perhaps for its proximity to Brussels.

None of these measures solved the relationships the two parts of the state would continue to have with one another. Each was merely given its own administration: the ministries were simply divided just as the country had been. A series of decrees resulted in the creation of two ministries each for Agriculture and Public Works, Sciences and Arts, Industry and Labor (May 5), Interior (May 12), Justice, Finances (June 9), Navy, and Post and Telegraphs (September 13). Each of the two regions received a *Verwaltungschef* charged with directing these services.

In short, such a separation was only a temporary expedient. It only affected administration. Clearly, it was conceived to last only during the occupation. Belgium's definitive status was left to the peace negotiations. The country did not disappear; it was simply cut in half.

But this decoupling was none the less a significant portent of Belgium's fate. Except within the Council of Flanders, the administrative separation was felt by all Belgians as a decision made by Germany to put an end to their nationality. No one accepted it. And this would soon become clear.

§ III. — The Administrative Separation

It was not enough merely to decree the administrative separation for it to become a reality. Without support from officials and from the people, the transformation could not be accomplished. The services Germany was dividing or doubling were those that the occupying power had left to Belgians to fulfill. It was vital for these agents to agree to continue doing their job under the regime imposed upon the country. But the obligation they had accepted from the occupier did not go as far as forcing them to collaborate in the destruction of their homeland. They were still bound by their oath of faithfulness to the King and of obedience to the Constitution and to the laws of the Belgian people.

It became clear immediately that they would not comply with the edict. Except for very rare exceptions, all department heads informed the German authorities of their desire to be made "inactive." Their salaries were immediately suspended. They had earlier discussed their response with members of Parliament who had not left Belgium. To resign en masse would mean plunging the entire country into anarchy or leaving it to the mercy of German officials. Thus they stuck to a form of passive resistance which involved the resignations only of the directors of the various ministry departments. This was enough to confront the measure with serious obstacles. The arrests of several officials who had resigned had no effect. On April 18, 1917, an official notice made it known that those who had withdrawn their declaration of loyalty would be deported to Berlin, and those arrested were sent to a prison camp.

On July 11, after several other officials had fled, an order was given that from then on "all ministry employees, so long as they do not fulfill their service duties, would be subjected to close surveillance," which meant appearing twice each day at their neighborhood German police station. All who were to be part of the Namur administration resigned en masse. Orders issued to summon them had no effect.

But the government in Le Havre feared that the resistance would increase disorder and suffering in the country. On May

1, it secretly sent a telegram to the leaders of the department of finances, asking all patriotic officials to retain their positions in order to monitor the separatist intruders who would be appointed to the offices by the occupier, to reduce their influence to a minimum, and to prevent the execution of any measure contrary to the national interests. "The financial administrators," it said, "would not be able to give a better demonstration of patriotism than by sacrificing their pride for the sake of the Belgian people, and not abandoning their positions. Instead they should resolutely fight to preserve national unity." Similar instructions were received a few days later by the staff of the other ministries. However, several of them did not heed them. They decided that they were in a better position than the Le Havre government to determine the appropriate conduct. And indeed, by following the government's advice, they would have put themselves in an awkward position, since they would have been obliged to sign a statement of loyalty toward the occupier. And so their opposition continued despite the anxieties and dangers it gave rise to.

In order to fill the new vacancies, the Governor General appointed notorious activists in Brussels. On June 15, as planned by the decrees, they took possession of the ministries of Industry and Labor, Agriculture, Public Works, and Science and Art. In Namur, however, the general unwillingness to participate made things more difficult. The makeshift premises hurriedly set up for the new administration in schools, in courts, etc., remained empty, as well as the housing assigned to personnel. There was no other option than simply to accept whoever showed up. The administrative separation was clearly leading to disorganization. When the German government introduced the initiative, it had clearly been thinking only of Flanders. By giving it Brussels as a capital, it provided it with an organization already in place. Vacant positions were easily filled. The ministries that had so far worked for Belgium simply continued to do so for half of Belgium.

In Namur, on the contrary, everything had to be created from scratch.

Indeed there was no movement in the Walloon half of the country that was comparable to Flemish activism. There was no trace of the discontent that had been triggered before the war by the linguistic quarrel. At best, a few exasperated Francophiles led an inconsequential campaign abroad for the annexation to France of the Walloon provinces. A few brochures signed with unknown names advocated in vain a federation of Wallonia and Flanders, both independent. Nobody responded to these appeals, which were obviously inspired by activism. Those leaders of Flemish separatism who had hoped to see Walloons join in their efforts were sadly disappointed. For the latter, national unity remained the only condition for future peace. Articles occasionally published by the German press about the Germanic origins of the Walloons were not read and had absolutely no influence. *L'Avenir wallon*, published in Brussels and paid for by Germany, desperately demanded that Wallonia have a distinct political existence, as well as a separate archbishopric from the one in Mechelen, but it was met with nothing but contempt or indifference. The population formed a united bloc against the invader.

The Governor General accepted this fact and confined himself to establishing a makeshift administration.[1] On July 11, the *Verwaltungschef für Wallonien* took over the barracks for the 13th infantry regiment in Namur, bringing along a secretary, a messenger, a typist, and a telephone operator. It was only in October that the improvised administration was functioning. It had been provided at this point with a propaganda office.

Almost all of the personnel of this singular Walloon administration were German. They were accommodated at the Hotel d'Harscamp, the best in town, complete with casino, reading rooms, and café. In January 1918, the *Verwaltungschef* noted that

---

1 On this subject I follow the report from M. Haniel, *Verwallungschef* for Wallonia, about the latter's organization, kept at the War Archives.

the difficulties in hiring native assistants were increasing day after day. There was a "general strike" by government workers against the recruitment efforts. The Flanders Council's advice to forcefully deport this new kind of striker from Brussels to Namur was not heeded, for fear of stirring up unrest.

However, owing to the efforts of "two Belgians whom the *Deutschfreundlichkeit* could not thank enough," it was possible to fill vacancies with a few candidates "who were driven by the difficult times to seek a living any way they could." Several of them turned out to be unfit for the task; others would definitely never have been hired had there been another choice. Little by little, new recruits showed up, either out of need or ambition. In order to better retain them, their pay was increased, their lodging and food were discounted, and they were provided railway passes to enable them to return to their families from Saturday to Monday.

Meanwhile, the *Verwaltungschef* dreamt that "the conviction of Germany's victory would spread through the Belgian people and do most of the work." As soon as they were convinced that the administrative separation was irrevocable, the undecided would be persuaded to seek a position in the administration. The acceptance by the "leader of Walloon separatism" of a position in the Ministry of Science and the Arts seemed to augur well. In any case, the administrative chief concluded, "time is working for us." But it was important to help the process along with propaganda that would popularize, in Germany and Wallonia alike, the idea that a division of Belgium into two parts was inevitable, to demonstrate the economic necessity of tight relations between Wallonia and Germany, and generally to induce Walloons to be more favorably disposed toward Germany. Nothing would be neglected to create a Walloon activism similar to the Flemish activism which is "so useful to us." But a different method was needed in Wallonia. The best way to destroy Belgian patriotism there would be to appeal to the Walloons' sense of superiority over Flanders, dominated as it was by reactionary clergy. It would also be necessary to "put it in their heads" that autonomy would result in material and financial advantages.

In short, the Germans focused on radicals and socialists. Brochures and *Flugschriften* went to great lengths to show how the peace treaty would liberate democratic Wallonia from clerical Flanders. However, care had to be taken not to upset the clergy, so as to still maintain a good relationship with the right-wing Walloon League. A paper, the *Peuple wallon*, was created in Brussels, though ostensibly published in Charleroi. Also planned was the publication of an illustrated satirical paper with a socialist perspective, which would be written partly in the Walloon dialect. Various means were proposed to weaken French influence: promoting local culture, publishing articles on Wallonia, subsidizing a Walloon dictionary begun by the region's literary association, organizing conferences on the originality of Walloon culture, enlisting the help of the University of Liège in these efforts, teaching Walloon folklore in schools and, if possible, in the local dialect, having the *Inselverlag* publish small books similar to the ones being distributed in Flanders, calling for philological studies in order to highlight the German influences that had shaped the Walloon dialects, pressuring Walloons to demand an organization similar to the *Raad van Vlaanderen*, and lobbying the German press to not mention the possibility of Germany ceding the Walloon provinces to France in negotiations for peace. At the same time, and in a significant contradiction with the claim of favoring Walloon nationality, *Deutsche Schulen* continued to operate in Verviers, Liège, Namur, Charleroi, and La Louvière.

These maneuvers resulted in complete failure. It could not have been otherwise. The administrative separation, which no one in Wallonia had asked for, and which was only demanded by a handful of Flemish extremists all the more loudly in so far as their numbers were so small, was nothing but a ploy of the German High Command. Its goal was to act ahead of the peace treaty in order to make the restoration of Belgium impossible. It completely disregarded the peoples' wishes, and aimed only to break the country in half by putting pressure on what seemed to be its weak point: the linguistic border. In fact, it was unenforceable, and the most lucid among German officials knew that full well. In July 1917, the civil administration leader, Herr von Sandt, resigned and was sent to Warsaw. The Governor General himself thought the separation premature and was only carrying out orders from Berlin.[1]

The very way in which it was applied showed that it was nothing more than a scheme to serve German war aims. Germany was careful not to alter the services it depended on. The organization of finances, railroads, justice, and the *Zentralen* was left untouched. In fact, it only affected the Ministries of Sciences and Arts, of Agriculture, and of Public Works. And it only succeeded there because the general paralysis affecting the country had virtually brought their activities to a halt.

On August 9, 1917, a decree made Flemish the official language within the entire administrative region of Flanders, including the Brussels urban area, "for the offices and officials' communication between themselves and with Wallonia, for their verbal and written communications with the public, as well as for public communications, notices, and records." French would be tolerated "until further notice" for communications with people who used French themselves, but only within the Brussels urban area. French translations would also be temporarily allowed for official communications. These measures extended to the *Société Générale*, *Banque Nationale*, *Caisse d'Épargne*, and all establishments, institutions, companies or people who provided public services.

The decree was too obviously incompatible with the state of things to be applied. Consider the linguistic situation of the Brussels urban area. Of its 910,963 inhabitants (in 1910),

---

[1] Von Köhler, previously cited work, p 42.

166,454 spoke exclusively Flemish, 203,988 exclusively French, and the rest (540,521) were bilingual.[1] And these numbers only give an approximate idea of the true picture. In any case, a simply quantitative estimate is not helpful. Qualitatively speaking, the importance of French goes beyond its numbers. It is the language for the entire upper class: business people, scholars, administrators. It was thus impossible to apply the decree without oppressing the most important part of the population, and without severely impairing local organization. It undoubtedly was nothing more than a political move rather than a measure of public utility. The area's burgomasters saw this clearly. The letter of protest they sent to both the Governor General and the ministers for Spain and the Netherlands, as well as the general consul for Switzerland, rightly condemns it. "Numerous clues," the letter reads, "lead one to assume that Germany plans or at least hopes to gain recognition through international treaties for some of the changes it has introduced in Belgium's internal structure. It would be extremely pernicious for the country if the invader were able to claim a fait accompli..." In such a situation, "the legitimate concern that the new regime would ignore or distort the intentions and will of the Belgian people" made resistance their duty.

For the first time, the country was no longer simply being occupied; it was being violated. "We can confirm," the burgomasters wrote a few days later (October 23, 1917), "that what injures and afflicts our people more than anything else is a regime that affects its deepest feelings, the rights it considers sacred, its freedoms—a regime forced upon it by a foreign power without our being consulted, without being given the opportunity to voice an opinion..."

On October 29, the Brussels Communal Council also issued, unanimously, a protest in the name of the entire people. "The Belgian people," it read, "wants to be its own master. It refuses to

---

[1] Survey of the usage of French and Flemish in the Brussels urban area (Brussels, 1919).

be bound by the measures the occupier has arbitrarily taken without consulting it. It is important that this desire be recognized as firm, unalterable, and irrevocable when the time comes to begin peace negotiations and when, to use the words of eminent politicians, the rule of law will be substituted for the temporary reign of force." And, after signing the document, the Council members renewed their oath of allegiance to the King and of obedience to the Constitution and to the laws of the Belgian people.

Their resistance was strengthened by the visible embarrassment of the German authorities. Obviously, the latter had not expected such an attitude. They were naïvely surprised at the "unwillingness" they were confronted with and did not hide their desire to reach a compromise that would allow them to retreat without sacrificing too much self-esteem. The linguistic measures went the way of the deportations. Imposed by the military, they placed the unfortunate officials in charge of enforcing them in an awkward position. The president of the Brabant civil administration did not dare send the Council's protest to the Governor General. "In the eyes of the military," he said to Mr. Steens, the Brussels *échevin* who was the acting burgomaster, "the word protest was synonymous with revolt." He resorted to concessions and threats, in turn, with the same lack of success. "You will be replaced," he would say, "if you do not obey, and local affairs will no longer be in the hands of a Brussels citizens, but of Germans or Flemish," that is activists.

However, he began to realize that no local authority would give in. On November 6, he tried to threaten the burgomasters by telling them that if they did not yield, he would replace them with "dictators."[1] But on the following day, he sent them a proposal for compromises "which would be applied with leniency." On the 9th, fifteen towns of the area rejected these proposals.

---

1 By November 5, the Brussels Communal Council had already taken measures to replace the *échivinal* cabinet if it was dismissed, and had even chosen individuals to substitute for members who might be arrested.

Local employees threatened to stage a general strike of all the services they were in charge of in the event the government didn't yield.[1] On November 10, at the matins service, Cardinal Mercier expressed his "admiration" for the Brussels *échevins*. Activists at a meeting held the following day at the Alhambra were greeted with boos from the crowd.

The chief of the civil administration was expected to take drastic measures on the 10th. He had announced that in case of a boycott "a thunderbolt would strike the Town Hall." The boycott came, but no thunderbolt followed. Finally, on November 17, the Germans backed off. The chief of the civil administration of Flanders wrote to the burgomasters that "so as to avoid hardships in the application of the August 9 decree, temporary measures would be taken." To conceal the failure, he pretended to regard French-speaking *Bruxellois* as Walloons. This was to falsify history. It is probable that the Chancellor of the Empire, to whom the burgomaster had addressed an appeal on November 8, had intervened. The chief of the civil administration at least indicated that these concessions satisfied the request sent to the Chancellor. No other innovations were attempted.

The measures taken had ignored the feelings of the nation, and thus failed. Clearly the resistance of the communal councils cannot be explained by their hostility toward the Flemish language. Among its members, several were notorious *flamingants*. On January 9, 1918, the city of Brussels declared itself ready to communicate in Flemish with local or provincial authorities which, "outside of Brabant," expressed a desire to use that language in their communications with it. It took the opportunity to state once more that it condemned the administrative separation. The decision was based on Article 23 of the Constitution and on respect for Belgium's unity and indivisibility, for the sake of

---

[1] Regarding the fears of the German authorities about this and the measures taken by it to face them, see *Bulletin des Archives de la Guerre*, t II, p 49 and following.

which it was important for Brussels, "as a bilingual city and capital of the kingdom, to consider the wishes expressed by Flemish-speaking Belgians."

The Germans themselves, in daily life, did not take any more notice of the linguistic regime imposed by the military than did the Belgians. The German companies that printed announcements in the *Verordnungsblatt*, whose official languages for Flanders were supposed to be German and Flemish, used only French. The posters for German firms that had branches in Brussels were also in French. In June 1917, as a result of steps taken by the union of Rhineland and Westphalian exporting firms, French-language communications with the *Étapes* zone had to be permitted!

What was responsible for the resistance to the administrative separation was that its obvious objective was to destroy national unity. The issue was not just about languages; it went well beyond that. In July 1917, the Antwerp local council justified its attitude this way: "While Antwerp proudly considers itself to be the city with the strongest Flemish sentiment in the country, it is no less proud of being, as a port and artistic center, one of Belgium's most powerful entities, and whose patriotism is exceeded by no other town. This patriotism regards the entire country and all of its citizens, Flemish and Walloon alike, with the same cordial affection. We know our people and have a right to speak in its name, and we can guarantee that our feelings are shared by most of our fellow citizens. Blind are those who do not see that a people has concerns other than the language question, however significant it may be."

It has been essential to dwell in some detail on the way the administrative separation was regarded, because nothing characterizes the Belgian reaction in the face of occupation more clearly. Strictly speaking, it was not a political opposition, but rather a social and national reaction which came from deep within the people. It was expressed through the only organizations that were still able to speak in its name: the local authorities. It was a direct consequence of the country's history. All the old instincts which, despite the language diversity, had united the people into a community attached equally to its autonomy, to its freedoms, and to the institutions it had created for itself, rebelled against foreign pressure. The nation's behavior was but a revival of what prompted it to rise against Spain in the 16th century, against Austria in the 18th century, and against the Netherlands in 1830. In opposing Germany, it called upon its Constitution as it had once called upon its historic privileges against its sovereigns. Flemish and French speakers alike agreed that they needed to protect their right to decide what regime they wished to live under, as had Catholics and Protestants under Philip II, statists and democrats under Joseph II, and clerics and liberals under William I.

This is what German officials did not understand. They were dumbfounded that their gifts were refused simply because they were imposed. The resistance seemed futile to them, and they stubbornly attributed it to deep-rooted Francophilia or to Walloonism opposing Germanism. They did not see that by meddling with the citizens' freedom, "they were touching," as Morillon said of the Duke of Alba in the 16th century, "the skin to which the fingernails are attached." They were astonished that for a reason that seemed nothing more than one of amour-propre, so many comfortable middle-class citizens were willing to be deported to camps, or jailed. Could it be that despite racial theory, there was such a thing as a Belgian people? A few were starting to realize this. For the nation to remain resilient after three years of occupation and amid general distress and growing pressure had to be the result of something other than childish vanity. Clearly, the idea that the population was terrified of the government in Le Havre, as official opinion had it, was too obviously impossible to be believed. Besides, the Belgian government was particularly accommodating. Did it not advise officials to remain in their positions? If they were so anxious to obey it, then why were those living under German rule not heeding its advice?

Why were the people being more Catholic than the pope, more Belgian than Belgian ministers? And above all, why were they not agreeing to the innovations proposed by the German authorities? Was something more than a simple language question at stake here? Was the notion of the oppression of the Flemish by the Walloons perhaps only a convenient myth?

A few German officials thought so and said so. Sounding out of tune in the middle of allegations from both the official and unofficial press regarding Belgium's artificial nature, a few papers recognized that neither of the two Belgian peoples dominated the other and that there was absolutely no animosity between them. At the end of 1917, Karl Kautsky rejected the doctrine that sanctioned the claims of a people in the name of its language and he pointed to the claims made for the affinity of the various ethnicities within the Empire. He rejected any correlation of the Flemish question with the Czech question, noted the antiquity of the peaceful penetration of French into Flanders, and of Belgium's unity despite the two languages, the result of common interests, institutions, customs, and destinies. Similarly, Adolf Grabowsky recognized that from a social standpoint Flemish and Walloons were alike: they shared the same individualism, the same love of liberty.[1]

These observations are undoubtedly explained by the vote of the Reichstag in July 1917 in favor of peace without annexations. This naturally encouraged Belgian resistance. It was made unshakable by the publication in early 1918 of President Wilson's "Fourteen Points," in which the complete restoration of Belgium's independence was explicitly demanded. The last months of the occupation, however, were about to put the nation through the harshest trials it would have to endure.

---

1 Karl Kautsky (1854–1938) was the leading Marxist theoretician after the death of Engels. He urged the SPD Reichstag members to abstain from voting for war credits in August 1914, then broke with the party ten months later in opposition to the government's annexationist aims. He substantiated these and German war guilt in a 4-volume collection of official documents he edited after the war. Adolf Grabowski (1880–1969) was a prominent German political scientist, and also helped found an opposition party in 1917.

CHAPTER IX

Activism

§ I. — Until the "*cès de justice*" (February 7–10, 1918)

In November 1917, Governor General Ludwig von Falkenhausen convened in Brussels a commission of German specialists charged with determining the status to be given to the autonomous administration of Flanders and Wallonia, following their separation (*Kommission zum Ausbau der Selbstverwaltung in den flämischen und wallonischen Landestheilen*). It is unnecessary to discuss its work, which was intended to create a Belgium that would be consistent with Germany's interests, in the event that the latter would emerge victorious. The war's vicissitudes forced the commission to turn to simple projects. These are of interest only to the extent that they allow a better understanding of the direction in which the occupying power was heading during the last year of its existence. Although members of the commission only ever expressed their personal opinions, they were in complete agreement about the essential issues, and the body did have a direct influence on the conduct of the Governor General, and also on the military authorities whose instrument he was.

It must be noted, indeed, that from General von Bissing to General von Falkenhausen, the position of Governor General for Belgium effectively, if not legally, was drastically transformed. Nothing was left of von Bissing's authority. He had reported directly to the Emperor. General von Falkenhausen was simply an official of the Reich, subordinate to the Chancellor, and even much more so to the German High Command, which gradually gained influence over German policy as the war progressed. This stranglehold by the military authorities over the Governor, against which von Bissing had fought for as long as he could, was exerted over his successor without any resistance on his part. His function was reduced to administering Belgium strictly according to Germany's war goals. The "conservative policy" was abandoned; the new policy was simply to prepare for the subordination of Belgium to Germany that would be imposed by the peace treaty.

It would of course be impossible simply to erase Belgium from the European map. Such a grave act could not be undertaken unilaterally. It could only come out of negotiations that would confer on it international recognition. Perhaps the country would be allowed to continue to exist. But in this case, it must only retain a semblance of existence, and its weakness must prevent it from ever emerging from the status reserved for it, that of a protectorate. The administrative separation was the first blow at Belgium's foundation. But its effectiveness depended on the way in which it was applied. If it only implemented dual public services, it would not lead to the destruction of Belgium. Von Bissing does not seem to have considered anything other than stipulating that government institutions in each region use exclusively the language of that region. The *Commission zum Ausbau der Selbstverwaltung* went much further. In accordance with the wishes of Chancellor Michaelis, it prepared measures to provide full autonomy to both parts of the country. Each was to become a distinct state within the Belgian state, which would then be reduced to a general administration.

Actually, of the two regions, only Flanders interested Germany. It was the "aspirations of the Flemish nation" that the Reich aimed to satisfy. Wallonia wished for nothing other than Belgium's independence; there was no pretext to intervene. But it was impossible not to grant it the privilege of autonomy which Flanders received. In fact, administrative separation was intended only to destroy Belgium. Wallonia was but a residue, without any value to Germany except economically.[1]

To carry out its plans, Germany found a collaborator in the *Raad van Vlaanderen*. Chancellor Theobald Bethmann Hollweg officially recognized the organization as the representative of the Flemish people. Of course, everyone was well aware that the vast majority of the people regarded the members of the Council as nothing but a handful of traitors. The *Commission zum Ausbau der Selbstverwaltung* recognized that "the Flemish movement would be annihilated in any election." But it was none the less essential to work with the activists, since their support could be used to justify Germany's anti-Belgian policies. The government turned to the *Raad* as an unofficial advisor in legislative matters. In January 1918, a decree allowed it to choose eleven of its own members to form a permanent commission, with the approval of the Governor General.[2] However, this committee could act only at the request of latter. It was necessary to keep up the appearance that these measures had the support of Flemish public opinion. Thus, on December 22, 1917, the *Raad* unanimously voted on complete autonomy for Flanders. It then decided to "end the mandate it had received from the Flemish National Congress" on the previous February 4 and to hold a new election which would let the people express their wishes regarding the separation of Belgium. The voters would be selecting provincial councilors along with members of the new *Raad*.

As a result, a meeting summoned the previous day gathered in Brussels on January 20, 1918 in the Alhambra room. It comprised

---

[1] Even from a linguistic standpoint, the balance was not even between both regions. In Flanders, the use of French was banned; however in Wallonia Flemish was allowed in relations between the administration and the citizens, J. Pirenne and M. Vauthier, previously cited work, p 109.

[2] They were named on January 5. Earlier, an *Oberkommission* made up of the office for the Council of Flanders and high-ranking German officials had fulfilled their duties.

about 3,000 activists who elected at once 22 deputies for the *Raad*, as well as 52 provincial councilors for the Brussels district, which included 220,000 voters and nearly a million inhabitants. Since a previous meeting on November 11 had been booed, people mostly refrained from celebrating the event in public demonstrations. But they were less careful in Antwerp. The German authorities had requested the stock exchange facilities for the election. Since the College of *Échevins* had refused, they were quick to requisition it "for German public utility purposes." The meeting took place on Sunday, February 3. It was set to end with a large procession. When this emerged under protection from troops, it was met with resounding boos; it was cut off in several places; the demonstrators' flags were ripped, their musical instruments torn away; they were showered with insults, hit, spat on, and the crowd's behavior became so threatening that they had to find refuge in hotels around the train station from which they escaped in small groups during the afternoon.

This conduct, from a city which deservedly bragged about being the most Flemish in the country, could not leave any doubt regarding the disapproval the activists elicited. They were met with the same indignation everywhere. In the *Étapes* zone, the military was able to prevent popular anger from manifesting itself. In Ghent, a ceremony that was mostly remarkable by the small number of its participants took place in front of the statue of Jacob van Artevelde.[1] Everywhere else, in Mechelen, Tienen, Leuven, Lokeren, activist demonstrations strikingly reproduced those which the Jacobins and the sans-culotte had staged under the protection of the conqueror's bayonets, during the country's conquest by the French in 1794. The composition of the new *Raad* naturally reflected the legitimacy of the elections that had conferred office on its members. Almost all were activist officials

---

1 *Jacob van Artesveld (1290–1345), a wealthy cloth merchant in Ghent, ruled the city the last eight years of his life. He expelled the Count of Flanders, who had sided with the French, and allied Ghent with the English at the start of the Hundred Years War.*

hired by Germany, or professors from the new University of Ghent.

Everywhere, however, protests arose. On January 28, 1918, the Ghent Communal Council "considered," it said, "that the actions of the committee named Council of Flanders are all the more shameful in so far as are carried out while the country is suffering from the yoke of foreign occupation and any free public demonstration of the population's true feelings is made impossible." "It is important," the Communal Council said, "to enlighten the German Empire regarding the true feelings of the Ghent population," and these were that "the Council of Flanders had no legal or de facto authority, and its actions betrayed the nation's most sacred interests."

The Leuven Communal Council condemned "the crime against truth that is being committed in Belgium." Those of Antwerp and Brussels addressed the German Chancellor in the same spirit. The Brussels College of *Échevins* spoke with the neutral ministers residing in the capital. The University of Brussels, the Ghent Court of Appeals, and the Flemish deputies who remained in the country joined the movement. Cardinal Mercier called the activists "a handful of traitors without a mandate." A manifesto signed by nearly 200 Flemish association presidents and managers, written by Louis Franck, one of the promoters of the bill submitted to the Belgian Chambers proposing the creation of a Flemish university, supported the protests and provided unimpeachable confirmation of the extent of the indignation. Finally, on February 11, the Brussels Communal Council met to receive delegations of each of the capital's associations, which came to personally hand the burgomaster protest letters they entrusted him to pass along in their name to the Chancellor of the Empire.

Opponents were too exasperated to fear punishment. They didn't have to wait long. On March 5, Franck and another deputy from Antwerp were deported to Germany under the pretense of having refused to provide the occupying authorities with the necessary personnel to operate the port's elevators. On the 19th, Brussels was fined 2 million marks for having participated in a "political demonstration."

The fermentation of the public spirit had to end in an explosion. On January 31, 91 deputies and senators, in an address handed to the presidents and councilors of the Brussels Court of Appeals, denounced "the acts of a group of men who, using the title of Council of Flanders, decided in a plenary assembly on December 22, 1917 on complete autonomy for Flanders, and were thus guilty of an assault with the objective of either destroying or changing the form of the government,…of the crime of usurping public functions, of the wicked and public attack against the King's Constitutional authority, and the Chambers' rights and authority…" On February 7, as a result of this complaint, the Court ordered the Attorney General to file suit against "any perpetrator, co-perpetrator, and accomplices" of the *Raad* "for endangering the state's safety." The following morning, the president of the Council of Flanders and one of the individuals who had spoken at the Alhambra meeting were arrested at their homes.[1]

The action of the Appeals Court was based on articles 104, 109, and 110 of the penal code, articles 2 and 3 of the July 20, 1831 decree, and the first article of the law of March 25, 1891, all laws that had formally been left in place by the Germans. It was also justified by the Constitutional principle of the equality of Belgians before the law, which did not allow perpetrators of crimes as severe as those that had been denounced to go unpunished. By not acting, the Court would have become their accomplice. But by acting, it struck a blow at the occupier's policy. A conflict was inevitable, and took place immediately. The examining magistrate had barely begun interrogating the accused when a German official arrived. He had been ordered by the Governor

---

1 P. L. Tack and August Borms

General to seize the dossier and free the defendants. Armed soldiers occupied the antechamber. All the magistrates could do was to protest and give in.

It was the first time since the country's invasion that the judicial power was violated. Until then, the German authorities had limited themselves to diminishing its authority in favor of military courts. They had respected the independence that had been guaranteed to the magistracy from the very beginning of the occupation. A letter from General von Bissing to the Supreme Court on March 22, 1916 had solemnly renewed the assurance. This time, not only was a legal procedure being impeded by violence, but judges were being punished who were guilty only of having fulfilled their duty. On February 9, the First President of the Court of Appeals and three Chamber presidents were arrested and then deported to a prison camp in Germany.[1] The Court counselors received orders to vacate their seats, having been associated with a political demonstration and having thus violated "the conditions under which Belgian officials could be allowed by the German administration to fulfill their functions." German policy was being pursued to its logical conclusion: justice was subordinated to politics. By siding with the enemies of the Belgian state, the occupier crushed the last remnants of autonomy which it had until then done its best to respect. But since it recognized the Council of Flanders as representing the Flemish people, how could it have tolerated criminal charges being filed against it? The Governor's measures had been suggested to him by the Council "to ensure the free expression of the popular will of Flanders." The occupation had come a full circle: it was once again, as it had been in the beginning, simply a regime of force.

Perhaps the Governor General believed that the example he had just made would suffice to ensure obedience from the magistrates. However, this example didn't frighten them any more than

---

[1] Only one was freed, due to his old age and his poor health.

the deportation of Adolphe Max had frightened the burgomasters.

The gravity of the circumstances and the character of the victims only made the coup more sensational.

On February 11, the Supreme Court, the highest judicial authority in the country, joined the resistance. Deeming, as did the Attorney General, that "words were no longer sufficient and action was needed," and after declaring that the violence used by the occupying government "constituted the negation of the freedom and independence of the judiciary," it decided, without surrendering its duties, to adjourn hearings. The following day, the Magistrates' Court adopted the same position. The Public Prosecutor's department followed suit, with all its personnel and its clerks. On February 13, the Commercial Court also ceased operations. The Bar joined in without hesitation. A courts strike meant a lawyers strike. Even the volunteer "Palace Guards," filling in for policemen who had left to join the army, suspended their work.

On February 21, General von Falkenhausen wrote a letter to the Court of Appeals in which, while he claimed to also be a supporter of judicial independence, observed "that it is unreasonable, in an occupied country, for the courts who deliver judgments under the authority of the occupying power to prosecute as crimes actions directed against authorities who have been stripped of power and against whom the occupying state is at war." At the same time, the Dutch newspapers published a note from the government in Le Havre which "recognizes the courageous attitude adopted by the judicial authorities, who did not hesitate to call for the application of the laws against the wicked citizens who were guilty, in complicity with the enemy, of pursuing the criminal scheme of dismembering the country." The Court of Appeals replied on February 25, opposing the Governor's argument with that of the separation of powers, from which derives the independence of the judiciary from the political power. The Court of Appeals denied that its actions made it guilty of hostility against the occupier.

The provinces followed the example of the Brussels judicial authorities. The president in Mons, the court members in Arlon, and the president of the Bar in Ghent, were all arrested or deported. However, the situation worried the Governor. He sought, through the Marquis of Villalobar, to arrange a deal. On March 9 and April 2, he offered to free the presidents if the courts resumed operations. But the court demanded a formal acknowledgement of its rights, as well as guarantees. An agreement could not be reached.

Thus the Belgian judicial authorities renewed the old national tradition of the *"cès de justice,"*[1] so often used when its privileges were violated. It opposed collaboration with the occupier. It acted in agreement with the spirit of the *Joyeuse Entrée*[2]. It did not yield to force; it crossed its arms just as did the deported.

But what would come of the suspension of justice in a country where misery led to crimes? While the population agreed with the judicial powers, it worried about public safety. Rumors grew that criminals who were arrested by the police would be released, given the lack of judges. And they would have been, indeed, if prosecutors had not resorted to a subterfuge in the interest of public safety: they took it upon themselves to deliver orders imprisoning arrested individuals and keeping in jail those against whom sufficiently serious charges were being pressed. If judgments had to cease, then those who ought to been judged would temporarily be rendered harmless.

Due to the judicial strike, the Governor General had to replace the Belgian judicial powers with a German substitute.[3] In April, he established German courts made up of penal and civil branches. Above them, a *Kaiserliches Obergericht* served as

---

[1] *The cessation or suspension of justice. A boycott by the bench in response to the abrogation of its authority, as in 1917.*
[2] This is the name of the old 1356 Brabant constitution which remained in effect until the end of the 18th century.
[3] J. Pirenne and M. Vauthier, previously cited work, p 113 and following.

an appeals court in Brussels. The proceedings of these successors were conducted in German, and the lawyers were replaced by "justice commissioners." If necessary, interpreters were called in. Belgians only used these as criminal courts. The civil jurisdiction was restricted to Germans and citizen of Germany's allies and neutral nations. Thus, the Belgian resistance resulted in the annihilation of the national judicial system. It forced the occupier to go much further than it would have wanted to. Its hopes to use Belgian institutions while controlling them through violence had been thwarted. It is also interesting to note that it was forced to violate the administrative separation that it insisted on forcing on the nation. The Brussels *Obergericht* served Wallonia as well as Flanders.

And so the administrative situation reached the same point as the economy. The long duration of the war and the desire to win it had eliminated all scruples. Belgium was now nothing more than a dominated and exploited territory. Its legal life turned out to be as impossible to preserve as its economic life.

And what was true of justice was true as well for municipal authorities. Here, also, a dictatorship was imposed when they did not respond to threats. In Ghent, the College of *Échevins* was deposed. The burgomaster and two *échevins* were deported. The former was replaced by a German, and the Communal Council was replaced by an activist council.

§ II. — Activism in Action

The January 1918 decree, which associated the *Raad van Vlaanderen* with the occupier's authority, can only be considered as a measure forced upon the Governor General by the German High Command. The collaboration of a non-German organization with the German civil administration would give rise to too many complications and difficulties for its chief to have wished for it. If the High Command did not recognize this, it was probably because it was deluded by the similarity of the activists' views to its own, and because it immensely overestimated the importance of this insignificant group. The generals believed or pretended to believe that not only did the activists represent the Flemish people's aspirations, but also that the *flamingants* were as convinced as they were of Flemish and German racial identity, just as persuaded of the virtues of *Deutschtum*, just as enthusiastic about *Kultur*, just as certain of Germany's providential role, and of the legitimacy of the hegemony it claimed over Europe. Moreover, the generals still viewed the Flemish question as exactly like the Polish or Czech questions. They assumed there had to be a deep-rooted national hatred between Flemish and Walloons, and that the former viewed the latter as foreign oppressors. They didn't wish to or were unable to notice that while there were differences between them, there was no hostility, and that the Flemish "*fransquillons*," unlike the Germans of Posen or Prague, were not the descendants of a conquering or oppressing people, but that their origin and history was much the same as that of their compatriots. If they spoke a different language, it was because, over the centuries, their close proximity with France, the prestige of its civilization, and the influence of its economy had Frenchified them, while they never ceased to belong to the Flemish nation.

No doubt the language of a few activists was responsible for these illusions. Some of activists, whether out of exasperation at the disapproval they met with or out of stupidity or servility, seemed to confuse their cause with Germany's and were ready to follow directions from Berlin. But overall, the men in the *Raad van Vlaanderen* wanted autonomy for Flanders above all else. They were enemies of the Belgian state more than they were allies of Germany.

Moreover, they did not all have the same goals. Some were content with dreaming of a sort of federalism, which would have left Belgium in a similar situation to that of Switzerland. Others, wanting to keep the monarchy and the dynasty, would have been satisfied with a simple administrative separation. They were fighting against the state's Constitution rather than against its very existence. They yearned for a reform that would liberate Flanders from the Belgian Parliament with regard to internal administration, and which would allow them to put an end to the country's traditional bilingualism, convinced as they were of the all-powerful ability of a national language to elevate a people they declared to have been bastardized.

The supporters of a completely independent Flemish state were relatively few. But at this time, these extremists were bound to prevail. Having irreversibly broken with the Le Havre government, they had to make common cause with Germany. Whether they liked it or not, the radicalism of their attitude put them at its mercy and, through a contradiction they would not admit to, these promoters of Flemish independence could only succeed by abandoning Flanders to the designs of Berlin. In order to deceive themselves to such a degree, they needed as much political inexperience as they did fanaticism. If victorious, Germany would obviously dictate their laws; if defeated, it would abandon them to its conquerors. Within the great tragedy that was being played out, they were nothing more than unknowing accomplices.

Germany used them, while despising them. It asked only that they help it destroy Belgium, reserving for itself alone the decisions regarding its fate once peace came. In the press, the German High Command presented them to the world as the voice of oppressed Flanders. It did not mention that these liberators were only speaking out thanks to the silence imposed on their opponents.

As mentioned, since January 1918, the *Raad van Vlaanderen* communicated with the German civil administration through authorized plenipotentiaries (*Gevolmagtigden*) chosen by it with approval from the Governor General. This body consisted of a president, a secretary-general, and representatives for Foreign Affairs, Interior, Agriculture and Public Works, Sciences and Art,

Justice, Finances, Industry and Work, National Defense, and Post and Telegraph.

And so it could be thought of as a council of ministers. But it had only a consultative role. It did not have any authority. While members could deliberate without any German intervention, the official reports for their sessions had to be sent to the Governor General, who could thus constantly monitor them. Their situation vis-à-vis the *Raad van Vlaanderen* was a little like that of the members of a parliamentary government toward the parliament. But this situation was doubly false. In the first place, the *Raad*, lacking any legal authority, just as the *Gevolmagtigden* did, had no way of imposing a course of action on them. Thus they found themselves almost continuously in conflict with the plenipotentiaries. But most of all, Germany's constant interference in their business, or more accurately the guardianship exerted by Germany over them, removed the national character without which there can be no parliamentary regime. These supposed authorized representatives of Flanders in fact were and could only be Germany's pawns.

They certainly felt this themselves, and sometimes would observe it with bitterness. In the official reports of their sessions, one finds protests, more than once, however timid, against the powerlessness they had been reduced to. The most candid of them went so far as to confess that Germany's goodwill toward them was not a result of any interest in Flanders, but simply because of the assistance they provided in fulfilling its war goals.

But while Germany had a tight grip on them, they still occasionally caused it some serious difficulties. Having publicly recognized them as the spokesmen of the Flemish people, Germany could not treat them too openly as a *quantité negligible* without disavowing itself. It had to discuss policies with them and at the very least feign to take them seriously. Had they not been so self-servingly malleable, the activists might have been in a very strong position. But they never dared to speak loudly and clearly, nor to confront the Governor General in a conflict in which he would probably have had to have given way to avoid the consequences of a break-up. They had neither the intelligence nor the courage to escape the situation they had accepted, and which provided them, in the midst of their compatriots' misery and servitude, with the satisfactions of money and influence.

It goes without saying that the incidents from the last year of the war had a decisive effect on both their conduct and that of the German government. Declaring Flanders autonomous was obligatory. But when and how? At first, the delegates sent by the chief of the civil administration showed a very understandable embarrassment. The Brest-Litovsk deliberations had just started and Germany had invited its enemies to take part in them. It could be dangerous, in these conditions, to go too far and become irreparably compromised vis-à-vis Belgium's allies. Courage returned when, on January 17, Richard von Kuhlmann reported in Brussels that since the delegates from the Entente never arrived, our "hands are free." But the chief of the Flanders civil administration, Dr. Schaibel, immediately intervened to avoid any excessive zeal that might compromise the government. He advised Berlin to limit itself to a declaration of autonomy, which would allow it to go further in the future, while permitting the Chancellor to claim, if necessary, that Belgium could still be restored.

Indeed, on February 17, a note was published stating that Flanders' independence did not necessarily mean that the Belgian state would disappear. A few days later, the delegates managed to agree on an ambiguous text claiming Flemish autonomy, either outside of Belgium or in a reformed Belgium (*vernieuwd België*). However, within the *Raad*, an agreement could not be reached between the moderates or unionists and the young Flemish (*Jong Vlaanderen*) who wanted nothing to do with any restoration of the past.

Chancellor von Hertling's February 25 speech, in which he declared that Germany had no plans to preserve Belgium, further complicated things. How to reconcile the *Raad*'s aspirations with Berlin's political fluctuations?[1] A thorny and delicate task, which obviously troubled the Brussels government. The *Verwaltungschef* proposed, to gain time, to combine activism with a peace movement and to try to rally socialists to it. On March 7, the Governor General affirmed on his side that it was impossible to specify what would become of Belgium, but that in any case Germany would not allow it to return to its pre-war status. In the meantime, and with unconscious irony, he asked the *Raad* to reconcile itself with the majority opinion in Flanders. And thus the *Raad* was deprived of its freedom to speak about Flanders without Germany's permission. Its president, who had dared mention (on March 28) that the word Belgium should disappear, was brutally called to order. It was intolerable that Flemings should present the Reich with a fait accompli. If they were going to indulge in such outbursts, the *Raad* would disappear. Feelings in Berlin, where a delegate was sent, were no more encouraging. Except for Pan-Germanists, public opinion left no hope for much support. Ertzberger[2] went so far as to say that Germany would have to reconcile itself to Belgium's continued existence. Even in Brussels, within the civil administration, there were worrying signs of bad faith. The Governor General refused to intervene with the Marquis of Villalobar when the minister for Spain ordered a delegation of activists out of his hotel and accused them of treason. In Ghent, German officers at an activist gathering refused to stand up during a performance of the *Willelmus van Nassau*.[3]

Thankfully, the German spring offensive on the French front opened up happier prospects. The proclamation of autonomy finally seemed imminent. On June 20, on the eve of the push

---

1 *Changes in the German attitude toward the Council were determined partly by secret negotiations for an armistice with King Albert, which resumed in early 1918.*
2 *Matthias Erzberger (1875–1921), a prominent Catholic Centre Party deputy, had as early as July 1917 proposed that Germany accept a peace without annexations.*
3 *The* Wilhelmus van Nassouwe *was then the unofficial Dutch national anthem.*

in the Champagne area, the *Raad* issued a manifesto proclaiming Germany's inevitable victory, condemning the Belgian government as the enemy of Flanders, and announcing the certain emancipation of the latter. The Governor General offered comforting assurances. However, the French front did not give way and the activists, like the troops, had to retreat. In July, Chancellor Hertling, who was going through Brussels, delivered only vague promises. His point of view, he said, regarding the Flemish question, remained the same as that of his predecessors. And so he continued the ambiguous policy. This was not a good omen. Nor were reports in the Berlin papers. In the Reichstag, a socialist deputy spoke of the "despicable conspiracy that is the *Raad van Vlaanderen*." In August, General Keim, although a notorious Pan-Germanist and annexationist, described the activists as a general staff without troops. Then, on September 12, Vice-Chancellor von Payer said that the Flemish question would be resolved by Belgian politicians. This was the official announcement of Germany's desertion of activism. With a military catastrophe now inevitable, it hastily abandoned its embarrassing ally.

The debacle for the *Raad* had begun in August. A member noted that the reaction against its policy was "taking giant leaps," and another added: "The Germans are mocking us." A few activists discussed sending a protest letter to the Governor General, reproaching him of having violated his commitments, in short to "show our teeth." Others proposed abandoning Germany and turning to England. But the days of the pathetic assembly were numbered. On October 5, the new Chancellor, Prince Max of Baden,[1] officially admitted the fiasco that was the Flemish policy had been foisted upon the government by the German High

---

1 With the collapse of the Western Front at the end of September, Prince Max (1867–1929) replaced von Hertling, the second of Bethmann Hollweg's successors. His was the first true parliamentary government in Germany, as it included members of the largest parties, including the SPD. He persuaded the Kaiser to demand Ludendorff's resignation, then unilaterally announced Wilhelm's abdication, before being forced out himself by the fear of a socialist revolution.

Command. Now it was crumbling, along with the Reich's military power. The peace treaty would have to restore Belgium's rights and re-establish its independence and integrity. The activists had placed a bet on Germany's victory and lost. Their newspapers admitted it, contenting themselves with begging Germany not to completely forget, during peace negotiations, the hopes it had awoken.

From September 26, a new organization had replaced the rickety alliance instituted in January. There were no longer any *Gevolmagtigden*. In their place, a commission of chargés d'affaires was instituted (*Zaakgelastigden*), named by the Governor General and answering to him only. Thus collapsed the façade of autonomy that had until then concealed Germany's stranglehold on activism. The *Zaakgelastigden* were considered "officials for the German army!"

The *Raad von Vlaanderen*, left to its own devices, still held a few sessions. It clung to the hope that Germany would at least not evacuate Belgium before peace. It even believed it could prepare for the latter. But on October 14, the victorious assault was launched by the Allies. Belgian troops entered West Flanders and the following day the *Raad* met for the last time. Its members, who had declared a few days before that they would die at their posts, could now think of nothing but flight. Starting on the 26th, equipped with money and passports, they made their way to Germany, one after another.[1] An address on the 31st was their last testament. It was full of hopes for autonomy and love of country.[2]

The idea of using the Flemish movement on behalf of Germany's war goals appears as a formidable psychological

---

1 Not all fled. The Catholic conservative August Borms, Minister of Defense, remained and was sentenced to death, along with 38 others. Fifteen activists received life in prison and 103 were sentenced to over ten years, including professors who lectured in Dutch at Ghent University, even if they were not involved in activist politics. Most who did flee went to the Netherlands, not Germany.

2 The chargés d'affaires would have wanted to settle in The Hague and seek relations with the "passivists." The German government did not allow them to. It is interesting to note, however, that a few days before leaving Brussels, the Governor General withdrew 10 million francs from the Belgian Ministry's funds, to be deposited in the Berlin *Reichsbank* in order to continue the *Flamenpolitik* after the war.

mistake. Its failure was certain in advance. The vast majority of Flemish nationalists were just as loyal to their country as were their opponents. They intended to have their grievances resolved in the Belgian state and by the Belgian state. They regarded with horror any collaboration with the enemy. Overtures from Governor von Bissing, who at first had hoped to rally them to his cause by strictly applying linguistic laws, were met with nothing but hostile silence. They had protested against the opening of the Germano-Flemish Ghent University. The administrative separation outraged them. And in the end, they had regarded the activists' behavior as treasonous.

The ground had to collapse under the latter's feet. Reduced to an insignificant faction in foreign pay, they persisted with growing zeal to impose on the masses who hated them the dictatorship that Germany wished to see them organize. For this, they could count on the Reich's continued support. It was eager to help them establish their prestige and influence. It used them to justify the administrative separation and to convince neutrals of their interest in the Flemish of Belgium. It was from the ranks of the activists that all of the higher officials were selected after of the administrative separation, and these nominations were almost always proposed by the *Gevolmagtigden*. In short, the activists behaved during the German occupation exactly as did the Jacobins after the annexation of Belgium to France in 1794. They showed the same hunger for domination, the same presumptuousness, the same radicalism, and the same fury in denouncing their enemies. Although a century apart, the activists regarded the "*fransquillons*" and patriots much as the Jacobins regarded the aristocracy.

Especially in the *Étapes* zone, the slightest sign of disapproval shown toward them was sufficient for the culprit to be deported. Enjoying all rights of free speech, of assembly, and of propaganda which were denied their compatriots, they used them to destroy and terrorize their enemies. On January 31, 1918, they demanded the Ghent Communal Council be shut down; on March 21, they asked the same for that of Brussels. In February, they proposed transporting to Germany a few people "who could be used as hostages to discourage possible attacks against activists." If it had been up to them, after the Brussels Court of Appeals intervened against the *Raad van Vlaanderen*, all of its members would have been deported. Their propaganda against Cardinal Mercier was particularly inflamed, though ineffectual.

In revenge, they used their influence to secure for individuals they favored all kinds of appointments and advantages. In August 1918, they proudly got the Governor to pardon five individuals who had been sentenced to death.

They managed to make July 11, anniversary of the Battle of Kortijk, into the national holiday. Thanks to the kindness of German troops, they were put in touch with the defeatist party (Frontparty), which was trying to encourage defections from the Belgian Army.[1] On May 10, 1918, two deserters were solemnly welcomed by them in a meeting attended by the *Verwaltungschef*, and which one of them pompously recognized as a historical event. In the entire Flemish region of the country, their meetings and their brochures constantly challenged public opinion. In November 1917, they boasted about having distributed 270,000 flyers and leaflets, and many more were issued during the next year.

The disapproval the group met with is all the more significant in so far as supporting activism was so profitable. It is incredible that in the midst of general misery, the number of adherents to such a clearly advantageous group remained so insignificant.[2] Among them were only the enemy's henchmen and war profiteers. They

---

[1] The Front Party was formed by Flemish soldiers unhappy about their treatment by the largely Walloon officer corps. Study groups and books were banned, they were discriminated against in the assignment of duties (orders were, of course, given only in French, and desk jobs assigned only to French speakers), etc. The frontline infantry was 70–80% Flemish. A catalyst was the refusal of the Le Havre government to promise that the University of Ghent would offer classes in Dutch after the war. Flemish soldiers, however, were as grateful as their Walloon compatriots that King Albert refused to allow the Belgium Army to participate in any of the Allied offenses until September 1918.

[2] Council members estimated the number of their supporters at only 15,000.

were well aware of the antipathy and the contempt they aroused. But how could they avoid it without breaking with Germany? The deportation of workers was, as *Raad* members conceded, a terrible blow to their "prestige." Among themselves, behind closed doors, they lamented such a cruel measure, so opposed to the *Duitsch Vlaamsche politiek*, and so fatal to their movement's progress. And yet, even though the military authorities were driving 14-year old boys and 60-year old men to the battlefront, all the while treating them "like livestock" (*als vee*), they never dared to speak up. They continuously felt the stick under which they agreed to bow. The *Zivilverwaltung* interfered in their business at every turn and without apologies. It prevented them from debating what they wanted, read their letters, and forbade them to control the *Gevolmagtigden*.

Clearly, Germany only supported them for its own sake. It blamed them for not managing to overcome public opinion despite the money it was spending on them. And the longer the war went on, the less Germany itself felt favorably inclined toward the activists. After the Reichstag came out in favor of peace without annexations or compensations, Berlin socialists no longer disguised their dislike for them.

Things might have been different if the activists had been a tight-knit and like-minded group. But internal disagreement further weakened it. Not only, as mentioned, were the *Raad* and its *Gevolmagtigden* bitter enemies, constantly bickering and insulting each other, but there were also within the *Raad* itself rivalries between individuals, and bitter opposition between factions. Most members had conservative beliefs, either out of personal conviction or to flatter the German "Excellencies" with whom they worked. On May 14, they proposed that burgomasters be selected from among the nobility. At University of Ghent, the almanac published by students sought to awaken in them a sense of social hierarchy by urging them to use titles reserved for ministers, high officials, and aristocrats. But with time, radical and demagogic tendencies surfaced among the party's younger members. As early as February 1918, many of the propagandists claimed to be revolutionaries. Others declared that the state of Flanders would be built on a democratic foundation. Manifestos demanded the confiscation of the Limburg mines. On February 20, a brochure distributed in Brussels demanded that the coal mines pay 40 million francs for the creation of Flemish schools. If they did not comply, "we will find the money in Avenue Louise[1] and in the banks." Unfortunately, the socialist party contemptuously rejected the offers made to it. The Ghent *Vooruit* refused to publish the program of a so-called *Vlaamsch Sociadistische Partij* which claimed to be organized in opposition to the *Raad van Vlaanderen*.

In such conditions, it was obvious that the movement was doomed. Besides, it suffered from a curious plethora of organizations acting side by side with no common discipline: the *Nationalistische Bond*, which sought to enroll youth by supporting musical bands, a women's league, lecture halls, and a commercial bank, as well as publishing the *Vlaamsche Smeder*. The *Bond* vowed to fight "any organization or persons who endanger the Flemish State and to take all the necessary measures to annihilate the influence of its enemies from within and without;" the *Vlaamsche Voorwachten*, which organized branches in Brussels, Antwerp, Leuven, and sixteen other towns, and whose goal was to prepare recruits for a Flemish army; the *Vrij Vlaanderen*, an association with social and Christian tendencies which claimed to be a substitute for the *Boerenbonden*; the *Vlaamsche Arbeiders Gemeenschap*, which sought to organize Flemish workers; the *Groeningerwacht*, founded in 1909, and the *Nationale Jong Vlaanderen Beweging*, which tried to incite desertion within the Belgian army and demanded the annexation of French Flanders

---

1 the broad thoroughfare in southern Brussels, something like the city's Champs Elysée, home to upscale restaurants and hotels, and corporate headquarters.

to the Flemish state. Despite their proliferation and their agitation, these groups were all much noisier than they were dangerous. Their membership was ridiculously small. In June 1918, the *Nationalistische Bond* only had 4,236 members, and the *Groeningerwacht* had 678.

In the midst of these disorganized efforts and of the recriminations they elicited, the *Raad van Vlaanderen* and the *Gevolmagtigden* tried to delude themselves regarding their importance by organizing the future Flemish State. They considered proposals for flags and stamps, debated the establishment of permanent representation in Berlin, the annexation of French Flanders, and the incorporation, at Wallonia's expense, of a strip of land to be used as a direct route between Flanders and Germany. They also organized a police force (*Rijkswacht*) which, for the sake of expediency, would wear the Belgian police uniform, "due to the respect the people have for it." There would also be a separate secret police (*Veiligheidsdienst*) in charge of monitoring citizen's behavior and their political convictions. Finally, a constitution drafted by a Leipzig University professor left only the facade of the original Belgian political system. From the freedoms borrowed from the list in the 1830 constitution, it took care to exclude the freedom of language[1] and it proclaimed freedom of education only if it were provided in the *landstaal* (national language).

All of this was nothing but a charade with which the Governor General contemptuously let the activists amuse themselves. The wisest of them noted this with bitterness. They were well aware that in the middle of a war and within an oppressed people, only the language policy of the Germans would be enforced. To enhance activist prestige, there would have to have been more substantial undertakings. The *Gevolmagtigden* would have wanted the German administration to give them the coal mines that had

---

1 *The vaunted "freedom of language" proclaimed in Article 23 of the 1830 Constitution in fact gave carte blanche to government officials, the judiciary, and the military to use exclusively French in Dutch-speaking regions.*

recently started production in the Campine. They campaigned in their papers to have them turned over to the Flemish state. But their interest clashed with those of the German industrialists who had immediately set their sights on this rich prey. A group of Rheno-Westphalian capitalists was in line to get the concession, or, to use the words of one of the *Gevolmagtigden*, to "steal them" from Flanders. Despite all their protesting, begging, and plotting, they never got anywhere. The adventurers who claimed to represent Flanders were simply not wealthy enough to prevail over the captains of industry across the Rhine.

A more promising idea was to try to take over from the *Comité National* the supplying of the Flemish part of Belgium. To be able to replace it would obviously divert for the benefit of the *Raad* the influence the *Comité* exercised and the gratitude it elicited from a people whose main concern was to get food on the table. The *Volksopbeuring* was founded in early 1918 with this goal in mind. It was an association in the form of a cooperative, whose capital came from contributions of 25 francs, and which included 70 branches, half of which were in the *Étapes* zone and the other half within the General Government. Understandably, the material benefits it promised helped immediately attract thousands of clients. For their part, the German authorities granted it the status of civil person (August 10, 1918), and assigned it a one-million franc grant, to be withdrawn from the Belgian budget. In the Netherlands, a *Nederlandsch Comiteit tot steun van Volksopbeuring* was founded, with the Archbishop of Utrecht as honorary chairman.

But it soon became clear that the *Volksopbeuring* was using charity only as a means of exerting pressure on behalf of activism. It demanded its members adhere in some form to the *Raad van Vlaanderen*, and it was soon discovered that it was involved in the initiative to organize desertion on the Belgian front lines. The neutral ministers protecting the *Comité* were obliged to intervene. They did so with great indignation. Enlightened by them, the Archbishop of Utrecht withdrew. The German administration, fearing that Britain would halt the shipments of grain, gave up on the fleeting idea of applying the administrative separation to the country's provisioning of food. It surrendered once more to the *Comité National.*

An attempt to divide the distribution of coal into two separate services, one for Flanders, the other for Wallonia, did not fare any better. Resistance from the coal mining industry proved fatal. Miners and owners did not want to become "an instrument of civil division and dissension," and threatened to strike if they were to be forced to join the new organization.

And so activism was just as powerless economically as politically. Belgian unity, which it was trying to end, triumphed over the joint efforts of both activism and Germany. The influence and prestige of the *Comité National* grew all the greater for the plots carried out against it. In November 1917, the civil administration had hoped to cause it to split by forcing it to use Flemish in its communications with Flemish provinces. Once again the measure had to be withdrawn, due to protests from the neutral ministers, and the Germans had to be content with a simple promise from the *Comité* to attach a translation to the official reports of weekly committee meetings that were sent to Flanders.

However, censorship enabled the activist press to attack and defame the organization. Activists furiously accused it of being nothing more than an association of schemers, profiteers, power-hungry politicians, and the enemies of Flanders, and begged the German authorities to clean out the stable. In September 1918, the neutral ministers felt compelled to speak out against "the campaign of malice and calumnies led by the activist party against the provisioning and assistance patronized by neutral governments, a campaign which enjoys, so we are told, support from some Imperial government officials." They complained that by tolerating and even encouraging attacks against the *Comité National,* the German censor was attacking its neutral nature.

"We are certain that our governments would be very upset to learn that the international humanitarian work they are protecting has turned into a political scapegoat in Belgium."

As a result, the *Gevolmagtigden* considered declaring that Spain and the Netherlands had ceased to be friendly powers.

But the chief of the *Politische Abteilung* promised the ministers to rein in the press. A note was sent to the papers chastising those who, "in the difficult circumstances the country is going through, systematically defame men who have selflessly devoted themselves for four years to relieving their fellow citizen, and who seek to destroy the trust they've earned and that people must place in them in order for them to successfully carry out the difficult task which they accepted purely out of a sense of social solidarity."

The *Comité National*, faced with its enemies' impotent rage, felt more than ever the importance of its mission. It was fully aware of its role when it declared itself as being, "currently, the only thing still linking the two halves of a country separated by criminal hands."

CHAPTER X
The Debacle

The administration imposed on Belgium by Germany was only a consequence of its victory. It was sure to collapse with defeat, and it did so precipitously. Of this great oeuvre, which had been so painstakingly and meticulously assembled, nothing was left. The occupier had proudly thought that the excellence of its organization would compel the Belgians to retain at least parts of it. But such was the hatred that had accumulated against Germany that it was demolished from its very foundations. The country's Constitution and administrative structure were restored in their entirety. There has perhaps never been such a long, systematic, and invasive occupation which ended up leaving so little behind. Materially, the country was ruined. Morally, it remained intact.

And to give credit to the German administration, it had no illusions as to the feelings it had provoked. In the final days of the war, it made no attempt to reach an understanding with the Belgians, to jointly decide the modalities of the evacuation, or to establish an interim regime. It left the country as one would leave a house one had squatted in. Its departure resembled a flight. While it communicated with the victors to facilitate the retreat of its troops, it ignored the national authorities who remained, that is the communal administrators.

As early as October 11, the German flags that had flown in front of public buildings since 1914 were removed. The government ordered those of its archives that could not be brought east to be burned, dismissed the Belgian officials who had served it, evacuated members of the Council of Flanders to Germany, closed the doors of its innumerable offices, and advised the University of Ghent, which had reopened on October 15, to end its classes.

On October 12, senators and deputies sent a message to Chancellor Max of Baden. Noting that this was a moment "when it seems a new Germany has arisen," it asked for "an end to the policy of conquest and oppression," an end to the "vain and detestable undertaking" of dividing Belgium between Flemish and Walloons, the abolition of the *Zentralen* and the requisitions, an end to the demolition of factories, and, finally, the return of the deported. All of these grievances disappeared by themselves. Without even waiting for the order, German agents abandoned their positions. No service remained in operation. The debacle was faster and more dramatic than the most optimistic had dared hope for. It was a collapse. Political prisoners saw their cell doors flung open; the deported came home to cheers, passing disbanded soldiers and military vehicles in the streets, heading for Germany.

However, the enemy's disarray made the situation particularly difficult. Forced back by the German retreat, pathetic groups of refugees and evacuees arrived from the Nord and Ardennes departments in France, and from Hainaut and Flanders. No measures had been taken about them. It was left to the *Comité National*, the communal administrations, and the charitable associations to work miracles to house them, feed them, hospitalize the sick, and take care of the elderly and the children.

The German revolution, which began in November, unleashed a catastrophe. Military discipline disappeared among the troops in the garrisons. The red flag was hoisted over barracks, and soldier councils attempted to seize power. For a while, they tried to rally Belgian socialists to their movement. But their reception at the *Maison du Peuple* in Brussels quickly dissipated their illusions. Faced with a Germany that was divided against itself, Belgians formed a united front. The unanimity of their resistance during the war lived on through peace. For a few days, surprised and bewildered, they witnessed street fights between rebel and loyal troops. The disputes among the papers sponsored by Germany, which suddenly started insulting the activists, hardly increased the disgust they had always aroused.

It's truly remarkable that order was generally maintained during the rout of the conqueror. The conduct of people's behavior at this time was as praiseworthy as it had been over the previous four years. Except for the looting of a few military trains in stations, the destruction of a few homes of notorious activists, and the punishment of women whose "Germanophilia" was considered scandalous, there were no incidents. The hatred that had accumulated in Belgian hearts did not result in violence. The supposed 1914 franc tireurs did not take advantage of the fugitives' disorganization to attack them. The communal councils, which were the only survivors of the destruction of the state, were sufficient, with the loyalty of citizens and thanks to the truce between the parties, to maintain public order until the Constitutional authorities returned.

CHAPTER XI

The Diaspora

One would have only an incomplete idea of the consequences of the German occupation of Belgium if one neglected to take into account the emigration it triggered. The importance of this event was such that one could almost say that, alongside the country, there existed an external Belgium between 1914 and 1918. What took place was really more than a simple emigration. It was a mass exodus, a diaspora.

It is very difficult to estimate its size with any precision. Records are missing, and besides, the number of emigrants continued to fluctuate with the vagaries of the war. The shortage of works on the subject makes covering it adequately, given its scale and importance, even more difficult. One has no choice but to provide only a rough sketch.

When the German armies suddenly swamped the country on August 4, holidays had just begun. Many rich or well off families found themselves in the countryside, by the sea, or abroad, and an invasion was so unexpected that, despite the mobilization, few had thought of interrupting their vacations. Furthermore, the sudden invasion of the Liège, Luxembourg, and Namur provinces resulted in their populations being immobilized there. In all occupied areas, it became impossible to move around. Even those who would have wanted to flee were unable to. In the parts of the country where the invader had not yet penetrated, inhabitants did not think of seeking refuge during the first few days. Confident that the Allies would be able to save them, blinded by the illusion that the French and British Armies would arrive promptly, they expected day after day to see the enemy's forward progress halted. It was only when they realized that the country would not be saved, when they learned that the Liège forts had fallen, then those in Namur, and finally that the Belgian army had retreated to Antwerp,[1] that they realized that the invasion would indeed go well beyond the Meuse.

At this point the fear of what would come and the desire to escape the shortages and sufferings inherent in war persuaded individuals to leave whose wealth enabled them to get out, or who were motivated by their timorousness, their egotism, or concerns about their health. The mass exodus did not begin until news broke about the horrors committed in Dinant, Andenne, Aarschot, and Leuven.[2] After that, there was a frantic flight. A contagion of terror spread ahead of the German troops, increasing as they advanced, and driving the distraught population toward the interior. First in Brussels, then in Ghent, thousands of unfortunates came pouring in, without any resources. All the roads were jammed with haggard crowds of people who needed to be accommodated, hospitalized, and fed, and who, when they had barely arrived, were immediately driven onward by the constant stream of terrifying news and rumors.

When Antwerp surrendered,[3] the panic-stricken population rushed, almost in its entirety, towards neighboring Zeeland. The Germans' advance beyond the Scheldt, after occupying Ghent (October 12, 1914), met with less excitement. The executions and arson having halted, fears decreased. There was no mass exodus. Besides, where would people flee to? The routes to both France and the Netherlands were now blocked by armies. Only the way

---

1 *The retreat was ordered on the evening of August 18th, and the army arrived in the forts on the 20th.*
2 *between the 19th and 26th of August*
3 *October 10th*

to England remained open. But the means of transportation was lacking. Almost all Belgians vacationing on the coast set sail to Dover and Folkestone.

However, with the occupation of Ostend, the country was encircled. For a little while, though, it was still possible to leave on trains and tramways headed north. But soon enough the German authorities took measures to monitor people's identities and places of residence. The carrying of identification cards and passports was made mandatory. In 1915, they constructed an electrified fence along the entire Dutch border, guarded by sentinels and military posts. Belgium was now entirely sealed off. From then on, to get out of the country, one had to pay a steep price for infrequently-granted authorizations, or risk one's life trying to slip between troops and under the deadly wires. Only those moved by tremendous courage and in good physical condition could face such obstacles. From 1914 to 1918, many young men wanting to join the Belgian Army exposed themselves to these dangers. An estimated 30,000 succeeded in escaping. It is impossible to know exactly how many perished, either shot by sentinels or electrocuted, or how many were arrested on their way or betrayed by their guides and were sent to prison camps in Germany.

During the last trimester of 1914, an estimated 1,056,000 refugees crossed into the Netherlands, a seventh of Belgium's entire population. But this enormous wave soon flowed back. The German government did not want to let such a considerable mass of Belgians escape its control. It feared, with reason, the damage to its reputation among the neutral powers, and the reinforcements the expatriates would provide to war industries, espionage networks, and to the Belgian Army. Germany officially announced that full freedom would be guaranteed those who returned, and that they would not have to fear either conscription in the army or deportation. They promised also that the tragedies that had bloodied the first stages of the occupation would not happen again.

For their part, the fugitives started missing their country after the original panic subsided, and for many the suffering of exile and the misery of daily life were too much to bear. A mass return followed the mass departure. In December 1914, the number of refugees still in the Netherlands was estimated at 200,000. In May 1915, that number had fallen to about 100,000, and this figure was not exceeded until the end of the war. Those who returned were back to stay, since escaping the country had become more or less impossible. However, the deportation of Belgian workers in 1916 and 1917 and the growing misery did trigger some departures. But these did not significantly affect the number of Belgians in the Netherlands.

Not all Belgians who left the Netherlands returned to their country. Many of them boarded ships for France and England. In France, their number at the end of the war was estimated at about 325,000, and in Britain, 162,000.[1] All in all, at the time of the armistice, at least 500,000 Belgians were living abroad, one fourteenth of the entire population.

Of these Belgians, most came from the Flemish part of the country. This is easily explained by the swiftness of the invasion in the Walloon provinces and the impossibility of escaping to France, where battles were being fought, or to reach the Netherlands through the German Army. The Flemish population, however, was very close to the Dutch border, and so individuals naturally sought refuge there. It is probably not an exaggeration to say that about two thirds of Belgian émigrés were Flemish.

Among the refugees, slightly more came from urban rather than rural areas. In the beginning, everyone undoubtedly fled pell-mell. But farmers, who knew they would get their land back, were more likely to decide to return than craftsmen or industrial

---

[1] On November 1, 1918, there were 325,298 Belgian refugees in France, 121,786 of whom were men, 116,995 women, and 86,517 children (*Bulletin des Archives de la Guerre*, t. I, p. 45 and following), spread across all departments, but most of whom were in the Seine (93,341), the Calvados (13,303), the Seine-Inférieure (35,396) and the Seine-et-Oise (12,650).

workers, who faced unemployment and food shortages..

Finally, it's worth noting that fewer poor returned than rich. This is probably because the latter were worried about their investments, and about the tax that Germany imposed on those who did not return by March 1, 1915, in order to encourage repatriation.

To maintain Belgian emigrants, various services and initiatives were organized. The Belgian government in Le Havre founded charitable agencies for all kinds of needs, including by age, profession, and social class.[1] On November 1, 1914, it established in Britain a Belgian Committee to advise all of the official and private British organizations which had been created to help the refugees. On March 10, 1915, a similar committee was established in The Hague. Various decrees created other organizations to help refugees obtain loans to provide for their daily needs. In September 1916, King Albert's Fund was established to build temporary housing. Teachers and professors set up boards in France and the Netherlands to enable students among the refugees and the military to take their exams.

It goes without saying that Belgian ministers and consuls throughout the world worked zealously to help relieve the suffering of their compatriots by organizing collections, fundraisers, and charitable associations, and by publishing articles and pamphlets.

Foreign governments also distinguished themselves. Some, such as France and Britain, could not ignore the fate of an allied people. They acted with energy and compassion. In most French *departments* regional commissions for relief were set up, at the urging of the Ministry of the Interior, as well as camps for students, etc. Among the neutral states, the Netherlands was most helpful. Camps were built for the refugees and for the soldiers who, after the Antwerp siege, had found asylum on Dutch soil,

---

1 See F. Van Langenhove, previously cited work, p. 33 and following

first in Hontenisse, then in Uden, Nunspet, Ede, and Gouda.[1] At the initiative of the city of Brussels, schools were opened and had, in 1915, 9,400 students and 358 teachers, and in 1916–1917, 16,000 students and 450 teachers.[2]

The sympathies of the British, too, were aroused by Belgium's misery and its resistance to Germany. Among the organizations set up in London were the War Refugees Committee, the Belgian Relief Committee, the Esperanza Circle for Belgian Sufferers, the Belgica, the Belgian Finance Committee, and the Belgian Orphan Fund. The archives of the Belgian refugees committees allow one to fully appreciate the extent of their charitable work.

It was similar in Paris and in the French *departments*. In Switzerland, there was a Commission for Assistance to Belgians Interned in Geneva, a Central Swiss Committee for Assistance to Refugees, and many more. In 1916, 2,500 Belgian children were looked after in the Confederation's various cantons.

Just like the emigrants from the French Revolution at the end of the 18th century and the Russian emigrants today, Belgians who had been chased out of their country by the Great War lived mostly among themselves, without interacting with foreigners. This is too natural to prevent. A lot of the wealthy and educated devoted themselves to the plight of their compatriots, either by joining the relief committees, or by giving classes or organizing conferences. Craftsmen and workers sought employment, albeit not always successfully. But dockworkers, tugboat captains, mechanics, and pilots were much sought after in France.[3] Many emigrants signed on as agricultural workers. The conscription of all able-bodied men had made farmers desperate for laborers. Mechanics found jobs in arms and ammunition factories, working either for the Belgian

---

[1] R. Verdeven, *België en Nederland. De vluchtoorden Hontenisse en Uden*. La Haye, 1920.
[2] P. Buysse, *Une experience d'éducation professionnelle et sociale de masses, Les écoles du travail pour soldats belges internes en Hollande*, Bruxelles, 1926.
[3] De Kerviler, *La Navigation intérieure en France pendant la guerre*, p. 34 (French series of this collection)

Army or for Allied armies.¹ In Britain, they had to be employed in special workshops, since their habits and procedures were too far removed from those of British workers.² ³

In the Netherlands, Le Havre, and Paris, as well as in London, Belgian journalists founded newspapers, both in Flemish and French, or revived papers no longer being published inside Belgium. In general, they respected the truce the parties had agreed to. The activists also started some organizations, with no success. Despite a few imprudent acts and some unfortunate words, patriotic feelings remained just as strong in the diaspora as within the country.

The spying and intelligence services, renowned for the number of heroic victims, naturally drew heavily on the emigrants. The Hague, Flushing, and Maastricht were the centers to which informants, at the cost of grave dangers, forwarded news about the movements of the German armies.⁴ At the same time, the outflow of political propaganda in newspapers, books, and brochures never ceased. In short, in every field, and despite the sufferings and bitterness of exile, "external Belgians" demonstrated the same energy as those within the country.

However, the emigrants knew that they were not popular, and that those who remained in the country resented them for abandoning them to their suffering. When they returned, misunderstandings were unavoidable. Both sides had not experienced events in the same way.

---

1 A. Breyre, *La Participation de Belges aux industries de la Défense nationale en France penant la guerre*. Bulletin de l'Association des Ingénieurs sortis des Écoles de Liège, 1920.
2 H. Wolfe, *Labour supply and regulation*, p. 81 (English series of this work).
3 Among the most famous was the one in Birtley in County Durham, where over 2000 workers manufactured shells. They and their families lived in a town constructed next to the factory called Elisabethville, and which was declared sovereign Belgian territory.
4 Von Bissing used to say that "*Der Belgier ist geradezu sportliebend in Bezug auf Spionage*." ("The Belgian absolutely loves the sport of espionage.") *Rapports et documents d'Enquête*, vol 3, t. II, p. 48.

INDEX

A

Aalst, 178
Aarschot, xlix, 62, 117, 200, 262
Abbaugruppe, 190, 194
Activism, 231, 240; (see: separation; languages)
Administrative separation, l, li, 35, 99, 106, 120, 191, 197, 216, 217, 219, 221, 222, 226, 227, 232, 233, 240, 242, 248, 254
Agneessens, 81
Agriculture, 15, 112, 114, 115, 116, 145
Albert I, 23. See king
Algemeen Nederlandsch Verbond, 198
Algemeen Vlaamschen Raad, 215
Alps, 7, 12
Ame belge (newspaper: l'—), 84
Amsterdam, li, 202
Andenne, 61, 262
Antoinistes, 11
Antwerp, xlvii, li, 11, 13, 14, 16, 17, 37, 40, 41, 44, 46, 47, 55, 57, 58, 59, 61, 62, 63, 66, 90, 94, 98, 117, 118, 123, 128, 132, 158, 167, 180, 181, 184, 196, 199, 200, 202, 203, 213, 217, 227, 234, 235, 251, 262, 265
Antwerpsche Tydingen (newspaper: —), 203
Appeals Court, 236
Archives de la Guerre, 106, 226, 264
Arlon, 8, 239
Armistice, 2, 126, 135, 142, 193, 245, 264
Artevelde, 81, 234
Atrocities, 54, 62, 71
Australia, 133
Austria, 18, 44, 205, 208, 228
Automobiles, 47, 111, 168
Autre Cloche (newspaper: l'—), 84
Avenir Wallon (newspaper: l'—), 220

B

Baden (Chancellor Max of —), 246, 258
Banks, 17, 98, 105, 110, 116, 123, 124, 125, 126, 129, 161, 168, 251
Belfried (magazine: —), 213
Belgian Army, 46, 56, 57, 59, 60, 78, 102, 158, 249, 263, 266
Belgian Constitution, 20, 21, 32, 49
Belgian emigrants, 169, 265
Belgian government, liii, 53, 55, 61, 75, 92, 97, 127, 134, 135, 155, 200, 203, 206, 207, 228, 246, 265

Belgian King, 91, 130
Belgian officials, 106, 141, 237, 258
Belgian people, lii, 49, 82, 83, 87, 97, 100, 103, 105, 106, 130, 135, 143, 144, 146, 151, 152, 160, 162, 165, 166, 173, 176, 218, 219, 221, 224, 225, 228
Belgian question, 71, 196, 197, 202, 212
Belgian state, v, xvi, 71, 92, 95, 99, 106, 108, 191, 196, 203, 205, 210, 211, 213, 214, 232, 237, 241, 244, 248
Belgian unity, xlii, 254
Belgian workers, l, 169, 175, 176, 179, 264
Berlin, l, 60, 70, 74, 98, 100, 105, 107, 126, 132, 136, 160, 161, 179, 181, 182, 188, 190, 205, 208, 213, 218, 223, 241, 242, 244, 245, 246, 247, 250, 252
Bernardiston (Colonel —), 71
Bethmann Hollweg, (Chancellor T. von —), 204, 233, 246
Beyens, (N. —), 61
Births, 115
Bismarck, 70
Bissing (M. von —), xlviii, xlix, lii, 93, 98, 100, 101, 102, 104, 137, 144, 145, 148, 149, 153, 161, 162, 164, 165, 175, 176, 177, 178, 180, 181, 182, 184, 185, 186, 187, 188, 189, 191, 195, 196, 197, 206, 209, 213, 216, 231, 232, 237, 248, 267
Bittmann (K. —), 100, 101, 172, 189, 211
Black market sales, 113
Blockade, 75, 100, 109, 110, 118, 127, 129, 131, 132, 158, 159, 176, 197
Boerenbonden, 17, 31, 35, 251
Bohemia, 9, 33, 205, 210, 211
Border, 7, 21, 43, 46, 48, 56, 57, 58, 74, 78, 79, 94, 113, 115, 130, 152, 181, 196, 216, 223, 263, 264
Borinage, 154
Boulogne, 57
Brabant, 11, 17, 57, 66, 94, 98, 99, 132, 158, 169, 180, 184, 208, 217, 225, 226, 239
Brest-Litovsk, 244
Breyre (Ad. —), 267
Britain, xlvii, 15, 25, 41, 75, 78, 109, 118, 130, 133, 143, 157, 158, 159, 164, 165, 166, 169, 186, 187, 254, 264, 265, 267
British Army, 158
Brouckère (H. de —), 22
Bruges, li, 11, 14, 178, 214

269

Brussels, xlvii, l, li, lii, 3, 4, 9, 14, 16, 17, 20, 22, 26, 35, 41, 42, 43, 44, 47, 57, 61, 62, 66, 67, 74, 75, 81, 84, 85, 90, 91, 95, 96, 101, 104, 105, 123, 129, 130, 131, 132, 133, 134, 140, 141, 142, 143, 144, 149, 150, 151, 153, 161, 162, 168, 172, 177, 180, 181, 187, 198, 199, 203, 209, 214, 215, 217, 219, 220, 221, 222, 223, 224, 225, 226, 227, 231, 233, 234, 235, 236, 239, 240, 244, 245, 246, 247, 249, 251, 258, 262, 266
Bulletin des Archives de la Guerre, 226, 264
Burgomasters, 26, 53, 107, 108, 152, 177, 184, 224, 225, 226, 238, 250
Butter, 113, 114, 166, 167
Buysse (P. —), 266

C

Caillaux (Madame —), 44
Caisse d'épargne, 114
Campine, 14, 28, 78, 119, 197, 253
Camps (concentration —), 79, 181, 183, 185, 228, 263, 265
Canada, 87, 133
Canals, 111, 118, 131, 150
Capital, iv, l, 12, 16, 17, 28, 39, 81, 90, 98, 113, 124, 125, 129, 163, 168, 188, 217, 219, 227, 235, 253
Cardinal Mercier. (see: Mercier)
Catholics, 11, 20, 23, 24, 25, 27, 30, 36, 37, 40, 70, 80, 82, 103, 180, 228
Cement (— industries), 187
Censorship, lii, 85, 183, 204, 212, 254
Centrals (*Zentralen*), 146, 147, 148, 223, 258
Cereal, 14
Cès de justice (February 7–10, 1918), 231, 239
Chancellor (of German Empire), liii, 196, 235
Charity work, 87
Charleroi, 15, 17, 36, 117, 121, 192, 222
Charles V, 7, 18, 82, 203
Children, xlix, 8, 33, 41, 54, 60, 61, 76, 86, 87, 129, 154, 175, 185, 258, 264, 266
Chlepner (B. S. —), 123
Cities (large —), 11
Civic Guard, 26, 52, 53, 54, 78
Civilian executions and massacres, xxii
Civilians, xxiv, xlix, 53, 54, 59, 60, 62, 89
Civil justice, 97
Classes for the unemployed, 148, 174
Coal, 13, 15, 28, 117, 119, 120, 121, 122, 154, 164, 165, 166, 169, 185, 188, 193, 197, 251, 252, 254
Cockerill (— establishments), 122
Collinet, 127

Comité National de Secours et d'Alimentation, li
Commission for Relief in Belgium, li, 3, 4, 127, 145, 146, 149, 163, 169
Congo, 23, 28, 74
Copper, 161, 167, 192
Cotton, 15, 118, 121, 161, 187
Council of Flanders, l, 4, 215, 217, 233, 235, 236, 237, 258
Council of Flanders delegates. (see: *Gevolmagtigden*)
Courts, ii, 91, 93, 97, 138, 162, 174, 175, 180, 189, 219, 237, 238, 239, 240
Cuvelier, J., 5

D

Dampierre (Gui de —), 119
Denmark, 14
Deportation, xlix, 4, 75, 76, 78, 79, 81, 96, 108, 152, 176, 178, 179, 180, 182, 185, 191, 206, 238, 250, 263, 264
Deutsche Kriegsrohstoffabteilung, 160
Deutsch-flämische Gesellschaften, 213
Deutschtum, 70, 200, 210, 241
Dinant, xlix, 61, 117, 262
Ducarne (general —), 44

E

Echo de Liège (newspaper: *L'*—), 75
Economic activity, 11, 38
Economic restoration, 2
Education, l, 24, 29, 30, 36, 37, 40, 68, 90, 112, 204, 206, 209, 252
Education (question of —), 36, 37
Egmont, 81
Einkaufgesellschaften, 165
Emmich (General von —), 56
Emperor of Germany, xlviii, 54, 92, 93, 177, 182, 183, 191, 215, 232
Erntezentrale, 146
Errera (P. —), 20
Ersatz, 188
Erzberger, 245
Étapes (zone of the —), 93, 94, 166, 178, 181, 183, 184, 200, 227, 234, 248, 253
Exportation, 47, 127, 136, 145, 152, 162, 166
Extraterritoriality, 66

F

Falkenhausen (von —), 93
Fallersleben (Hoffman von —), 198
Famine, 113
Farmers, 14, 17, 31, 113, 114, 116, 154, 167, 183, 264, 266

Fertilizer, 112
Finances, 95, 217, 243
Fines, 178
Fires, 168
Fischer (Otokar —), 198
Flambeau (newspaper: Le —), 84
Flanders, i, ii, iv, v, l, 4, 7, 8, 9, 10, 11, 15, 32, 33, 35, 62, 63, 66, 91, 93, 94, 98, 119, 121, 132, 157, 158, 178, 183, 197, 198, 200, 201, 203, 205, 206, 207, 208, 209, 210, 212, 213, 214, 215, 216, 217, 219, 220, 221, 222, 223, 226, 227, 229, 231, 232, 233, 234, 235, 236, 237, 240, 241, 242, 243, 244, 245, 246, 247, 251, 252, 253, 254, 258
Flemish nationalist movement, xxv, 34, 198, 199, 233, 247
Flemish people, 199, 205, 209, 210, 211, 214, 215, 216, 233, 237, 241, 243
Flemish police force, 252
Fleurus (battle of —), 7, 65, 89
Flour, 87, 128, 131, 153
Food supplies, 145
France, liii, 7, 9, 12, 16, 17, 18, 26, 33, 37, 38, 39, 43, 45, 51, 55, 63, 65, 66, 72, 74, 78, 94, 103, 127, 132, 134, 135, 146, 154, 157, 158, 169, 183, 184, 190, 195, 202, 203, 205, 210, 212, 213, 215, 220, 222, 241, 248, 258, 262, 264, 265, 266, 267
Franck (Louis —), 235
Francqui (Émile —), 129
Francs-tireurs, 61, 62
Fransmannen, 39
Fransquillons, 33, 199, 241, 248.
  (see: languages)
Freemasons, 180
Free-trade, 13, 41
French army, 46, 57
French (General —), 51
Fumay, 94
Furnes, 114
Furniture (— industries), 122

G

Gay (George —), 131
Gazet van Brussel, 212
Geneva, 10, 42, 148, 266
German Army, xlix, 55, 56, 57, 59, 70, 98, 121, 193, 195, 264
German Constitution, 72
German government, 4, 82, 94, 102, 125, 136, 139, 143, 144, 195, 196, 197, 203, 209, 219, 244, 247, 263

German High Command, xlviii, 57, 176, 179, 183, 201, 207, 222, 232, 240, 242, 246
Germania (magazine), 34, 198
German militarism, 73
German military authorities, xxv, 4, 75, 76, 85, 113, 115, 120, 124, 133, 136, 137, 143, 149, 152, 171, 218, 225, 226, 229, 234, 237, 253, 254, 263
German ordinances, 93, 97
Germany, ii, v, xlviii, xlix, liii, 1, 2, 4, 7, 12, 16, 32, 33, 34, 37, 38, 40, 41, 43, 44, 46, 49, 51, 54, 59, 61, 62, 65, 69, 70, 72, 74, 75, 76, 77, 78, 79, 86, 91, 94, 99, 101, 102, 103, 104, 105, 109, 113, 118, 121, 122, 123, 125, 128, 129, 130, 132, 133, 136, 140, 141, 143, 144, 145, 148, 149, 152, 153, 154, 156, 157, 158, 159, 160, 162, 163, 164, 165, 166, 168, 170, 172, 173, 174, 175, 176, 178, 179, 181, 182, 184, 185, 186, 187, 188, 189, 190, 191, 193, 196, 197, 198, 200, 201, 202, 203, 204, 205, 206, 207, 208, 210, 211, 212, 213, 214, 215, 217, 218, 220, 221, 222, 223, 224, 228, 231, 232, 233, 235, 237, 240, 241, 242, 243, 244, 245, 246, 247, 248, 249, 250, 252, 254, 257, 258, 259, 263, 265, 266
Gevolmagtigden, 242, 243, 247, 248, 250, 252, 253, 255
Ghent, xlvii, li, 4, 10, 14, 15, 16, 17, 30, 35, 39, 58, 85, 86, 117, 122, 170, 200, 201, 202, 203, 204, 206, 209, 211, 214, 234, 235, 239, 240, 245, 247, 248, 249, 250, 251, 258, 262
Gille (L. —), 108
Givet, 94
Glass factories, 121
Goltz (von der —), 144
Goutte de Lait (*La* —), 154
Governor General, xlviii, li, 84, 85, 92, 93, 95, 96, 97, 98, 100, 102, 120, 124, 125, 133, 137, 144, 145, 146, 148, 153, 156, 162, 163, 165, 167, 172, 173, 174, 175, 177, 179, 180, 182, 186, 187, 189, 191, 193, 195, 204, 205, 206, 211, 214, 215, 216, 219, 220, 223, 224, 225, 231, 233, 236, 237, 239, 240, 242, 243, 244, 245, 246, 247, 252
Grabowsky, (A. —), 229
Grey (Sir Edward —), 145
Groeningerwacht, 251

H

Haelen, 57

Hainaut, 13, 15, 31, 57, 62, 63, 93, 94, 117, 121, 132, 169, 178, 183, 184, 209, 217, 258
Hamburg, 14
Hapsburg, 7, 18, 72
Henry (Albert —), 2
Hertling (Chancellor von —), 244, 246
Heyse (Th. —), 204
Hindenburg (General P. von), 177, 181, 191
Höcker (P. O. —), 60
Hoene (General von —), 181
Hohenzollern, 69, 70
Hoover (Herbert —), xxiv, 127, 130, 131, 132, 193
House of Representatives, 20, 35
Human Rights (— violations), 4

I

Imports, 28, 112, 113, 127, 131, 132, 143, 153, 161, 165, 186, 187
Indies Company, 12
Industriebüro, 172, 173, 174, 185
Industry, 2, 11, 12, 13, 14, 15, 29, 31, 39, 40, 69, 75, 86, 105, 109, 110, 112, 117, 118, 119, 121, 122, 126, 161, 163, 164, 165, 169, 174, 175, 184, 185, 186, 187, 188, 189, 190, 191, 192, 193, 194, 253, 254
Information Agency for War Prisoners, 147
Information (newspaper: *l'*—), 75
Inselverlag, 222
Intellectuals, xlix, 59, 71
Invasion, xlviii, xlix, l, liii, 2, 43, 44, 45, 46, 48, 52, 56, 60, 62, 63, 71, 72, 73, 89, 97, 102, 103, 109, 110, 115, 117, 118, 119, 123, 127, 128, 129, 135, 138, 149, 160, 164, 168, 169, 179, 195, 203, 237, 261, 262, 264
In Vlaanderen Vlaamsch, 32, 35
Italy, ii, 28

J

Jews, 11
Jong Vlaanderen, 244
Junkers, 69

K

Kautsky, (K. —), 229
Keim (General —), 246
Kerchove (Ch. de —), 2
King Albert's Fund, 265
Kohlenzentrale, 120, 165
Köler (L. von —), 3
Kommandantur, 200, 201, 214

Kommission zum Ausbau, 231
Kortrijk, 15
Kriegsministerium, 161
Krieschefs, 96
Kuhlmann (R. von —), 244
Kulturkampf, 40, 70

L

Lace, 12
Lambert (Baron —), 130
Lancken (Doctor von der —), 105, 166, 182
Langenhove (F.G. van —), xlix, 2, 59, 68, 265
languages (question of —), vi, xxvi, xxvii, xxxi, xli, xlvii, xlix, l, li, 8, 9, 10, 16, 18, 32, 33, 34, 35, 36, 38, 47, 49, 60, 68, 71, 90, 104, 180, 198, 199, 200, 202, 203, 204, 205, 209, 210, 211, 212, 214, 216, 223, 224, 226, 227, 228, 229, 232, 241, 242, 252
Lannoy (Ch. de —), 127, 137
Lanrezac (General —), 57
La Panne, 8, 66, 83
Laruelle, 81
Leener (G. de —), 114
Le Havre, 1, 57, 66, 67, 68, 95, 97, 106, 128, 202, 203, 218, 219, 228, 238, 242, 249, 265, 267
Leman (General —), 56
Lemonnier (*l'échevin* —), 67
Leopold I, 13, 23
Leuven, xiii, xxix, xliv, xlix, li, 17, 55, 62, 63, 85, 103, 117, 131, 180, 200, 217, 234, 235, 251, 262
Liberal (Party —), 20, 30, 31, 38
Liberty, 22, 49, 69, 81, 103, 179, 229
Libraries, xvii, 85, 104, 149
Libre Belgique (newspaper: La —), 84
Liebknecht, (K. —), 101
Liège, v, xlvii, xlix, 10, 13, 15, 16, 17, 31, 35, 37, 41, 43, 46, 48, 50, 51, 52, 56, 57, 58, 59, 60, 61, 62, 75, 85, 86, 94, 121, 123, 128, 132, 158, 180, 184, 192, 196, 197, 209, 217, 222, 261, 262, 267
Lierre, 77
Limburg, 52, 62, 94, 132, 184, 217, 251
Linen, 12, 15, 87, 121, 161, 187
Livestock, 47, 112, 113, 136, 146, 179, 250
Lkkeu, 102
London, xv, xxxviii, xliii, li, 41, 123, 130, 131, 132, 136, 146, 165, 202, 266, 267
Los van Havre, 205
Ludendorf (General E. von —), 191
Lumm (von —), 104, 105, 124
Luxembourg, l, 52, 62, 93, 94, 113, 132, 142, 170, 178, 180, 183, 184, 217, 261

M

Machines, 162, 163, 170, 186, 188, 189, 190, 192, 193
Maeterlinck, (M. —), 39
Magistracy. (see: justice; courts)
Mahaim (Ernest —), 2
Man (Henri de —), 102
Manifesto of German intellectuals, 71
Markets, ii, iii, 13, 28, 29, 45, 119, 128, 178
Marne (battle of the —), 57, 58, 158
Marx (K. —), 40
Max (A. —, burgomaster), v, xv, 81, 90, 108, 129, 238, 246, 258
Mayence (F. —), 82
Mechelen, xlix, 61, 63, 83, 117, 122, 123, 180, 220, 234
Meldeamt, 78, 178
Mercier (Cardinal —), 81, 82, 83, 103, 180, 181, 182, 203, 226, 235, 249
Messenger de Bruxelles (newspaper: *Le* —), 75
Metallurgy, 13
Metternich, 22
Meuse, 8, 37, 51, 55, 57, 198, 262
Michaelis (Chancellor —), 232
Militärgouverneur, 96
Mines, xvii, 14, 25, 117, 121, 122, 131, 135, 164, 165, 169, 188, 251, 252
Ministries, ministers, 26, 27, 44, 47, 53, 67, 68, 103, 218
Mobilization, 44, 261
Mons, 15, 57, 104, 117, 121, 123, 180, 239
Morality, 180
Mot du Soldat (*Le* —), 79
Municipalities, 25. (see: towns)

N

Namur, xlix, l, 37, 46, 51, 52, 57, 58, 61, 62, 94, 132, 158, 184, 217, 218, 219, 220, 221, 222, 261, 262
Nationale Jong Vlaanderen Beweging, 251
Nationalistische Bond, 251
Nederlandsch Comiteit, 253
Netherlands. (see: The Netherlands)
Neutrality, xxiii, 1, 19, 24, 27, 37, 41, 43, 44, 46, 49, 54, 59, 72, 99, 155, 157, 161, 176
Neutral (— powers), xxi, 7, 75, 95, 101, 104, 130, 133, 139, 140, 141, 145, 146, 148, 153, 157, 159, 166, 181, 193, 196, 208, 211, 235, 240, 253, 254, 263, 265
Newspapers, 17, 30, 36, 39, 44, 45, 50, 54, 71, 75, 80, 83, 150, 164, 202, 203, 238, 247, 267
Nieuwpoort, 14, 58
Ninove, 178

Noot (van der —), 207
Nord (*department*), 39

O

Obergericht, 239
Oberkommando, 93
Okkupationsgerichte, 97
Olbrechts (R. —), 115
Olzentrale, 166
Ooms (A. —), 108
Ostende, 125
Ougrée Marihaye (— establishments), 192

P

Page (W. H. —), 130
Palais Nationale, 66
Pan-Germanism, xxxvii, 198, 201
Paris, ix, xiv, xix, xxii, xxvii, xxxix, xliii, xliv, xlv, 17, 20, 38, 39, 40, 44, 126, 132, 215, 266, 267
Parliament. (see: Chamber); Flemish — (see: Council of Flanders)
Passelecq (Fernand —), 2
Passivists, 247
Passports, 247, 263
Patrie (newspaper: *La* —), 84
Patriotism, xxi, xxxi, xxxiv, 49, 71, 73, 76, 77, 80, 120, 137, 147, 172, 173, 219, 221, 227
Payer (Vice-chancellor von —), 246
Permanent delegations, 48
Peuple Wallon (newspaper: *Le* —), 222
Pine plantations, 14
Pirenne (Henri —), 86, 208, 215
Pirenne (Jacques —), 2
Poland, liii, 9, 33, 158
Police, 53, 78, 79, 84, 96, 97, 106, 107, 140, 206, 215, 218, 239, 252
Politics, xi, xviii, 8, 18, 20, 26, 27, 30, 38, 43, 68, 135, 237, 247
Poll tax, 21
Poor, xxvii, xxxiv, 14, 51, 129, 169, 170, 171, 173, 237, 265
Pope, 40, 81
Ports, 11, 13, 14, 165, 196
Posters, 172, 174, 199, 227
Potatoes, 14, 47, 113, 145, 146, 154, 166
Press. (see: newspapers)
Priests (executions of —), 61
Prison, xxi, 77, 78, 79, 174, 175, 189, 218, 237, 247, 263
Prisoners, xxvi, 78, 148, 192, 258

Propaganda, xxv, 11, 30, 31, 34, 83, 85, 108, 174, 203, 211, 220, 221, 248, 249, 267
Protectionism, 12, 13
Protestants, 11, 228
Provinces, xlvii, xlix, l, li, liii, 7, 8, 9, 17, 18, 25, 31, 32, 33, 34, 48, 52, 62, 67, 68, 91, 94, 96, 98, 99, 113, 126, 132, 136, 143, 152, 167, 184, 196, 198, 209, 217, 220, 222, 239, 254, 261, 264
Prussia, 22, 60, 68, 69, 70, 208

Q
Quarries, 121, 122, 169
Quotidien (newspaper: *Le* —), 75

R
Raad van Vlaanderen. (see: Council of Flanders)
Railroads, 13, 14, 28, 43, 111, 118, 128, 131, 150, 169, 183, 188, 197, 223
Rathenau plan, 188
Rathenau (Walther —), 161
Rationing, 143, 166
Raw materials, iv, 12, 13, 15, 29, 109, 111, 117, 118, 119, 121, 160, 161, 162, 163, 164, 165, 166, 169, 170, 186, 187, 190
Red Cross, 79, 148, 174
Reed (H. —), 20
Refugees, 63, 147, 266
Reich, lii, 4, 40, 68, 69, 71, 72, 98, 104, 105, 118, 143, 146, 158, 163, 165, 170, 173, 175, 182, 184, 188, 196, 198, 203, 208, 213, 232, 245, 247, 248
Reichenbach, 208
Reichstag, 49, 92, 182, 204, 208, 229, 246, 250
Religion, xxxvii, 20, 24, 37, 40, 60, 103
Repatriation, 265
Reports from the Commission of Inquiry on the Violation of Human Rights, 62
Requisitions, 73, 90, 98, 107, 111, 118, 121, 128, 160, 162, 163, 165, 167, 168, 170, 183, 184, 186, 258
Reserves, 182
Revolution, iii, xxviii, xxix, 9, 13, 18, 19, 21, 23, 24, 30, 36, 80, 129, 194, 208, 246, 258
Rice, 114, 131
Ridder (A. de —), 5, 22
Roads, 13, 14, 47, 58, 59, 111, 121, 150, 170, 178, 262
Rohma, 190
Rotterdam, li, 14, 131

Rotterdamsche Courant (newspaper: —), 75
Russia, 28, 44, 158

S
Sainte-Adresse, 1, (see: Le Havre)
Sambre, 57
Sandt (Dr. von —), 90, 223
Sarajevo, 44
Schaibel (Dr. —), 244
Scheldt, 8, 12, 13, 58, 119, 262
Schwertfeger (Colonel —), 54
Senate, 20, 24, 67
Serbia, 44
Shaler (M. K. —), 130
Slavic people, 8
Smet (J. de —), 99
Socialism, socialists, x, xlii, 11, 30, 31, 35, 39, 101
Société Générale, 124, 125, 126, 223
Solvay (Ernest —), xvii, xxii, 129, 156
Soup kitchens, 147
Spain, lii, 7, 18, 28, 95, 130, 135, 181, 224, 228, 245, 255
Speech (February 25, 1918 —), 244
Spies, 75
Stahl, 127
Strikes, 30, 154, 157
Studienkommission, 206
Süddeutsche Monalshefte, 101
Sugar, 13, 28, 145, 146, 166
Sweden, 159
Switzerland, 8, 10, 152, 159, 166, 224, 241, 266

T
Taici (Monseigneur —), 61
Tamines, 61
Textile (— industries), xi, 117, 121, 122, 192
The Hague, xix, 42, 132, 174, 247, 265, 267
The Netherlands, vi, xxxi, xxxvi, xliv, lii, 7, 9, 13, 18, 19, 25, 26, 44, 63, 94, 95, 106, 120, 123, 129, 135, 152, 159, 164, 166, 186, 193, 198, 201, 202, 203, 211, 224, 228, 247, 253, 255, 262, 263, 264, 265, 267
Tienen, 234
Times (newspaper: *The* —), 83
Tirpitz (Admiral von —), 213
Toorts (journal —), 211
Tournai, 61, 178

Towns, ii, iii, v, xxiv, xlvii, liii, 16, 52, 62, 63, 65, 94, 96, 107, 108, 115, 117, 124, 126, 128, 129, 132, 135, 136, 137, 139, 141, 152, 153, 158, 170, 171, 172, 174, 177, 184, 209, 225, 251
Treaties, xlii, 7, 8, 19, 27, 43, 46, 51, 55, 224

U

Ultimatum, 45, 46, 47, 49, 51, 62, 143, 157
Unemployment, lii, 2, 80, 86, 107, 110, 114, 115, 121, 122, 168, 169, 170, 171, 172, 175, 176, 178, 187, 188, 265
Unions, x, 17, 30, 31, 112, 167, 173, 180, 182
United Provinces, 7, 12, 119
United States, xxxiv, 72, 87, 95, 130, 132, 134, 136, 137, 149, 181, 208
Universal suffrage, xi, 21, 24, 30, 101, 102
Universities, 17, 40, 69, 85, 180, 204
Utrecht (archbishop of —), 253

V

Vandervelde (E. —), 67
Vannérus (J. —), 4
Vauthier (M. —), 2
Verdeven, (R. —), 266
Verhaeren, (E. —), 39
Vermittelungstelle, 133
Verviers, xlix, 4, 8, 15, 56, 117, 121, 122, 196, 222
Verwaltungschef, 217, 220, 221, 245, 249
Villalobar (Marquis of —), 135, 146, 155, 182, 239, 245
Visé, 8, 56
Vlaamsch Socialistische Party, 32, 35, 251
Volksopbeuring, 253
Vollenhove (van —), 135, 155
Voorit, 30
Vrij Vlaanderen, 251

W

Waentig (H. —), 144
Walloons, vi, 8, 11, 16, 17, 32, 34, 35, 104, 120, 180, 202, 205, 210, 211, 215, 220, 221, 222, 226, 229, 241, 258
Walloon separatism, 241. See separation; activism
Walther Rathenau, 161
War contributions, liii, 98, 126, 163
War Ministry's commissioner, 164
Waterloo, 19
Weapons (— factories), xxxii, 13, 61, 159, 177
Wheat, 14, 112, 113, 118, 127, 128, 129, 146, 153, 154

Whitlock (Brand —), lii
Wilson (President Woodrow —), 193
Wolfe (H. —), 267
Women, xlix, 60, 61, 77, 87, 114, 154, 183, 251, 259, 264
Wool, 13, 15, 119, 161, 167, 187
Workers' trains, 16
Workforce, 115, 174, 177
Working class, 29, 31, 51, 102, 110, 112, 114, 170, 180, 181
Wumba, 190, 192

Y

Ypres, 114
Yser, xlvii, 1, 58, 65, 66, 67, 93, 100, 110, 112, 115, 117, 132, 158, 195, 200, 204

Z

Zaakgelastigden, 247
Zeebrugge, 14
Zentrale, 146, 166
Zentraleinkaufgesellschaft, 166
Zivil Arbeiter Betaillone, 181

www.ingramcontent.com/pod-product-compliance
Lightning Source LLC
Chambersburg PA
CBHW032032150426
43194CB00006B/251